THE
BURNLEY FC
MISCELLANY

THE
BURNLEY FC
MISCELLANY

Written and compiled by
DAVID WISEMAN
(Who got by with a little help from his friend Dave Thomas
and dozens of other Burnley fans!)

breedon **books**
PUBLISHING

Dedicated to Burnley fans everywhere, with whom I have sat, stood
and travelled, laughed and cried, cheered and been cheesed off…
all by this remarkable club.
Including, not least, my son Christian.

First published in Great Britain in 2009 by The Breedon Books Publishing
Company Limited, Breedon House, 3 The Parker Centre, Derby, DE21 4SZ.

A catalogue record for this book is available from the British Library.

ISBN 978-1-85983-717-7

Printed and bound by TJ International Ltd, Padstow, Cornwall

CONTENTS

FOREWORD

Who was Albert Hungerdunger? Or Jimmy Slimsack? Here is a clue. According to one who should know, they both played for Burnley, in the first team and in the First Division. And if you do not believe it, then the source of the information was none other than the Burnley captain!

There have been numerous excellent histories about our beloved Clarets, but never one quite like this. Here are the quaint, quirky and downright queer events in the history of our football club.

Why was Bert Freeman never cold? Did you know that Andy Lochhead was once the manager of a hair salon? Who was known as the 'flying wardrobe'? Which Claret played at Wembley when he was 51 (and was on the winning side)? Whose picture was on the Burnley captain's bedroom wall?

I could go on. Which member of Burnley's Championship team in 1960 was told: 'If your brains were made of dynamite and I put a match to them, they wouldn't blow your cap off!' Who missed kicking someone's head and instead scored the goal of a lifetime? Who was the subject of a question on *Mastermind*?

Do you want more? Which Claret starred with Pelé? How many pies do they sell in a season at Turf Moor? What have zebras got to do with the Clarets? What position did Blackadder play in the Clarets team? And who scored with a 90-yard shot?

By the way, I forgot to mention Herbert Portgornie. What an inside-forward he was!

Of all the teams that have ever won the First Division, Burnley are from the smallest town and have, almost certainly, the smallest attendances. You could say the same about the FA Cup as well. Here at Turf Moor we have seen it all – League titles, FA Cup winners, Footballer of the Year, *twice* within a hair's breadth of losing our place in the League. (And even the most faithful Burnley fans thought it only happened once – against Orient.)

Many of the stories included here are quotes from people who were there at the time. My favourite is 'Glorious inconsistency – thy name is Burnley!' That says it all.

I hope that you enjoy these tales, which I have collected for every Claret fan. I have laughed a lot as I read them and I hope that you do too.

David Wiseman

P.S. And what has a 'tatterdemalion scarecrow' got to do with the Clarets?

ACKNOWLEDGEMENTS

My thanks and appreciation go out to many, both mentioned here with thanks and unmentioned with apologies.

My first acknowledgement must go to my good friend Dave Thomas, whose idea this book was in the first place, and which he then left me with. His numerous pithy comments have helped considerably. My appreciation also goes to Peter Seddon, whose superb book on Derby County inspired this much lesser effort.

My readers will realise my indebtedness to earlier football writers and reporters, who belonged in previous years to the *Burnley Express*, the *Burnley Gazette* and the *Burnley News*. This brings me nicely to the staff at Burnley Library (especially the Rosegrove branch, where I have spent the last 12 months researching in the cellar). There have also been many other newspapers, like the *Sunday Express, Daily Express, Daily Mirror, The Sun, Lancashire Evening Post* and the *Newcastle Sunday Sun*, all of which have helped in my research.

I have been greatly assisted by writers Peter Fyles, Ria Hopkinson, Pauline Pratley, Mervyn Hadfield, Dave Alton, Andrew Proctor, Bill Evans, Stephen Cummings, Stuart Hall, Jack Rosenthal, Andrew Firmin and Martin Barnes. It is a vague dividing line between such writers and fellow fans like Tom Jackson, Jonny Smith, Mrs Binns, Mrs H. Walton, Kevin Wolski, Andrew Lupton and Fred and Christine Noden, but they are all part of my efforts here. There are even some fans who have helped out and who do not live in Burnley, Colne or Nelson, like Darrell Barnes in China and Atle Normann in Norway.

I have read and quoted players and managers far too many to mention, but which include Paul Fletcher, Stan Ternent, Steve Cotterill, Jimmy Greaves, Jimmy McIlroy (thanks Jimmy for your thoughts and memories), Jimmy Adamson and Tom Finney. I have a very good library of 'Burnley books' and these have all proved extremely helpful. At this point I should make a special mention of my friend Ray Simpson and his 'Clarets Chronicles' colleagues.

Every day for over 12 months I have browsed websites like 'ClaretsMad', 'The Longside' and my indispensable Clarets companions 'When the Ball Moves' and 'Something to Write Home About'. Many thanks guys, your efforts are much appreciated. And, of, course, my thanks go to Steve Caron and his editorial team at Breedon Books for their skills, guidance and encouragement in helping to get this book into your hands.

And there, every step of the way, every day of my life, Burnley Football Club. What would we do without it?

Chapter One

A–B

(From Accidents and Accrington Stanley to a Burnley tale and the Bus conductor)

A

Only three players for Burnley have had both Christian names and surnames beginning with the letter A. They are:

⚽ Albert Alderman (who played in the 1930s)

⚽ Anthony Arins (who played in the 1970s)

⚽ Adeola ('Ade') Akinbiyi (who has played in more recent seasons)

⚽ If this were a competition, the prize would go to Albert Alderman, who was born in Alvaston!

THE 'A' TEAM

		Adams		
	Aird		Angus	
	Armstrong	Adamson	Attwell	
Abbot	Akinbiyi	Anderson	Adebola	Atkinson

ACCIDENTS

⚽ Mitchell Thomas was once nearly responsible for the early demise of Chris Waddle and Glen Hoddle. Thomas was accompanying Hoddle and Waddle on a Bermuda golf excursion and was the golf buggy driver. Deciding to drive down a steep slope, he discovered that it ended in a cliff edge. At the last minute Hoddle and Waddle jumped clear and the buggy ended up embedded in a tree.

- After he had left Burnley, ex-player-manager Chris Waddle was still ballooning shots over the bar at non-League Worksop. One shot flew right over the stand and smashed the windscreen of teammate Darren Brookes's motor van, leading to a £239 repair bill.

- Jamie Hoyland was nicknamed 'panda' by his colleagues, on account of the two black eyes he received in a car accident.

ACCRINGTON STANLEY

- Despite their close proximity, Burnley have never played against Accrington Stanley in either League or Cup competitions.

- There was a different club called Accrington, who were co-founders, alongside Burnley, of the Football League in 1888–89. Over the five seasons the clubs met honours were even, with each team winning three times and drawing the rest. Even the goals scored were 17 all.

- The Clarets played a friendly at Peel Park in the 1950s to christen the Accrington floodlights, and since the 1990s they have frequently played pre-season friendlies.

ALBION ROVERS

About 20 years ago, the Revd David Wiseman found himself preaching at the Congregational Church in Coatbridge, Lanarkshire. After the morning service, as he was greeting the local worshippers outside the church, he saw some floodlights across the road. Being a curious fellow, he asked whom the football ground belonged to. 'Ah, that's the Wee Rovers!' came the reply. On further questioning, David discovered that the 'Wee Rovers' were Albion Rovers, a Scottish Third Division team.

And though David never returned to Coatbridge, and though he has never seen the 'Wee Rovers' play, he was smitten. He now writes in the club programme every week – yes, a Burnley historian writes regularly for a Scottish team. It is a mixture of Lancashire and Lanarkshire football chat – Clarets and Coatbridge all in one.

Here are a few excerpts:

- 'How about this for a Clarets–Scots team, formed of entirely Scottish players who have played for our Burnley team while I've stood and worshipped. Adam Blacklaw (Aberdeen), Jock Aird (Jeanfield Swifts), Jock Winton (Jeanfield Swifts), Bobby Seith (Coatbridge), Jim Thomson (Provanside Hibernians), Ian Britton (Dundee), Willie Morgan (Fishcross), Peter McKay (Newburgh), Andy Lochhead (Renfrew Juniors), Ted McMinn (Castle Douglas), Tommy Hutchinson (Alloa Athletic) and res. Doug Newlands (Aberdeen). The places in brackets refer either to their birthplace or their previous club. And yes, in the early 1950s we did actually have a pair of very good full-backs from Jeanfield Swifts!' *September 2007*

- 'I was moved by a message on the Albion Rovers' website from 'Nanook', who lives in the Shetlands and supports the Wee Rovers. He's only seen two games this season. A bit like my friend, Andrew Morris, who supports Burnley. Andrew lives in New York but still has a season ticket at Turf Moor. He usually manages about six games a season! Just imagine, travelling 3,000 miles each way, the meals, the cost, the time involved? Still, his Mum back in Burnley is always glad to see him. I haven't the courage to tell her who he has actually come home to see! But after a lifetime of allegiance to the Clarets, I reckon she knows!' **November 2008**

- '"Well, we did it! WE DID IT!" my son Christian shouted down the phone to his mother at 10.30pm from Stamford Bridge at the final whistle. "WE WON!" The Chelsea supporters have never suffered, never cried and couldn't accept being beaten. Over four seasons they've lost only four times at home. Just imagine, Albion Rovers fans going to Glasgow and beating Celtic or Rangers in the Cup, and you can share my feelings right now!' **November 2008**

- 'I wish all my fellow Wee Rovers fans all the best for this afternoon – I still have every confidence in a Play-off place at the end of the season for both the Clarets and the Rovers (and it's not Blackburn I'm talking about!)' **August 2008**

'ALIENS' PLAYING FOR BURNLEY!

Dear Sir,
The ridiculous extent to which professional football is now pushed is yielding fruit in widespread disgust. It is laughable to hear of the supreme struggles which are entered upon to secure the services of some Scotchman or other alien to serve in the ranks of the Burnley team. It is contemptible to place these distinguished outsiders in the team, and fight Burnley's battles with foreigners. 'Good gates' are the great objects which the committee appears to have in view. It does not matter to them who sails under Burnley's colours, so long as they can put sensation into the game, give it a 'sporting' flavour and obtain splendid 'gates'.

All this importation of 'kickers', etc, is done under cover of furthering the cause of recreation. The system adopted, is to my mind, dishonest, unhealthy and demoralising, and the sooner there is put into operation a purification process, and the game of football encouraged on true lines, so much the better for Burnley and its reputation.
    Yours truly,
    HONESTY
Burnley Express,1890s

ALL-ROUNDERS

Within Burnley FC the record of Andy Farrell, a player in the 1980s and 1990s, takes some beating. He played in every shirt then available from numbers one to 12 and

14 during his six-year Turf Moor career. He also scored at least one goal in each shirt, except numbers one and nine. His time as goalkeeper came in 1991 when goalie Chris Pearce was sent off.

Outside of football, the best-known person in Burnley in the late Victorian era was Walter Place. Burnley-born and bred, Walter first played for Burnley in 1886–87. Altogether, he played in 129 games for the club and scored nine goals.

He would compete in any sport and do it well. He was one of the fastest sprinters in Burnley and he specialised in running backwards too. He was a roller skater, a snooker player, a swimmer and a champion marksman with the rifle. He also played cricket for Burnley and was a leading local bowler. Few people could match him at any of these sports. He bred and flew pigeons and won competitions at that too.

However, he was maybe best known off the football pitch for his exploits in the wrestling ring. In 1904 he fought the Russian champion Hackenschmidt and won, thereby gaining the reputation of being the best wrestler in England. Walter Place was a true Burnley legend.

ALLITERATION

Over the years, local newspapers (especially in Victorian and Edwardian days) specialised in headlines involving alliteration. Here are a few to illustrate the point:
'Turfites towelled at Toffeeopolis'
'Turfites topple over at Teesside'
'Bolton batter baffled Burnley'
'Shocking Show by Second String'
'Bully for Burnley, Bitter Beer for Burton'
'Masterful Manoeuvring Methods – Magnificent Marksmanship' (3–0 versus Wolves)
'Waiting for Whistle Wielder' (when the referee was late!)
'Triumphant Turfites turn tables on Tykes' (beating Hull 4–2)
'Lancashire lads lick Lincoln!'
'Praise for Players – particularly Parker!'
'Stiff Struggle with Southerners for Supremacy'
'Turfites triumph over Trinity at Trentside'
'Cheese County Contingent Completely Conquered!' (After a 3–0 win over Stockport)
The newspapers were not averse to praising the opposition either:
'Butler's brilliancy baulks Burnley boys!' or
'Gould gets good goal for Glossop!'
The shortest and maybe the best was 'Reserves receive reverse!'

ANIMAL ANTICS

⊛ Unable to keep his pet greyhound in his lodgings, 1950s full-back Harold Mather, along with his colleague Arthur Woodruff, once kept his dog underneath the Cricket Field Stand at Turf Moor. It never won a single race, probably because it was overweight. It was a great favourite with the other players, who fed it too many scraps and titbits.

⊕ One day Harold and Arthur raced the dog at Blackburn and bet all their money in the hope that it would win: it lost. Having lost all their money, they walked the long trudge all the way back to Burnley along the canal towpath with the dog. They were utterly miserable and fed up with a dog that was completely useless. 'Let's chuck it in't canal' said Arthur. Harold thought for a minute, 'Nay, ah can't do that ter't poor bugger…let's just run away and leave it. It'll never bloody catch us up!'

⊕ In more recent times, Paul Weller and Glen Little co-owned a greyhound, but did not keep it under the Cricket Field Stand. And while on the subject of 'pets', 1960s star Brian O'Neil was never happier than when he was rearing his pigs on an allotment in Towneley.

⊕ Burnley once received an addition to the team when centre-forward Joe 'Andy' was given a monkey wearing the Burnley colours as a mascot. For several games the monkey would come on to the pitch before the game and climb on to the crossbar to perform various tricks.

ANAGRAMS OR MANARAGS OR GRANMAAS OR RAGAMANS

It is amazing what you can do with the names of a few Burnley players. Try these out for size:

AGREE WET RIFE GOLD

A DON ROBS MINT

TEN BE FARMER

CODS DOME PIERS

JEAN NOD ROSE

YON REAR PIT

ALERT! WE WAVER

SPOT RASH LACE

LET TILLY BOIL!

BE ROUGH ALTERS BEECH

LITTLE BY BINS

TREE BRACE JAMS

GROW LIME NAIL

BLINKING 'P' RATION

AVOIDING TERM 'RD'

BILLION 'L' MATH

FEATHER 'C' PULL

TILL GENTLE

GUAGE SLAP COIN

CRADLED WISH

LOANS AN EVENTS

BARELY HURL MAT

TEMPER 'E' ROLL

SOUND WE GLAND

ANNIVERSARIES

100th year as a Football League Club…1988
50th year as a Division One Team…1975
100th season in the Football League…1999
50th anniversary of winning the Division One title…2010
50 years since Jimmy McIlroy came to Burnley…2000

22 years since the 'Orient' game...2009
96 years since Burnley won the FA Cup...2010
128 years since the club's formation...2010
33 years since the club last played in Division One...2009
100 years since Burnley adopted claret colours...2010

APPRENTICES

Young Burnley footballers in the 1960s (Willie Irvine, Dave Thomas, etc) had a list of duties they were expected to fulfil, besides their daily training schedule. They had to clean out the Turf Moor public toilets, often with a shovel, paint barriers and turnstiles, clean dressing rooms and staff and player toilets, sweep the terraces, take playing kit to the laundry, cut grass and clean the boots of other players. (The boots had to be 100 per cent right, checking studs, polishing and checking laces.) The job they hated the most was pitch repairing on a Monday after a Saturday game, replacing divots one by one!

It is all a far cry from the current style of young professional footballers.

AFTER BURNLEY

Bobby Seith became a chiropodist.
Trevor Steven became a TV pundit.
Alan Stevenson became commercial manager at Coventry City.
Jimmy Strong had a poultry farm.
Jim Thomson became a brewery sales manager.
Jock Winton had a coal merchant's round.
Ian Wright became a well-known TV personality.
Dave Thomas became a gardener and then a PE teacher.
Billy Ingham became a Burnley bus driver.
Adie Randall became a postman.
Willie Irvine, among other things, had a window cleaning round.
Jimmy McIlroy became a *Burnley Express* journalist.
Les Latcham became an insurance representative.
Brian Pilkington became an estate-agent.
Trevor Meredith became a schoolteacher.
Steve Kindon became an after-dinner speaker.
Colin Waldron became a bookie.
John Connelly ran a fish and chip shop.
Billy Morris ran an off-licence.
Derek Scott became a policeman in Burnley.
Eddie Mosscrop became a schoolteacher.
Brian Miller owned a newsagent's shop.
Paul Fletcher was involved in football stadia design.
Peter Noble ran a sports shop in Burnley market.

Arthur Bellamy was a milkman.
Albert Cheesebrough ran a butcher's shop.
Ralph Coates became a Leisure Centre manager.
Billy Hamilton had a sports shop.
Billy Rodaway worked as a lorry driver and a scaffolder.
Jack Hillman had a sweet shop.
Joe Jakub became a journalist.
Willie Morgan became involved in marketing and promotions.
Geoff Nulty became a property developer.
Full-back Jock Aird emigrated to New Zealand, while Doug Collins went to Australia.
Both Arthur Bellamy and Billy Gray became groundsmen; Arthur at Burnley and
Billy at Nottingham Forest.

MOST APPEARANCES (League games only)

Jerry Dawson	522
Jimmy McIlroy	439
John Angus	438/1
Alan Stevenson	438
Tommy Cummings	434
Jimmy Adamson	426
Martin Dobson	406/4
Fred Barron	400 (in the years when there were only 34–38 League games)
Brian Miller	379
George Waterfield	371
Billy Watson	346
Leighton James	331/5
Joe Taylor	323 (in the years when there were only 30–38 League games)
Adam Blacklaw	318
George Beel	316
Colin Waldron	308
Harold Mather	301
Brian Pilkington	300

MOST FIRST-TEAM APPEARANCES
(League, Cup, Friendlies, etc)

Jerry Dawson	569
Alan Stevenson	543
John Angus	520/1
Jimmy McIlroy	497
Martin Dobson	495/4
Jimmy Adamson	486

Tommy Cummings	479
Brian Miller	455
Fred Barron	423
Leighton James	397/6

MOST APPEARANCES IN ONE SEASON

Joe Jakub	65 games (1990–91)	(46 L, 3 FAC, 4 FLC, 12 others)
Marlon Beresford	62 games (1993–94)	(46 L, 4 FAC, 4 FLC, 8 others)
Chris Pearce	62 games (1987–88)	(46 L, 1 FAC, 4 FLC, 11 others)
Mike Phelan	61 games (1982–83)	(42 L, 7 FAC, 9 FLC, 3 others)
David Eyres	61 games (1993–94)	(45 L, 4 FAC, 4 FLC, 8 others)
Andy Farrell	61 games (1987–88)	(45 L, 1 FAC, 4 FLC, 11 others)
Steve Davis (1)	61 games (1990–91)	(46 L, 3 FAC, 3 FLC, 9 others)
Adam Blacklaw	60 games (1960–61)	(41 L, 7 FAC, 7 FLC, 5 others)
John Francis	60 games (1990–91)	(45 L, 3 FAC, 4 FLC, 8 others)
Roger Hansbury	60 games (1983–84)	(46 L, 5 FAC, 2 FLC, 7 others)

AS THE CROW FLIES

(In the 1880s players could only play for clubs which were within six miles of where they lived.)

'Burnley v Accrington protest'

'Lofthouse played for Accrington in a Cup tie at Accrington. The only objection was that Lofthouse had not lived within six miles of Accrington for two years last past month. At the protest meeting, an ordnance map was produced which showed that the distance from No. 2 Piccadilly, Accrington, to No. 17 Dixon Street, Witton (Lofthouse's birthplace) was five miles four and a half furlongs, this being according to the crow-fly, while the distance to the ground was over six miles. Because Major Mandarin of the FA was not prepared to go into the issue any further, he went along with the crow-fly distance, and the protest by Burnley was disallowed.'

Burnley News, November 1887

ATTENDANCES (Highest at Turf Moor to watch a Burnley game)

1.	v	Huddersfield (FA Cup)	1923–24	54,775
2.	v	Arsenal (FA Cup)	1936–37	54,445
3.	v	Liverpool (FA Cup)	1951–52	54,031
4.	v	Sunderland (FA Cup)	1952–53	53,105
5.	v	Blackpool (League)	1947–48	52,869
6.	v	Manchester United (FA Cup)	1953–54	52,847
7.	v	Bradford City (FA Cup)	1959–60	52,850

8.	v Newcastle United (FA Cup)	1953–54	52,011
9.	v Blackburn Rovers (FA Cup)	1959–60	51,501
10.	v Arsenal (FA Cup)	1952–53	51,025
11.	v Everton (FA Cup)	1961–62	50,514
12.	v Liverpool (FA Cup)	1962–63	49,827
13.	v Blackpool (League)	1949–50	49,815
14.	v Port Vale (FA Cup)	1949–50	49,692
15.	v Aston Villa (FA Cup)	1956–57	49,436
16.	v Middlesbrough (FA Cup)	1946–47	49,244
17.	v Sheffield Wednesday (FA Cup)	1960–61	48,894
18.	v Arsenal (League)	1947–48	47,958
19.	v Manchester United (League)	1959–60	47,696
20.	v Birmingham City (FA Cup)	1934–35	47,670
21.	v Hamburg (European Cup)	1960–61	47,000
22.	v Spurs (League)	1961–62	46,810

HIGHEST-EVER ATTENDANCES TO WATCH BURNLEY

1.	Wembley FA Cup Final (v Spurs)	1961–62	100,000
2.	Wembley FA Cup Final (v Charlton)	1946–47	98,215
3.	Wembley Sherpa Van Trophy Final (v Wolves)	1987–88	80,841
4.	Goodison Park Division One (v Everton)	1960–61	74,867
5.	Stuttgart Euro Fairs Cup (v Stuttgart)	1966–67	74,000
6.	Crystal Palace FA Cup Final (v Liverpool)	1913–14	72,778
7.	Maine Road FA Cup semi-final (v Liverpool)	1946–47	72,000
8.	Hamburg European Cup (v Hamburg)	1960–61	71,000
9.	Villa Park FA Cup semi-final (v Spurs)	1960–61	70,000
10.	Maine Road Division Two (v Manchester City)	1946–47	69,463
11.	Maine Road Division One (v Manchester City)	1959–60	65,981
12.	Old Trafford Division One (v Manchester United)	1959–60	62,673
13.	Stamford Bridge FA Cup (v Chelsea)	1926–27	62,238
14.	Highbury Division One (v Arsenal)	1947–48	62,125
15.	St James' Park Division Two (v Newcastle United)	1946–47	61,255
16.	Old Trafford Division One (v Manchester United)	1947–48	61,100
17.	Naples Euro Fairs Cup (v Napoli)	1966–67	60,000
18.	Villa Park FA Cup semi-final (v Fulham)	1961–62	59,989
19.	Old Trafford Division One (v Manchester United)	1975–76	59,726
20.	White Hart Lane Division One (v Spurs)	1960–61	58,737

LOWEST-EVER ATTENDANCES TO WATCH BURNLEY

1.=	Burnley v Barnsley (Division Two)	1900–01	400 approx
1.=	Burnley v Gainsborough Trinity (Division Two)	1901–02	400 approx

3.=	Burnley v Glossop (Division Two)	1902–03	500 approx
4.=	Burnley v Blackpool (Division Two)	1901–02	600 approx
4.=	Preston N.E. v Burnley (Division Two)	1901–02	600 approx
4.=	Blackpool v Burnley (Division Two)	1902–03	600 approx
4.=	Burnley v Burton United (Division Two)	1902–03	600 approx
8.=	Burnley v Leicester Fosse (Division Two)	1901–02	700 approx
9.=	Burnley v Doncaster (Division Two)	1901–02	800 approx
10.=	Stockport v Burnley (Division Two)	1900–01	1,000 approx
10.=	Birmingham v Burnley (Division Two)	1909–10	1,000 approx
10.=	Burnley v Bradford City (Division Two)	1903–04	1,000 approx
10.=	Newton Heath v Burnley (Division Two)	1901–02	1,000 approx
10.=	Burnley v Bristol City (Division Two)	1901–02	1,000 approx
10.=	Notts Co. v Burnley (Football League)	1889–90	1,000 approx
10.=	West Brom v Burnley (Football League)	1892–93	1,000 approx
10.=	Burslem Port Vale v Burnley (Division Two)	1900–01	1,000 approx
10.=	Burnley v Chesterfield (Division Two)	1901–02	1,000 approx
10.=	Burnley v Burslem Port Vale (Division Two)	1901–02	1,000 approx
10.=	Burnley v Barnsley (Division Two)	1902–03	1,000 approx
21.=	Wolves v Burnley (Football League)	1891–92	1,200 approx
21.=	Burnley v Burslem Port Vale (Division Two)	1902–03	1,200 approx
21.=	Burnley v Preston (Division Two)	1902–03	1,200 approx
24.	Torquay v Burnley (Division Four)	1985–86	1,335
25.=	Burnley v Burslem Port Vale (Division Two)	1904–05	1,500 approx
25.=	Burnley v Stoke (Division One)	1895–96	1,500 approx
25.=	Burnley v Chesterfield (Division Two)	1905–06	1,500 approx
25.=	Burton United v Burnley (Division Two)	1906–07	1,500 approx
29.	Hartlepool v Burnley (Division Four)	1987–88	1,506
30.	Newport County v Burnley (Division Four)	1984–85	1,689
31.	Burnley v Colchester United (Division Four)	1986–87	1,696
32.	Burnley v Cardiff City (Division Four)	1986–87	1,717
33.	Halifax v Burnley (Division Four)	1986–87	1,735
34.	Aldershot v Burnley (Division Four)	1985–86	1,744
35.	Derby Co. v Burnley (Division One)	1894–95	1,750 approx
36.	Scunthorpe v Burnley (Division Four)	1986–87	1,770
37.	Burnley v Exeter City (Division Four)	1986–87	1,792
38.	Wrexham v Burnley (Division Four)	1987–88	1,821
39.	Cambridge United v Burnley (Division Four)	1986–87	1,874
40.	Burnley v Hereford (Division Four)	1986–87	1,961

HIGHEST AVERAGE ATTENDANCES AT TURF MOOR

1. 33,621 in 1947–48   First season back in Division One, ended the season in third place
2. 31,535 in 1920–21   Championship-winning season

3. 30,290 in 1948–49   Second season back in Division One
4. 28,480 in 1952–53   Sixth in Division One
5. 28,296 in 1950–51   10th in Division One
6. 28,151 in 1953–54   Seventh in Division One
7. 27,631 in 1949–50   10th in Division One
8. 27,125 in 1961–62   Runners-up in Division One
9. 26,978 in 1959–60   Championship-winning season
10. 26,624 in 1951–52   14th in Division One
11. 25,856 in 1946–47   Division Two promotion season
12. 25,180 in 1962–63   Third in Division One
13. 25,094 in 1954–55   10th in Division One
14. 23,827 in 1960–61   Fourth in Division One
15. 23,733 in 1958–59   Seventh in Division One

LOWEST AVERAGE ATTENDANCES AT TURF MOOR

1. 1,500 in 1902–03   Bottom of Division Two. Re-elected. Worst gates in England!
2. 2,225 in 1901–02   Division Two.
3. 3,204 in 1985–86   First season in Division Four. Bottom half of the table.
4. 3,275 in 1900–01   First season in Division Two after relegation.
5. 3,342 in 1986–87   Worst season in the club's history: third from bottom in Division Four.
6. 4,100 in 1903–04   Division Two.
7. 4,125 in 1897–98   First season in Division Two. Champions!
8. 4,177 in 1984–85   Division Three. Bottom four. Relegated.
9. 4,260 in 1904–05   Mid-table in Division Two.
10. 4,975 in 1905–06   Mid-table in Division Two.

BEST ATTENDANCES IN DIVISION FOUR.

It was a sad day for the Clarets when they were relegated to Division Four in 1985. However, it became good news for the other clubs in the League. Though the Turf Moor gates were dismal and the lowest for 80 years, they were still pretty good for Division Four. Indeed, even in their first season the Clarets were the fifth-best supported team in the division, with an average of 3,204. The next season, 1986–87 (the grim fight against relegation), saw the average gate at 3,342 (seventh best in the division).

The club revived in 1987–88 and so did the attendances. The average gate rose to 6,282 (second only to Champions Wolves).

For the following four seasons Burnley led the way in the entire division for average home attendances. In 1988–89 the average Turf Moor attendance was 7,062. This was by far the best attendance figure in Division Four and even topped 20 teams in Division Three and five in Division Two (Hull, Oxford, Birmingham, Walsall and Shrewsbury)!

In 1989–90, though the average attendance at Turf Moor fell to 6,222, that figure topped 19 teams in Division Three and one Second Division club (Oxford United).

In season 1990–91 the Turf Moor average rose to 7,882. This was better than all the clubs in Division Three (except for Stoke), five Second Division clubs (Plymouth, Charlton, Hull, Bristol Rovers and Oxford) and even a First Division club (Wimbledon)!

In 1991–92 the Clarets at last won promotion and, despite their success, the other Division Four teams must have been sad to see them go, as with the travelling supporters the Clarets usually gave their opponents their best home gate of the season. Their average gate of 10,521 gave them the title of the best-supported team in the Fourth Division and topped all Division Three teams (except Stoke, West Brom and Birmingham). They also beat 14 Second Division clubs and even two in the First Division (Luton and Wimbledon).

GOOD AWAY FORM?

'There has been much discussion in town this week after Burnley's away win at Derby County. People have been asking just how many games have Burnley won away from home? The record is as follows – 1888 Bolton, 1889 none, 1890 Stoke and 1891 Derby.'
Burnley News, 1891.

Ed – on reference to Burnley records, the reporter at the time has omitted to mention an away win at Sunderland in 1890. Here is the complete record for the first nine seasons:

1888–89   Bolton 4–3
1889–90   Stoke 4–3
1890–91   Sunderland 3–2, Derby 4–2
1891–92   Derby 1–0, Darwen 6–2
1892–93   Everton 1–0, Accrington 4–0, Aston Villa 3–1
1893–94   Preston 2–1, Sheff Wed 1–0
1894–95   Liverpool 3–0, West Brom 1–0, Derby 2–0
1895–96   West Brom 2–0, Bury 4–3
1896–97   Aston Villa 3–0, Liverpool 2–1

Altogether, just 18 away wins in the first nine seasons!

In 1920–21 the club only lost five away games. This record was equalled in 1981–82, but by far the best season for away form has been 1972–73, when the Clarets only lost twice.

WORST AWAY FORM

Between 21 December 1901 and 10 October 1903 Burnley played 31 consecutive League games away from home without winning. They drew five and lost 26!

A TO Z OF BURNLEY

⊕ **A**lbert Alderman came to Turf Moor from Derby County in 1933. He scored his first goal in 1933–34 against Barnsley.

- Barnsley was the club from which Tommy Boyle came to Turf Moor in 1911. While at Barnsley, he had captained the team beaten by Newcastle in the 1910 Cup Final at Crystal Palace.

- Crystal Palace was the scene four years later in 1914 when Burnley won the FA Cup thanks to a goal by Bert Freeman. One of the great stories that day was how Jerry Dawson voluntarily stood down from the team.

- Dawson played in the Burnley first team for 22 seasons, from 1907 to 1929. He also played for England when he was in his 30s.

- England's leading forward in the early 1920s was the magical Bob Kelly. At Turf Moor in 1914, Kelly scored in his first game when partnering Bert Freeman.

- Freeman was the top scoring centre-forward of his day, creating records at Arsenal and Everton before coming to Burnley. In all he scored 115 goals for Burnley.

- Goals were what made George Beel famous. He is the club record scorer, with 188 in 337 club appearances to his credit. He was the top Burnley goalscorer for six seasons. This record was never equalled, but Billy Hamilton came close.

- Hamilton (Billy) was the next Burnley player to top score for at least four seasons. An Irish international, Hamilton played in the 1982 World Cup for Northern Ireland. Over the years, the Irish team has featured many Clarets, including Irvine, Elder and McIlroy.

- Irvine (Willie) scored 97 goals for Burnley in 144 games. Irvine came into the Burnley team in 1963, just two months after Jimmy McIlroy had been transferred.

- Jimmy McIlroy, one of the most famous of all Clarets, is the only player to stand comparison to the immortal Bob Kelly. Both inside-forwards. Both internationals. Both legendary.

- Kelly was by far the most outstanding Burnley player in the 1920s. In the 1930s it was probably Tommy Lawton who stole the local headlines.

- Lawton began his career at Turf Moor. Tommy, later an England international, was a Bolton boy and went to the same school as Harold Mather.

- Mather (Harold) was a fine full-back, playing in over 300 League games. He signed on in 1938 and played his last game 16 seasons later, aged 34. He was one of the oldest full-backs at Turf Moor until Keith Newton.

- Newton came from Everton and was already an international full-back. When he played his last game for Burnley he was in his 37th year! In his last season one of the Overson brothers (Richard) made his debut.

⚽ Overson (Richard and Vincent) are the last brothers to have played for Burnley. Brother Vinnie made his debut the same month as Paul Fletcher made his last appearance for the Clarets.

⚽ Paul Fletcher was Burnley's top scorer in 1972–73, the year the Clarets won promotion back into Division One. Runners-up that memorable season were Queen's Park Rangers.

⚽ QPR had chased Burnley for the title all season. The Clarets stayed in Division One for three seasons, before being relegated again in 1976.

⚽ Relegation in 1976 was followed by relegation again to Division Three in 1980. And promotion in 1982. And relegation again back to Division Three in 1983. One player who stayed at Turf Moor during this entire period was goalkeeper Alan Stevenson.

⚽ Stevenson played in 543 games for the Clarets, playing with the likes of Trevor Steven in 1983, and right back to Dave Thomas in 1972.

⚽ Thomas was the youngest player ever to play for Burnley in the First Division when he played against Everton in 1967. In those days Dave played under manager Harry Potts.

⚽ Under Harry Potts the club played in the Cup Final in 1962. Twenty-five years later they had to be victors in the last game of the season to stay in the League.

⚽ Victors they were in a never-to-be-forgotten last game against Orient. Since then, the old club have battled back to the Championship, helped by many great players, including Glen Little and Ian Wright.

⚽ Wright came to Turf Moor in 2000 and helped secure a famous promotion from Division Two with four memorable goals in the last few games. It was an exceptional season, finishing with four consecutive victories. Four draws (X) would not have been enough!

⚽ X for the fan usually means a draw, which is often not enough. We needed to win at York in 1992.

⚽ York was the place where Burnley won promotion from Division Four in 1992. 'They came to York in their thousands; they're going home as Champions!' Was that the zenith?

⚽ Zenith? Not yet!

THE 'B' TEAM

Beresford
Bamford   Basnett
Brown (A.)   Boyle   Bray
Bruton   Britten   Beel   Brocklebank   Biggins

Subs: Billingham, Branch, Brass and Brown (J.)

BALLS

In the 1945–46 FA Cup Final the ball burst. Prior to the 1946–47 Final, which involved Burnley, the referee was asked what the odds were for the ball to burst again. 'About a million to one', the referee replied, smiling. The ball burst during the game!

BBC

'Records from the BBC Written Archives inform us that on at least six occasions the BBC visited Turf Moor from 1947–52, and only once did such an outside broadcast result in defeat, this being the opening game of the season, 1950–51, against Arsenal. Not surprising really, as the Gunners had not lost at Turf Moor since 1926. Apart from this blemish though, listening to Kenneth Wolstenholme and the Clarets in the immediate post-war years was five wins out of six.'
Burnley's Greatest Goal, Peter Fyles

BEDROOM GOLF

'After signing for the Clarets I was introduced to my new roommate Peter Noble. On our first trip away from home we played in London and stayed at the Great Western Hotel, Paddington.

"What do you normally do after dinner?" I asked Nobby. "Play golf" was his reply. "Can you play?" he enquired. At the time I was playing off a seven handicap at Pleasington Golf Club and like many other professional footballers I had become quite addicted to the game, but the idea of playing at 8.30 in the evening in the centre of London the night before an important game seemed ridiculous.

"Where do you play?" I asked. "In Paul Fletcher and Alan Stevenson's bedroom" came the reply. I must admit I was intrigued to find out about this bedroom golf. But absolutely flabbergasted when the door opened to the Fletcher/Stevenson room. There they stood, both completely naked except each was wearing a jock strap, golf shoes (rubber soled!), golf glove, flat cap and Alan Stevenson was pulling a Jack Nicholas golf bag….on a trolley with one club, a putter, in it!

"What the bloody hell is going on?" I asked Alan Stevenson as he did a few warming-up exercises – like golfers do. So he explained. Twelve months earlier he had bought a second half hickory shafted putter from a second-hand shop in Praid Street, across from the Great Western. When he got back to the room he and Fletch started putting on the carpet in the hotel room.

They would have a contest to see who could hit the "pot" (toilet), then flip the ball into the waste paper bin in the least number of shots. Then another few "holes" were added, then the etiquette and correct dress developed. They called the game "POT BIN" with hole number one always being a dog-leg down the room into the bathroom and the last "hole" always the bin. The game was played as a Stableford with all four "teeing off", then each team picking the best "drive" and playing alternate shots.

Great tournaments were played, always named by Stevo. "The Great Western Open", "The Swindon Post House Masters", "The Norwich Moat House Classic". The club was even taken on tour and the "Bermudan Medal" and the "QE2 Celebrity Am" were played for. Stevo and Fletch challenged every pairing at the club. Apart from myself and Nobby, Waldron and Collins, James and Ingham, Thomson and Rodaway, even a Miller and Holland pairing tried their luck. And nobody ever won! This was mainly because Stevo and Fletch were the biggest cheats I have ever come across. They always had some trick up their sleeves. After struggling to flick the ball into the bath you would find it to be half full of water. "Water hazard, one shot penalty!" Stevo would shout. "How is it that the bath was empty when you were in here?" I would ask. "There must have been a storm!" came the reply from Fletch.

On another occasion in the middle of a tense game we rang down to reception for coffee and sandwiches. The young maid nearly dropped the tray as she walked into the room with all four of us wearing only our golfing attire. "Put the tray on the fourth green, and mind you don't step into the bunker" said Stevo as she placed the tray upon the bed...'
(as told by Keith Newton in *BFC & Me*)

BEDROOM WALLS!

'Alan Morton – the only one in existence! The smallest forward in the Scotland team, but the artfullest, trickiest, cutest little bit of foot devilry ever set loose among an England defence. He is admired all over the kingdom and he has a framed portrait hanging on the bedroom wall of Jack Hill, captain of Burnley and England.'
Glasgow Evening News 1925

BEE HOLE END

One end of the pitch has long been called the Bee Hole End, named after the Bee Hole Coalpit. It first began to be used in 1908 when the *Burnley Gazette* wrote, 'An additional gate has been provided at the Bee Hole End for the convenience of people residing in that part of the town.'

It is only behind the goal – not in another country – 'in that part of the town indeed!'

BEFORE BURNLEY

Alan Brown was a policeman.
Jerry Dawson was a blacksmith.
Jimmy McIlroy was a bricklayer.
Willie Irvine was a grocery delivery boy.
George Halley was a plasterer.
Peter Noble was a painter and decorator.
John Connelly was a joiner for the NCB.
Brian Miller also worked for the NCB.

BEGINNINGS

⚽ In an issue of the *Burnley Express* dated 12 August 1882 the subject of 'Football' is given four lines alongside much larger articles regarding 'The Burnley Tramways', 'The Results of Slippery Pavements', 'The Proposed Extension of the Abattoirs' and the 'Burnley Floral and Horticultural Show'.

⚽ A month later the football news had seven lines on the Burnley versus Brierfield match. The club was still in its infancy, as witnessed by the fact that half a page was given to match reports on Blackburn Rovers versus Liverpool, Accrington versus Haslingden, Blackburn Olympic versus Witton, Darwen versus Padiham and Church versus Clitheroe! And all this in the *Burnley Express*!

⚽ In the 1880s the *Burnley Express* set out articles in alphabetical order, and so it was that 'Football' appeared sandwiched between 'Farming' and 'Funeral Arrangements'! For many years the news of the local football team in Burnley appeared on the same page as 'Draughts Problems' and 'Chess Corner', and though the accepted and long-established sport of cricket was often on page three, eventually football news became relegated to the back page (where it still is today).

⚽ As late as 1910 football reports shared the same page as rabbit coursing, starling shooting, knur and spell and pigeon shooting. This was until the Esperanto Column appeared on the same page, which limited football coverage even more.

BEST ATTACK

⚽ In 1960–61 Burnley scored 102 League goals in 42 games, an average of 2.42 goals per game. Added to this League record, they scored 37 further goals in Cup ties (FA, League Cup and European Cup) in 19 games.

⚽ The following season,1961–62, they scored 101 League goals (plus 16 FA Cup goals).

- On only three other occasions have the club averaged more than two goals a game (in a 42 or 46 match season).
  1959–60 – 85 goals
  1926–27 – 91 goals
  1925–26 – 85 goals

- However, in 1897–98, when there were only 30 League games, the club scored 80 League goals (an average of 2.66 goals per game).

BEST DEFENCE

- Without a doubt, the best defensive record for the Clarets was the 29 they conceded in 1946–47 when they had the 'Iron Curtain' defence – Strong, Woodruff, Mather, Attwell, Brown and Bray (0.69 goals per game).

- In 1972–73 (promotion to Division One) the club conceded just 35 goals.

- In Championship year 1920–21 'Halley, Boyle 'n Watson' conceded only 36 goals.

- Certainly worthy of a mention is that in 2004–05 the Burnley defence only conceded 39 goals in 46 games at an average of 0.84 goals per game.

BEST CUP RUNS

- The best Cup run was in 1913–14 when the club played eight FA Cup ties, winning six and drawing two, on their way to winning the FA Cup at Crystal Palace. This could be extended to 10 games unbeaten, as they won the first two rounds the following season!

- Similarly, if the previous season, 1912–13, is added, the club played 16 consecutive FA Cup ties between 1912 and 1915 and only lost once. Between 1959 and 1962 Burnley played 22 consecutive FA Cup ties and only lost twice.

BEST SEASONS?

This is a matter of personal opinion, but here goes:
1. 1959–60   League Champions and quarter-finals in FA Cup
2. 1920–21   League Champions and last 16 in FA Cup
3. 1913–14   12th in League and FA Cup Winners
4. 1961–62   Runners-up in League and FA Cup Finalists
5. 1919–20   Runners-up in League and last 32 in FA Cup
6. 1946–47   Promoted from Division Two and FA Cup Finalists

7. 1960–61   Fourth in League and FA Cup semi-finalists
8.= 1965–66   Third in League and last 32 in FA Cup
8.= 1962–63   Third in League and last 32 in FA Cup
10. 1914–15   Fourth in League and last 16 in FA Cup
11. 1973–74   Sixth in League and FA Cup semi-finalists
12.= 1921–22   Third in League and last 64 in FA Cup
12.= 1947–48   Third in League and last 64 in FA Cup
14. 1897–98   Champions of Division Two and FA Cup quarter-finalists
15. 1972–73   Champions of Division Two and last 64 in FA Cup

BETTER LATE THAN NEVER

Bobby Seith had to wait 40 years to receive his League Championship medal for being in the 1959–60 team. He left the club before the end of the season and the club refused to award him a medal, allegedly because of a fall-out with chairman Bob Lord.

When Barry Kilby became chairman years later the omission was put right. On 23 October 1999, Bobby received his medal to a standing ovation from the Burnley fans, many of whom had never seen him play. Justice was done. And to make the story even better, Bobby actually stayed overnight in Bob Lord's old house, now with new owners.

BELIEVE IT OR NOT

- When Burnley beat Loughborough 9–3 in 1897–98 it was the club's highest-ever League score. Jimmy Ross scored five, including a hat-trick within 14 minutes (the League's quickest?). 'King James', as he was known, had earlier in his career scored eight goals for Preston North End when they beat Hyde United 26–0 in an FA Cup tie.

- Alan Taylor only ever played one FA Cup tie for the Clarets, and scored a hat-trick in the game, against Penrith.

- In the final match of the 19th century at Turf Moor Edgar Chadwick scored a hat-trick as Burnley beat Glossop 3–1. In the final match of the 20th century at Turf Moor Andy Payton scored a hat-trick as Burnley beat Oxford United 3–2.

- The first player to score a hat-trick in the Football League was Walter Tait of Burnley. On 8 September 1888, he scored three in a 4–3 win over Bolton.

- Peter Kippax played in the 1948 British Olympics game versus Yugoslavia when Boris Stankowic became the first player ever to be sent off at Wembley.

- Players who knew him have told of how Alan Brown would sometimes hit his head against the woodwork of the changing room door before a game. It appeared to get him in the right frame of mind.

- While returning on a cruise ship from an American tour, Tommy Cummings said 'Anyone fancy a game of snooker?' At once Brian Miller replied 'I'm up for it!' (Think about it!)

- Martin Buchan, who was Burnley's manager very briefly, is the only player to captain both English and Scottish FA Cup-winning sides: Aberdeen in 1970 and Manchester United in 1977.

- John Murray, one of the 'Burnley Babes' of the late 1960s, became the first player to score a Football League hat-trick on 31 March 1973, for Bury at Doncaster, and then be sent off.

- Before a match in the 1960s most players limited themselves to a light lunch, such as a piece of fish or toast. Ray Pointer, meanwhile, would tuck into steak and chips!

- When Frank Saul was sent off for Spurs at Burnley on 4 December 1965 he was the first Spurs player to be sent off in a League game for 37 years.

BIBLICAL BURNLEY

Over the years there have been numerous players with Biblical names at Burnley – here are just a few:

Old Testament:
Daniel (Friel), Samuel (Hargreaves), Bethel (Robinson), David (Eyres), Jonathan (Cretney), Benjamin (Green), Reuben (Grice), Joshua (Harris), Abraham (Hartley), Jeremiah (Dawson), Adam (Blacklaw), Nathan (Dyer), Micah (Hyde), Joel (Pilkington).

To sum up – one place, one king, six books of the bible, one son of a king, two sons of Jacob, one prophet, one father of the nation and Adam himself.

New Testament:
Simeon (Lord), John (Aird), Thomas (Cassidy), Matthew (Heywood), Zacharias (Carr), Joseph (Taylor), James (Crabtree), Andrew (Haddow), Peter (Dougall), Philip (Eastwood), Levy (Thorpe), Stephen (Heys), Cornelius (Hogan), Paul (Bradshaw), Mark (Allen).

To sum up – eight disciples, three prophets, two apostles, one Roman centurion and the father of Jesus.

BISHOP'S BLESSING!

'Now we must begin to think of football. It will be a pleasure to visit Turf Moor on Saturday afternoons and see what there is to be seen. I hope that Burnley people will support their club win or lose for it is a sporting effort in which both directors and players are engaged, to keep the flag of the club flying in such very hard times.

I could wish that football crowds showed a little more sportsmanship than is sometimes the case.'
Bishop of Burnley, September 1932

BIZARRE

✪ The *Burnley Express* reported in 1983 that 20 minutes into the game against Crewe and with the score at 1–1 a large group of Burnley fans tried to climb OUT of the ground. One was caught and fined £20 for damages to turnstiles.

✪ Chris Woods, who was Burnley goalkeeper for a short while when Chris Waddle was manager, suffered the bizarre injury of a badly cut finger while trying to undo the string of his tracksuit bottoms. It forced him to miss an England game.

BINGO

Paul Fletcher tells the following tale, 'While travelling back from a tour of the Caribbean on the *QE2* in 1975, the players would gather at 4pm in the afternoons to play bingo in the Queen's Ballroom. We would gather in "Mick McNally's bar" on the second tier of this beautiful room along with 500 to 600 other holidaymakers trying to win one of the first prizes which would be equivalent to about a thousand pounds today.

After 15 numbers had been called, Colin Waldron had not had one single number up, so in frustration he crossed out every single number….except 15 and 28. At this moment Brian Flynn arrived (he'd been in his cabin playing with his Action Man…he was only 17 at the time!). Waldron said to Flynn, "Keep an eye on this card while I go to the loo" and he promptly vanished around the corner.

Needless to say, within a few minutes out came numbers 15 and 28, which sent Brian Flynn into a wild frenzy of delight. Not only the team but the rest of the passengers started cheering and screaming as Flynny made his way down the long, spiral staircase to the centre of the ballroom. After he signed a few autographs and had done a 10-minute interview on stage (the caller was a big Burnley fan), before being presented with the cheque, the caller checked his card…'
BFC & Me

BLACKADDER

And yes, the Clarets have had a player signed on for them, once upon a time, called Blackadder. Bill Blackadder was a local lad born in Padiham in 1899. In 1922 he signed on for Burnley as a promising left-half, but he was overshadowed by established first-teamers like Billy Watson and Alf Basnett and so never managed to make the first team at Turf Moor. He left Burnley in 1924 when he was transferred to Accrington Stanley, where he made 11 first-team appearances.

BLACKBURN
(Be it Rovers, Olympic, Witton, Lancs FA or what have you.)

'Not as well up as might be desired!' Burnley v Blackburn Rovers 0–10, 28 October 1882

'A match played between two teams of Burnley and Blackburn Rovers took place at Calder Vale on Saturday last. The Rovers had the game in their hands throughout, and won by 10 goals to none. In justice to the Burnley players, it must be stated that this is their first season of playing Association rules and consequently they are not as well up as might be desired. Nevertheless, they played very creditably, especially Chase (goalkeeper) and Brown (centre).'
Burnley Express

'Bad taste' – Burnley v Blackburn Olympic, 1883

'By the bye, from what I hear, some of the Olympians sounded their Paeans of Praise as their defeated adversaries passed them in the street after the game. This shows bad taste and is only on a par with a party of juveniles winning a game of marbles. There's a lot of the schoolboy about it!'
Burnley Express

'Hothouse plants!' – Burnley v Witton, 1883–84

'The game was played in anything but pleasant weather with a strong wind blowing and rain falling in torrents. At half-time, the Witton players refused to continue and they left the ground amid hooting and cries of "summer footballers!" and "hothouse plants!" from the Burnley spectators.'
Burnley Express

'Clearly overstretched' – Burnley v Blackburn Olympic, 1884

'Blackburn Olympic were clearly overstretched and seemed to lose heart considerably, the climax being reached when three or four of the Olympians left the field through the intense wildness of the weather. The match was then abandoned, the game being given in a win for Burnley by 3–0.'
Burnley Express

'Not bothered Rovers' – Burnley v Blackburn Rovers 1–1, October 1885

'Considerably after the time announced for the commencement of the match, only six of the Rovers players had put in an appearance. Eventually three more players showed themselves and after the contest had commenced, a 10th man joined the ranks of the visitors and this was the number that contested the game.'
Burnley Express

'Hard lines?' – Burnley v Blackburn Rovers 2–0, December 1885

'As I said before, the Rovers played their full strength team, while Burnley on the other hand were without the assistance of McLintock in goal and Friel in the centre. The

Manchester Courier in a report of the match, no doubt sent in from Blackburn, says the Rovers had hard lines. Had not Burnley hard lines on more than one occasion?

The fact is that the team who exhibited the best play won the match. Then why not say so? When a team holding the position of Blackburn Rovers is beaten on merit, there is every reason that the team which inflicts the defeat should have every credit for so doing, but I find that this is not always the case.'
Burnley Gazette

Rovers player and ref were brothers

In 1890, when winning 1–0 against the Rovers at Turf Moor, Burnley had a goal disallowed by the referee. Eventually, the Rovers won the game 2–1, thanks mainly, said the *Burnley Gazette*, to the referee, a Mr Richard Horne of Accrington. In the game the Rovers' goalkeeper was a player called John Horne, and naturally Burnley's suspicions were aroused. It turned out that the referee and the Blackburn goalkeeper were brothers and so naturally Burnley lodged a protest to the League.

However, the Rovers had already appealed to the League, objecting about the threatening Burnley crowd after the game, saying that the referee had been intimidated. Both appeals were dismissed but the Burnley club were warned to keep their crowd in better conduct.

The day Burnley won the Cup (v Rovers)

If 1889–90 was a season to forget(19 consecutive League games without a win), it was also a season remembered for many years as the club reached their first major Cup Final. It was the Lancashire Cup Final, played at Accrington, and Burnley came up against 'the old enemy' Blackburn Rovers.

It was typically the Rovers' seventh Lancashire Cup Final, while Burnley before that season had never even won a Lancashire Cup First Round tie! Up to that season they had been beaten in round one four times; once they had scratched without playing, twice they had received a bye, while in the other their opponents had scratched. What a success story! No one expected Burnley (second from bottom in the League) to even exist on the same field as the mighty Rovers (third from the top), but that day Burnley rose to the occasion with a great 2–0 victory.

Of course, one must not expect that Blackburn took the defeat lying down and they lodged a protest. But the protest came to nothing and the *Burnley Gazette* summed up their attitude in the following couched terms, 'The Rovers captain lodged a protest against the encroachment of the spectators, though how he could possibly expect to succeed with it is rather hard to understand. The only encroachment of note occurred three or four minutes before the finish, and the game was stopped till the crowd were put back. It would be interesting to know how many Blackburn people were among this band of encroachers, and whether they received no encouragement from the losing team?'

'A fair hearing?' March 1894

'We at Burnley are at present represented on the Lancashire FA by a Blackburn gentleman and Dr Morley from Blackburn. Another Blackburn man has a vote, and

I do believe that yet another Blackburn man is in the Association. Other things being equal, what chance have we for a fair hearing?'
Burnley News

Because of the extreme cold
It was not until the meeting at Ewood Park in December 1891 that Burnley managed to gain a point at the expense of the Rovers. That day Burnley found things going all their way and at half-time the score was 3–0 in their favour. But midway through the second half Rovers player Lofthouse kicked Stewart, who at once struck back. Both men were immediately sent off by the referee and shortly afterwards all the Blackburn players, with the exception of Herbie Arthur their goalkeeper, walked off the field.

Down the field stormed Burnley once again, and Arthur claimed that they were all offside! However, the referee stopped the game and awarded it to Burnley. The Blackburn team insisted after the game that they had left the field neither because they were losing, nor because Lofthouse had been sent off, but because of the extreme cold!

Toe to toe
A year later, again at Ewood, five minutes from the end, Lang, the Burnley captain, was knocked down and kicked. Getting up, he butted Southworth, the Rovers centre-forward, in the face. Soon they were standing toe to toe and the referee ordered both of them off the pitch. As the Burnley players left the field at the end, they were met with a shower of stones and mud and several players were struck.

FA Cup semi-final victory 1913
'It was something more than a cheer which followed the referee's final whistle. It was more like a roar from the ocean, and it was kept up for fully 10 minutes. From the cheering and the waving of hands, hats and sticks which ensued, there seemed to be as many Burnley enthusiasts in that vast crowd in Blackburn as there were supporters of the Rovers. It was a slow march back into Blackburn. Trams and motor cars were held up by the throng as the jubilant Burnley host poured into the town.'
Burnley News, 1913

Burnley v Rovers 6–2 (East Lancashire Charity Cup 1921)
'People who say that Burnley have gone stale have not seen the Rovers. They were the slowest and stiffest side the Turfites have met this season. Their half-backs were too slow to catch a funeral, and the Burnley forwards had a bit of a picnic.'
Burnley News

Burnley v Rovers 5–1 (East Lancashire Charity Cup 1922)
'But when Kelly commenced his "leg-pulling", the Rovers began to think about trying to play football. Bob tried one or two jokes on them, and a sort of amazement settled on the faces of the Rovers players and they went for him. Only to find that they had a will o' the wisp to deal with, and instead of catching the ball, they caught but air. It was

merry enough in all conscience, as Kelly could do almost what he liked with the ball, and he kept the crowd roaring with laughter at the trickery he exhibited.

And apparently he did it with so little exertion – swerving, swaying, dodging and dribbling. It was a scream. An unwritten comedy which will long be remembered.'
Burnley News, **1922**

Many players have played for both Burnley and Blackburn, but Jackie Bruton is the only player to play and score for both sides, for Burnley against Blackburn and Blackburn against Burnley.

BOOTS

'During the match an experiment was tried, Crabtree wearing a pair of boots with a patent sole made of India rubber or some such material, and those who saw his performance were able to report most favourably. This was done with a view of obtaining boots for the team in case the frost continued, so that such fiascos as that at Bolton should not be repeated. Had the boots been got before, or some other material used in order to keep the players on their feet, the same as the Bolton players kept on theirs. While the Turfites were slipping and falling all over the field, the Trotters went about as though they were playing in the most favourable of conditions. Clearly the committee are to blame for Burnley's defeat as much as the players.'
1890s

Liverpool v Burnley 4–0, 1895
'The ground was in a very sloppy condition. It transpired that Burnley wore the same material on their boots as in the Rovers match with the addition of two spikes, while the visitors were shod in the ordinary manner. That Liverpool kept on their feet much more than the Turfites was apparent to everybody. Their superior football was so palpable that there was a suspicion that Liverpool had something improper on their boots. The Burnley captain asked the referee to examine the Liverpool players' boots at half-time. The examination revealed nothing objectionable and the game was resumed.'
Burnley News, **1895**

Prior to the FA Cup Final
'Coupons much needed for new boots for the players are being received from all parts of the country, and officials are very gratified with the response to date.'

BRIBERY

⊕ Director John Turkington promised manager Stan Ternent a new Bentley if he could get Burnley into the Premiership after they won promotion to Division One. Unfortunately, Stan did not quite manage it!

⊛ Burnley fan, Dr Lance Knight offered £1,000 worth of cosmetic dentistry to any Burnley player who scored against Norwich on 20 January 2007, during a run of games when Burnley just could not score. The game was postponed.

BURNLEY BOOKS

Stan Ternent's dislike of all things Neil Warnock is well documented – or is it? In his book *Stan the Man* there is a page where he writes, 'If I am alone with him for just one minute' and there is a blank half page with the message 'THE FOLLOWING PASSAGE HAS BEEN DELETED FOR LEGAL REASONS!'

A veritable Clarets' library
My book on the history of the club *Up the Clarets!* written in 1973 opened the floodgates for a veritable library of Clarets books. Here we list a few more to ask your local librarian about:

Vintage Claret (1976, David Wiseman)
The Best Ground in the Fourth Division (1991, Andrew Procter)
Burnley's Greatest Goal (1999, Peter Fyles)
A Good Year for Claret (2000, Bill Evans)
Burnley were back!! (1996, Stephen Cummings)
It's Burnley not Barcelona (2003, Dave Thomas)
The Clarets Collection (1996, Ray Simpson)
The Rivals (2005, Mike Holgate)
No Nay Never (2004, Dave Thomas)
Forever and ever (Tim Quelch)
Burnley: A Complete Record (1991, Edward Lee and Ray Simpson)
East Lancashire Derbies (2001, Dean Hayes)
Burnley Centenary Handbook (1982, Burnley FC)
Russians Don't Land Here! (2007, Dave Thomas)
No Nay Never Volume Two (2008, Dave Thomas)
A Pictorial History of the Clarets (1988, Tony Durkin)
The complete A to Z of Burnley FC (1999, Dean Hayes)
Burnley Football Club 1882–1968 (1999, Ray Simpson)
1959–60: A Season to Remember (2002, Bill Evans)
Champions! 1992–93 Yearbook (1993, Ray Simpson)
It started with a cup! 1993–94 Yearbook (1994, Ray Simpson)
BFC & Me (1988, Paul Fletcher)
Willie Irvine Together Again (2005, Dave Thomas)
The Legends of Burnley (2006, Mike Jackman)
Promotion, the Wembley Way 1994–95 Yearbook (1995, Ray Simpson)
Clarets Blues 1995–96 Yearbook (1996, Ray Simpson)
A Case of Vintage Claret (2006, David Wiseman)
The Clarets Chronicles (2007, Ray Simpson)

Stan the Man (2003, Stan Ternent and Tony Livesey)
Triumphs, Trophies and Turf Moor Legends (2007, BFC)
Harry Potts, Margaret's story (2006, Dave Thomas)
The Greatest Burnley Team of All (2004, Geoff Crambie)
The Glory Years Remembered (2000, Mike Prestage)
The Pride and Glory (2002, Edward Lee and Phil Whalley)
The Longside; end of an era
Pictorial Guide to Programmes & Ephemera (2008, L. and M. Davidson)

And let us not forget the monthly flow of material from the Burnley fanzine *When the Ball Moves* and the magazine of the London Clarets, *Something to Write Home About.*

This book appears to be the 38th publication in the last 36 years, and I know for certain there are another half a dozen in the pipeline, which will help to swell the 'Clarets library'. They may not be the best football team, but they have some of the best-read football supporters.

When I wrote *Up the Clarets!* in 1973 I said in the introduction, 'What I have always wanted to see is a book to record for everyone the history of what is a most remarkable club. I have waited long enough – for well over 20 years – so I decided that I had better do something about it. This is the result.'

My thanks as a Burnley fan goes to all those others who 'decided to do something about it'.

'THE BIRMINGHAM BEAUTY SHOW!'

After Burnley had beaten West Brom 5–0 in 1892–93, the *Birmingham Daily Mail* reported, 'The Burnley men played a rough game and Basnett and the other West Bromwich players were badly shaken.' Another report at the time said, 'Burnley footballers have the most repulsive faces I ever saw!' The *Burnley Express* commented, 'I don't know who the writer is, but I can imagine he is of Midlands origin?'

The report was prefaced by the following poem:

> 'I used to think that teams were meant to play,
> And not picked for their handsome faces gay
> That for their speech it mattered not a jot
> But now a smart man down at "Brum" says "Not!"
> His criticism is so fine indeed,
> He pooh-poohs football, skill, or play, or speed –
> In fact the game he never can have seen –
> And yet upon poor Burnley vents his spleen.
> He wants fine faces, courtly talk and gait.
> Well, if I'm any judge – he'll have to wait!'

BOTTOM (or lack of it)

Burnley v Notts Forest 8–2, November 1922
'To have three goals scored against them in the first 16 minutes was enough to knock the bottom out of any side – if there had only been much bottom to knock!'
Burnley Express

BURNLEY BROTHERS

On only two occasions have two brothers played in the same Burnley League team. These were David and Jack Walders (37 games together in 1904–06) and Richard and Vince Overson (five times in 1979–80).

In 1927–28, brothers Billy and Peter Dougall played in the Burnley first team, though never in the same match. This was because they played in the same position (inside-forward) and on six occasions Peter stood in for his brother Billy.

Of course, brothers have often played against each other and these include George and Des Thompson, who were opposing goalkeepers several times for Preston and Burnley in the 1950s; and Willie and Bobby Irvine (Stoke City goalkeeper). Willie even scored against his own brother in 1965–66!

BURNLEY LAD WINS THE DOUBLE

James Crabtree was born in Burnley in 1871 and made his League debut for Burnley when he was only 18. By the age of 22 he was an English international and in 1896 he was transferred for an English record fee to Aston Villa.

At Villa Park, James Crabtree captained the team that won the double, winning four League Championships and two Cup Finals (he even scored the winner in his first FA Cup Final!), and he captained England too. Loyal to the core and afraid of no one, Crabtree played in all five defensive positions for England. With this sort of record it is no wonder that he has been described on several occasions as the greatest footballer of all time.

A BURNLEY TALE (or a 'shaggy Claret story!')

1. **Tommy Boyle** was born in **Hoyland.**
2. On his debut **Jamie Hoyland** replaced Steve Davis, who had been **injured.**
3. Also **injured** that day was **Ted McMinn,** who had come to Turf Moor from Birmingham City.
4. **Ted McMinn** had won the **Scottish Premier League title** with Glasgow Rangers in 1987.
5. Another Burnley player who went on to win the **Scottish Premier League title** with Glasgow Rangers was **Trevor Steven** – in 1990, 1991, 1993 and 1994.

6. After those successes, **Trevor Steven** was transferred to **Marseille** for £5.5 million.

7. **Marseille** was the same club for which **Chris Waddle** had played in 1991.

8. **Chris Waddle** became the Burnley manager in July 1997. He followed **Adrian Heath.**

9. **Adrian Heath** became the first **Burnley manager** ever to play in a competitive game for the club.

10. The last **Burnley manager** who had also played for the club – though at different times – had been **Frank Casper.**

11. **Frank Casper** was transferred to Burnley from **Rotherham United** for £30,000 in June 1967.

12. **Rotherham United** had drawn 1–1 at Turf Moor in a Cup tie in 1964 when Frank had scored for Rotherham. The Burnley player who scored that day was **Andy Lochhead.**

13. **Andy Lochhead** scored five goals for Burnley in one game: the 7–0 victory over Bournemouth in 1966. This was the second occasion that he had done it. The first time was the five he scored against **Chelsea** in the 6–2 League victory in 1965.

14. Older fans will always remember the FA Cup tie and four replays that the Clarets had with **Chelsea** in 1956. **Brian Miller** made his debut in the first replay.

15. After 455 appearances for the first team, **Brian Miller** made his final appearance for the club at Aston Villa in April 1967. Burnley won that game 1–0, thanks to a Villa **own-goal.**

16. The last occasion when an **own-goal** had decided a match was the previous season when **Alex Elder** scored at the wrong end (Bee Hole!) for Leeds United to win 1–0.

17. **Alex Elder** had arrived at Turf Moor from **Glentoran** in January 1959.

18. **Glentoran** was the same club which produced **Jimmy McIlroy** in 1950.

19. **Jimmy McIlroy** succeeded **Harry Potts** as inside-left for his first game for the Clarets at Sunderland, 21 October 1950.

20. **Harry Potts** was the first Burnley player to be transferred to Everton since **Tommy Lawton** had left Turf Moor in December 1936.

21. **Tommy Lawton** scored a **hat-trick** in his first professional game at Turf Moor, against Spurs in 1936.

22. **The hat-trick** was performed nine times within three years at Turf Moor by **George Beel,** 1926–29.

23. After scoring 188 goals for the Clarets within nine years (1923–32), **George Beel** was transferred to **Lincoln City.**

24. The previous Burnley player to be transferred to **Lincoln City** from Burnley had been half-back **Alf Basnett** in 1926.

25. During his time at Burnley **Alf Basnett** regularly deputised for George Halley, Tommy Boyle and **Billy Watson**, in all three half-back positions.

26. Left-half **Billy Watson** came to Turf Moor from the same club at Southport, which also produced left-winger **Eddie Mosscrop.**

27. **Eddie Mosscrop** played his first game for Burnley as an outside-right in September 1912. It was only the following season that he switched to the left-

wing, where he played for England and won League and FA Cup-winners' medals. Eddie Mosscrop took over on the right-wing from **Johnny Morley**, who had played there for four seasons.

28. **Johnny Morley(1908–12) and Tony Morley(1976–79)** are the only two players called Morley to play for the Clarets in 125 years.

29. **Tony Morley** cost Burnley £100,000 when he came from Preston in February 1976. He was sold to **Aston Villa** for £200,000 three seasons later.

30. At **Aston Villa** he won every honour in the game, except a Cup-winners' medal at **Wembley.**

31. The only Burnley player to have played for the club twice at **Wembley** is **Andy Farrell** – Sherpa Van Final in 1988 and Play-off Final in 1994.

32. In season 1990–91 **Andy Farrell** occupied four different numbered jerseys: four, five, seven and 11. The last player to have played in so many different positions in one season was **Roger Eli,** the previous season 1989–90. Actually, Roger played in five different positions: two, four, five, eight and 11.

33. **Roger Eli** had come to Burnley in 1989 and made his **debut** against Rochdale in the first game of the 1989–90 season.

34. Also making his **debut** that game was **Peter Mumby.**

35. **Peter Mumby** played just 36 games for the Burnley first team. His previous club was **Leeds United.**

36. The last player to come to Turf Moor from **Leeds United** had been **Kevin Hird** in 1984. Kevin scored over 30 goals from midfield within two seasons at Turf Moor; however, because of the club's financial state in the summer of 1986, his contract at Turf Moor was terminated.

37. Besides **Kevin Hird**'s departure that summer due to a lack of finance, forward **Alan Taylor** also left the club.

38. **Alan Taylor** had been in the West Ham team in 1975 when they **won the FA Cup** against Fulham.

39. When Burnley **won the FA Cup** in 1914 their famous captain was Tommy **W.** Boyle.

40. The **W** in Tommy Boyle's name stands for **Wilkinson.** Curiously, the club have never had a first-team player called Wilkinson!

BUS CONDUCTOR

I never met or knew Tommy Lawton but my Dad did. In the mid 1930s, my Dad was a bus conductor for the BCN (Burnley, Colne and Nelson Joint Transport). George Wiseman knew his passengers very well and served them every day. Tommy Lawton was one such passenger every day on Dad's Brunshaw Road bus, and over the next few months, Dad befriended the young boy called Tommy Lawton who travelled on his bus.

Within a year the whole of Burnley would know his name, and in the next decade the entire world of football would flock to their stadiums to see him. But Dad always remembered him catching his bus to the Turf every day!

Chapter Two

C–D

(From Caps and Captains to Doing a Jimmy Mac and Dougall the dentist)

THE 'C' TEAM

Crichton

Crabtree   Caldwell

Chaplow   Cummings   Cook

Cochrane   Collins   Conroy   Casper   Cargill

Subs: Conway (H.) and Cross

OR

Coyne

Cox   Camara

Cretney   Cahill   Cassidy

Chew   Cheesebrough   Cooke   Coates   Connelly

Subs: Chadwick and Comstive

CAPS

⚽ Jimmy McIlroy has won the most international caps while playing for Burnley – 51 in all.

⚽ The Burnley player to win most caps in one season is also Jimmy McIlroy, who played 10 times for Northern Ireland in season 1957–58.

⚽ The Burnley player to have played most international games at Wembley is John Connelly – six times.

⚽ The youngest Burnley international player is Leighton James. When he played for Wales versus Czechoslovakia in October 1971 he was still four months short of his 19th birthday.

- The oldest Burnley international player is Jerry Dawson, who was 34 when he played for England versus Scotland in April 1922.

- The Burnley player who has scored most international goals is Jimmy McIlroy, who scored 10 goals for Northern Ireland.

- The highest number of Burnley players in one international team is three. This happened twice in 1966 when Elder, Irvine and Todd all played for Northern Ireland against Mexico and England, and again on four occasions in 2006–07, when Duff, Jones and Lafferty all played for Northern Ireland against Finland, Denmark and Liechtenstein twice.

CAPTAINS

During one spell in 1928 the Clarets played four consecutive games with four different captains. Jack Hill led the team against the Rovers on 20 October, while Andy McCluggage took his place on 29 October against Derby County. Forward George Beel took over against Everton on 3 November and eventually George Parkin became captain against Huddersfield on 10 November. No wonder they finished in the bottom four!

CHAIRMEN

During their 125-year history the club have had 16 chairmen:
1882 Albert Jobling
1883 John Rawcliffe
May 1885 John Bradley
March 1887 B.Wyatt Granger
May 1896 Charles E. Sutcliffe
June 1899 Edwin Whitehead
June 1909 Harry Windle
March 1930 William E. Bracewell
January 1932 Edward J. Tate
July 1934 Tom Clegg
June 1948 Ernest D. Kay
October 1952 Wilfred Hopkinson
June 1955 Robert W. Lord
October 1981 John E. Jackson
May 1985 Frank J. Teasdale
May 1998 Barry C. Kilby

Old 'bollock chops'
Most football fans of a certain age will surely have heard of the Cobbold brothers, who were chairmen of Ipswich Town in their heyday and presided over the club's

greatest triumphs. The Cobbolds were Old Etonians, very wealthy, very plummy and great characters, and their great wealth was based on the family brewing business. They loved a drink, well, more than a drink; in fact they were great jokers and pranksters and their idea of a crisis was not when the team lost, but when they ran out of Chablis! They plied all their players with drink and it is a wonder that Ipswich ever won anything at all. When the ground was flooded one year their only response was to say 'Well, at least we shall have water for our whisky!'

They were the very antithesis of Burnley's Bob Lord, who was dour, blunt, serious and often kept the boardroom drink cupboard closed when the Cobbolds arrived. Thus they christened him 'old bollock chops' and Turf Moor became their least favourite place to visit. One year, finding the drinks cupboard closed, they simply opened it and helped themselves. Lord was not amused.

Of course, it went down like a lead balloon when Ipswich snatched the Championship from Burnley in 1962, and at the celebratory banquet Bob Lord said in his speech that Ipswich had only won it because Burnley had handed it to them. This made them even closer friends.

GIVE US A CHEER!

'One is afraid that the Burnley crowd is too well educated sometimes – and it sees all the good there is in the opposition and sees so much of the bad that is in their own side, that it does not give it all the credit for the good. It is easy to forgive opponents for making bad misses in front of goal, because they do not hurt us – but it is difficult to forgive similar misses by Burnley men, because they do hurt.'
Burnley News, 1927

'CHEESY!'

Mr Watts had a butcher's shop near St Luke's Church in Brierfield and was a very keen Burnley supporter. One Saturday in the 1950s he noticed young Albert Cheesebrough stood at the bus stop across the road, waiting for a bus to take him to the match. 'Cheesy' was playing in the first team that afternoon. The Burnley buses were going through one after the other, packed with fans heading for the match. Time was getting on.

So, in a moment of inspiration, Mr Watts shut his shop and went home to his garage where he got out his car and returned to the bus stop outside his shop. He picked up young Albert, took him to the match and returned to the shop. He re-opened the shop for a while and then, looking at his watch, he decided it was time to go to the match.

Catching the bus, he went off to Turf Moor, where he watched 'Cheesy' play for the Clarets. Would it happen today?

An afterthought: after retirement from football, Albert Cheesebrough became a butcher in Southport!

CHRISTMAS

- For me, the best day of the season in the 1940s and 1950s, was always Christmas Day. Church in the morning, Christmas dinner with grandparents, parents, aunts, uncles and cousins, followed by the four of us off to Turf Moor(Grandad, Dad, Uncle and me) – three generations, representing over 60 years at Turf Moor, all proudly stood together in the old Enclosure.

- The brass band played Christmas carols, the men smoked cigars for the only time in the year, and people could be seen putting quantities of whisky into their flasks of coffee!

- From 1893 until 1957 League games were often played on Christmas Day, and from 1893 until 1924 Burnley played all their Christmas Day games at home! (Curiously, during 60 seasons the Clarets only played three Christmas Day games away from home.) They were usually local derbies against Lancashire teams like Blackpool, Preston, Liverpool and Bolton.

- From 1905 until 1913 Burnley played eight games on Christmas Day against Blackpool, winning five and drawing three. (Of course, thanks to Father Christmas, they were all played at home.)

- The traditional Christmas was three games in four days: Christmas Day, Boxing Day and the nearest Saturday. Many times in the 1910s and 1920s the club played three games in three days.

- The happiest Christmases were in 1893 when the club won all three games (in four days), 1921–22 (three wins in four days) and 1964–65 (three in eight days).

- In 1924–25 the club lost all three games in seven days, in 1975–76 all three (in eight days) and again in 1984–85 (in eight days).

- More recently, games at Christmas are at the most two in a week.

- Among the memorable Christmas period games there was the Christmas Day of 1951 when the Clarets were beaten at home 2–0 by Preston (Billy Elliott versus Willie Cunningham – say no more). There were often 'turnarounds' of results between Christmas Day and Boxing Day. One of these occurred in 1927 when Leicester City beat Burnley 5–0 at Leicester, followed the day after by Burnley beating Leicester 5–1 at Turf Moor!

- Then there was Boxing Day 1963 when the Clarets 'won' 6–1 against Manchester United, only to be beaten the following day at Old Trafford, 5–1. (That was the day that George Best made his League debut.)

⊕ Another Christmas turnaround was in 1960 when Burnley were beaten 3–0 by Everton at Turf Moor on Boxing Day. However, the following day the Clarets won 3–1 at Goodison.

⊕ A similar Christmas was in 1965 when Stoke City beat Burnley 3–1, only to lose to the Clarets the following day 4–1.

P.S. For the younger readers I will reprint the 1951 report of the Christmas game against Preston:
'This game will be remembered for the clash between right-back Cunningham and left-winger Billy Elliott. (It developed from a duel, one-sided in Elliott's favour, to a 'battle'.) It started with Elliott, elbowed on each side, trying to get to the ball before Gooch, who dived at his feet and was injured. Cunningham showed his feeling then, and had to be pulled away. Subsequently, Elliott was kicked when the referee's back was turned. Later Cunningham was carried off, returning to continue aggressive action to such an extent that Preston captain Tom Finney ordered him out of his position over to the other side of the field at left-back!'
Burnley Express, **1951**

CLARET CHURCH

In the 1970s, I was minister of the United Reformed Church at Poulton-le-Fylde. One year it was decided to decorate the church and one of our members, who was a professional painter and decorator, was employed for the job. We decided to allow him to choose the colours and all he asked was that he be left alone for a fortnight to get on with the job.

The day came when we were allowed in to see the finished work and there it was in all its glory. A claret and blue church! All four walls and the ceiling. It only needed a big number eight behind the pulpit and it would have reminded you of Jimmy McIlroy's jersey!

Was all this a reflection of how often I mentioned Burnley Football Club in sermons?

CLEAN SHEETS

⊕ In the 1946–47 season Burnley only conceded 29 League goals. Of these, Jimmy Strong recorded 19 clean sheets and also stopped their opponents from scoring in six FA Cup ties. We think that these 25 clean sheets in one season is a Burnley record.

⊕ Similarly, Alan Stevenson recorded 19 clean sheets in the 1972–73 season (18 League games and one FA Cup tie).

⊕ Jimmy Strong had a season of 17 clean sheets in 1947–48 (all League games) and again in 1949–50 (all League games).

⊕ In 1920–21 Jerry Dawson recorded 15 clean sheets (all League games).

CLUB SHOP

Anything and everything connected with Burnley FC and claret and blue is sold at the club shop next door to Turf Moor. There you can purchase anything from dog leads (in claret and blue) to golf tees, from clocks to Christmas baubles – all of course in claret and blue.

COINCIDENCE

- What is it about 30 March? On that date Burnley lost to Stoke 5–1 in 1894–95, Cardiff 5–1 in 1922–23, Wolves 6–1 in 1959–60, and Tottenham 5–0 in 1967–68!

- Ray Hankin, Joe Jakub and Dave Merrington all made their Burnley debut on 24 April.

- Ralph Coates, Neil Grewcock and Dave Merrington all share the same birthday: 26 April.

- Gordon Harris and George Waterfield were both born on 2 June.

- Andy Farrell and Chris Pearce both made their debut on 1 August.

- John Deary and Keith Newton both made their debut on 12 August.

- Frank Casper and Billy Gray both made their debut on 19 August – Peter Noble's birthday!

- Seven players – Jimmy Strong, Harold Mather, Harold Spencer, Jackie Chew, Peter Kippax, Harry Potts and Alan Brown – all made their Burnley League debut in the same game – v Coventry City, 31 August 1946.

- Similarly, Chris Pearce, Shaun McGrory, Peter Daniel, Andy Farrell, George Oghani, Paul Comstive, Peter Zelem and Steve Gardner all made their Burnley League debuts in the same game – v Colchester, 15 August 1987. This was a club record (eight players).

- John Angus, Marlon Beresford and Adam Blacklaw all share the same birthday – 2 September.

- Hat-trick Saturday! Billy Gray (1953–54), Arthur Bellamy (1963–64), Willie Irvine (1965–66) and Billy Hamilton (1982–83) all scored hat-tricks on 7 September!

- Tommy Hutchinson, David Smith and Sammy Todd were all born on 22 September.

- Jimmy McIlroy shared the same birthday as his trainer and coach, Billy Dougall, 25 October.

COLLAPSE OF GOALPOSTS

Crash! Bang! Wallop! – Burnley v Barnsley 2–2
'If the crowd did not have more than five minutes of decent football, they saw one thing which they will probably not see again, and that was the whole framework of the goal at the Beehole End crashing to the ground.

Ten minutes after the start, Curran, the Barnsley outside-right, put in a high dropping ball, the bounce of which Sommerville misjudged – a soft goal by the way – and the ball rose over his head and went underneath the bar. Harvey raced in and jumped up in an endeavour to reach it with his head. Instead of that, he struck the post with great force and the post snapped clean off at the base, bringing the whole of the framework toppling down.

Immediately following the collapse, the players left the field, the crowd indulged its humour as fresh goalposts were being placed in position, and the workers who had to run across the slippery field in ordinary boots, came in for many jocular gibes. The referee, Mr Warburton, superintended operations and measured the height of the bar before allowing the game to proceed.'
Burnley Express, 18 March 1931

COLOURS

Colour clash 1 – Burnley v West Ham United, 1924–25
'West Ham United played until half-time in their own colours which were pale blue bodies and red sleeves, while Burnley were in red bodies and pale blue sleeves. After the interval, West Ham played in blue and white.'
Burnley Express

And it happened again…
Colour clash 2 – Burnley v West Ham United, September 1934
'Spectators rubbed their eyes at Turf Moor on Monday afternoon when West Ham turned out in the same colours as Burnley, claret and blue, only with the claret predominant, like Burnley's old strip. The referee soon waved his wand however, and there was a complete transformation scene, West Ham disappearing to reappear a minute later in white jerseys and white knickers. Before he ordered the visitors to change, Mr Wood had both captains Bellis and Barrett stand side by side a few yards away from him, while he eyed them up and down. He came to the conclusion that there was a possibility of confusion arising, and the spectators seemed to agree with him, for they cheered his decision.'
Burnley Express

Double sponsorship
On New Year's Eve 1994 Southend United came to Turf Moor. For some reason there was a colour clash and Southend had failed to bring a change strip. So Burnley lent them theirs. Obviously there was no colour clash, but both teams were sponsored by Endsleigh Insurance – good value for sponsorship money.

BEST COMEBACKS (in the last 50 years)

1. After losing 0–2, Burnley came back to beat Arsenal 4–2 away at Highbury in 1959–60.
2. After losing 0–1, Burnley came back to beat Spurs 4–1 away at Tottenham 1982–83.
3. After losing 0–2, Burnley came back to beat QPR 4–2 away at Loftus Road in 2007–08.
4. After losing 0–1, Burnley came back to win on penalties away at Chelsea in 2008–09.
5. After losing 0–2 at home to Wrexham, Burnley won 5–2 in 1985–86.
6. After losing 0–2 at home to Crystal Palace, Burnley won 4–2 in 1969–70.
7. After losing 0–2 at home to Sheffield Wednesday, Burnley won 4–2 in 1969–70.
8. After losing 0–2 at home to Crystal Palace, Burnley won 4–2 in 2008–09.
9. After losing 0–2, Burnley came back to beat Cambridge United 3–2 away in 1984–85.
10. After losing 1–2, Burnley came back to beat Spurs 3–2 at White Hart Lane in 1973–74.
11. After losing 1–2, Burnley came back to beat Arsenal 3–2 away at Highbury in 1962–63.
12. After losing 0–1 at home to Stoke, Burnley won 4–1 in 1965–66.
13. After losing 0–1 at home to Aston Villa, Burnley won 4–2 in 1966–67.

And a famous draw.......

14. After losing 0–4, Burnley came back to draw 4–4 against Spurs at White Hart Lane in 1960–61.

COMEDIAN COATES

'At the moment, I'm under the hairdryer, sat next to Andy Lochhead; we use the same hairdressers, have done for years. Here we both are, remembering the crosses I used to send over after battling my way down the wing – and all those missed chances squandered by Andy and his partner in crime, Willie Irvine!

One or two memories of my time at Burnley are still very clear. Like the occasion we played at Chelsea. I was outside-left. Willie Morgan was at outside-right. (If any youngsters are reading this you will have to ask your Dad to explain these strange positions!) Willie was being marked – all over – by Chelsea full-back 'Chopper' Harris. This chap would kick anything that moved. After being chopped and kicked by Harris a few times, Willie decided he would change wings and asked me to swap over. Needless to say, I wasn't over the moon about this and no matter how hard manager Harry Potts shouted and went blue in the face, I stayed put. I think it was the only occasion in the club's history that they played with TWO left-wingers!

Memory number two is very clear. On Saturday 27 November 1966 Gordon Harris finally gave me a pass straight to my feet! And just as clear is the occasion in 1968 when I witnessed Brian Miller buy a round of drinks!

I still live here in London, and if you are wondering what I am doing now, I'm pleased to tell you. I run a hair salon and gymnasium. My staff are: Salon Manager – Andy Lochhead. Dietician – Adam Blacklaw. Accountant – Brian O'Neil. Body Building – Arthur Bellamy. Between us, we've invested the profits in a race horse. It's called KINDON and true to form, he keeps running through the fences instead of over them!'
Ralph Coates (from *BFC and Me*)

COMPARATIVE SUCCESS

Considering their population as a town, the Clarets have had a comparatively successful history. For instance:

Burnley have won the old First Division title twice
Teams which have won the title only once include:
Ipswich Town, Sheffield United and West Bromwich Albion.
Teams which have never won the title include:
Birmingham City, Blackpool, Bolton, Cardiff City, Charlton, Coventry City, Crystal Palace, Fulham, Hull City, Leicester City, Middlesbrough, Southampton, Stoke City, West Ham and Wigan.

Burnley have won the FA Cup once
Teams which have never won the FA Cup include:
Birmingham City, Crystal Palace, Fulham, Hull City, Leicester City, Middlesbrough, Stoke City and Wigan.

Burnley have played in the European Cup
Teams which have never played in the European Cup include:
Birmingham City, Blackpool, Bolton, Cardiff City, Charlton, Coventry City, Crystal Palace, Fulham, Hull City, Leicester City, Middlesbrough, Portsmouth, Preston, Sheffield United, Sheffield Wednesday, Southampton, Stoke City, Sunderland, West Brom, West Ham and Wigan.

CLARET CONDOMS!

'Clarets fans can wear their colours with pride' said the *Burnley Express*. This was the heading for the story that Burnley FC and the Condom Collective were joining forces to try to make condoms more available to young people. Free condoms were given away as supporters left the home game against Preston North End in September 2008. Rumour had it that they even came in claret.

'I'd rather have had a free pie!' said the fan sat next to me.

'CONSISTENT BRILLIANCE'

'In passing review of the principal figures in the game during the last 14 or 15 years, I cannot recall one who stands out so distinctively as Burnley's left half-back Billy Watson for consistent brilliance. It is a very rare thing indeed for Watson to play even an indifferent game, or even rarer for him to be absent from his place in the side.

I do not think he has exactly received adequate recognition from the authorities because he is a more complete artist than any other left-half of his time, equally good

in defence and recovery as in attack. He is cleverer than Grimsdell, less showy than Bromilow, more polished than Bobby McNeal, Sturgess, Utley, or any of those who have flattered for the moment and flashed in and out of the representative side. His virtue of quiet workmanship veils some of his real strength.'
Lancashire Daily Post, **December 1922**

CONSECUTIVE SEQUENCES

Unbeaten League run
In the 1920–21 season the Burnley team played 30 consecutive League games without losing – from 6 September until 25 March – winning 21 and drawing nine.

Winning streak
In 1912–13 Burnley won 10 consecutive League games.
November 16 Fulham (h) 5–0
           23 Barnsley (a) 4–1
           30 Bradford (h) 5–1
December   7 Wolves (a) 2–0
           14 Leicester Fosse (h) 5–1
           21 Stockport County (a) 1–0
           25 Blackpool (h) 4–0
           28 Glossop (a) 3–1
January   4 Clapton Orient (h) 5–0
           18 Lincoln City (a) 3–1
They also won an FA Cup tie on 15 January at Leeds City 3–2, which would make the run 11 consecutive victories. (In these 11 victories, Bert Freeman scored 15 goals.)

Winning home sequence
Between March 1911 and January 1913 Burnley were unbeaten in 34 consecutive League games at Turf Moor.
In 1920–21 Burnley won 17 home games on the trot.

Unsuccessful home sequence
Stretching over two seasons, 1978–79 and 1979–80, Burnley went 11 consecutive home League games without winning. (If you were to be especially doom-ridden, you might add an extra League Cup home game, which was drawn.) So call it 12.

Unbeaten away sequence
During the 1920–21 season the Clarets played a sequence of 14 consecutive away matches without losing.

Losing away streak
In 1902–03 Burnley lost 16 consecutive away games. The only away game not lost that season was the first one, away to Burton United 0–0.

Between 7 December 1901 and 24 October 1903 Burnley played 33 consecutive League games away from home without winning.

Worst start to a season
In 1970–71 the Clarets did not win till until their 15th game, while in 1979–80 the team did not register a victory until their 17th game. Back in 1889–90 it was in their 18th game that the team eventually won a match.

Best start to a season
In 1897–98 Burnley did not lose until their ninth game of the season. This happened again in 1966–67. But by far the best start was in 1972–73, when the Clarets did not lose until their 17th game.

Deserves a mention
In 1979–80 the Clarets did not win any of their first 16 games, nor did they win any of their last 16 games. Thank goodness for Christmas.

CONTRASTS

Club programmes
Different costs: 1912 – 1d; 1927 – 2d; 1962 – 4d; 1980 – 25p; 1991 – £1; 2009 – £3.

Goals!
In 1960–61 the Clarets played five consecutive games in October and scored 24 goals: Fulham (5), Cardiff (4), Blackburn (4), Manchester United (5) and Chelsea (6). Ten years later, in 1970–71, it took the team the first 36 games of the season to score the same number of goals.

Failure and Success
In 1920–21 the team lost their first three League games and were bottom. From then they went 30 League games undefeated and finished Champions.

CORNY HUMOUR

'With reference to the man who asked "Why was Weaver Cross?" and answered himself "Because he saw Watson Boyle Basnett!", the execution has been fixed for next week!'
Burnley News, 1922

CRICKET versus FOOTBALL

❸ Cricket was a well established sport in Burnley long before the advent of football in the 1880s. So it was that football writers such as 'Hawkeye' in the *Burnley*

Express wrote in April 1883, 'As the legitimate football season is drawing to a close, and as you Mr Editor will want the space you have placed at my command for the purpose of chronicling cricket matches, I am compelled to bring my notes for this season to a finale'. After that there was silence from 'Hawkeye' until September.

⊕ Sometimes, the rugby club of Burnley Rovers would use the cricket ground at Turf Moor for their games. Witness this plaintive cry from a cricket lover in 1883: 'Rugby plays havoc with cricket grounds!'

⊕ Things getting nasty? 'The football players have been told over and over again that if they will come to us, we will hand over the keys immediately after our last match, thus giving them the winter months and us the summer'. *Burnley Express*, 1883.

⊕ 'The Pipe of Peace'. 'This week the Burnley Cricket Club Annual Dinner will take place at the Bull Hotel. It is hoped that a large contingent of the football club will see fit to be present and smoke "the pipe of peace" with their fellow workers at Turf Moor'. *Burnley Express*, 1883.

CLARET CRICKETERS

Countless Burnley footballers have also played cricket at a high standard:

⊕ Arthur Bell, a leading amateur footballer, was captain of Burnley CC, which won the Lancashire League three seasons in succession from 1906 to 1908.

⊕ Jerry Dawson played for Burnley CC for many years.

⊕ Walter Place (Snr) played many seasons with Burnley CC.

⊕ Jackie Chew was captain and a leading batsman with Rishton CC.

⊕ Peter Kippax played many years for Burnley CC. In 1958 he topped the entire Lancashire League batting averages.

⊕ Tommy Lawton topped the batting averages for Burnley CC when he was only 16. (He is the only person recorded to have broken St Mary's Church window with a mighty six.)

⊕ Leighton James played for Burnley CC, Martin Dobson for Read CC and Albert Cheesebrough was a regular with Lowerhouse CC.

⊕ At a higher level, Albert Alderman played for Derbyshire and Frank Sugg once played for England.

CROWDS

'As the crowd grew, there developed the most wonderful of all sounds and the most inspiring of sights – the murmur of thousands of human voices and the banks of human faces. The former reminded one forcibly of a walk on the seashore at night, the waves rolling over the shingle, somewhere out there in the darkness. The latter can be likened to nothing – for there is no other thing like it.'
Kestrel, *Burnley News*, February 1924, commenting on the Burnley v Huddersfield Cup tie, which set the figure for record attendance at Turf Moor.

CUP DRAW

On a Monday morning in November 1927, the day of the England versus Wales international match, which was to be played that afternoon at Turf Moor, the FA Council met at the Bull Hotel in Burnley in order to make the draw for the second round of the FA Cup. (Afterwards, they went to look around Towneley Hall in Burnley before making the short journey to Turf Moor).

CURIOUS CONNECTIONS

⊕ When Burnley played Barnsley in the FA Cup in February 1911 Tommy Boyle was captain of Barnsley. He handled the ball and gave Burnley a penalty. Who should be chosen to take it but Jerry Dawson! His shot was saved but Burnley went on to win 2–0.

⊕ John Connelly was in Walter Winterbottom's last England team.

⊕ John Connelly was in Alf Ramsey's first England team.

⊕ Martin Dobson was in Alf Ramsey's last England team.

⊕ Martin Dobson was in Don Revie's first England team.

⊕ The only Burnley player to play for his club twice at Wembley is Andy Farrell, in the Sherpa Van Final of 1988 and the League Play-off Final against Stockport in 1994.

⊕ Burnley have played in all four of the old Divisions against just six teams – Blackpool, Cardiff, Bolton, Carlisle, Preston and Leyton Orient.

⊕ While still an Everton player Dave Thomas was interviewed by John Motson, who asked him on *Match of the Day* what his ambitions were. Motty expected a football answer, but was surprised when Dave replied 'to meet gardener Geoffrey Smith'. Motty fixed up the meeting.

⊕ While on the subject of Dave Thomas, his grandfather was David 'Ticer' Thomas, who was a member of the 1909 West Auckland team that played in the 'World Cup' in Turin. This was the Lipton Trophy and they were one of four European teams invited to play – from Italy, Germany, Switzerland and England. West Auckland became the English representatives because the FA refused to nominate a team.

⊕ In Burnley's last game of 2001 at Manchester City the official away following was recorded as 2,002.

CONSECUTIVE RESULTS (League only)

Consecutive wins
1.   10 wins in 1912–13
2.   9 wins in 1991–92
3.= 7 wins in 1958–59
3.= 7 wins in 1961–62
4.= 6 wins in 1968–69
4.= 6 wins in 1911–12
4.= 6 wins in 1920–21
4.= 6 wins in 1971–72
4.= 6 wins in 1981–82

Consecutive draws
1.= 6 draws in 1930–31
1.= 6 draws in 1966–67
3.= 5 draws in 1901–02
3.= 5 draws in 1928–29 and 1929–30
3.= 5 draws in 1946–47

Consecutive defeats
1.= 8 defeats in 1889–90
1.= 8 defeats in 1894–95 and 1895–96
1.= 8 defeats in 1994–95
4.   7 defeats in 1904–05
5.= 6 defeats in 1931–32
5.= 6 defeats in 1895–96
5.= 6 defeats in 2001–02 and 2002–03
5.= 6 defeats in 2005–06

CURSE OF THE WISEMANS!

In 1988 we moved to Bournemouth from Lancashire. My son Christian, then aged six, had never seen Burnley win. And though we watched them in quite a few games while in the south we never saw them win. We came up to Burnley to see them play Torquay (1–1), we went to Exeter (lost 1–4), Portsmouth (0–2), Bournemouth (1–1, 0–1, etc) and I could go on.

By January 1994 I had gone six seasons without seeing the Clarets win and Christian 12 seasons. And then Burnley reached Wembley, where they met Stockport in the Play-off Finals. I was in France for a church conference, Christian was in Northampton at a church youth weekend. Neither of us could go to Wembley. It was heartbreaking, and I wrote to the *Burnley Express* to share my frustrations.

Of course, the Clarets won but the Wisemans were not there to see it! The next week a group of Burnley fans wrote to me and thanked me (and Christian) for not going to Wembley. They even sent me the video of the game as a gift for not spreading the Wiseman curse at Wembley.

The following season Christian and I went up to Swindon to see the Clarets. It was now November 1994, and we still had not seen them win! Again I wrote to the *Burnley Express* to share my hopes and fears as a Claret 'exile'. While sat in the 'Burnley end' of the stand at Swindon I got into conversation with the lady sat next to me; she had a pub in Accrington and she and her husband had come down to Swindon for the evening.

'Where do you come from?' she innocently asked, and I as innocently replied 'Bournemouth.' 'You're not that vicar who hasn't seen them win for seven years are you?' she asked suspiciously, and I had to reply in the affirmative. 'Hey, Eric' she said, turning to her husband. 'You know that letter I read to you from that vicar in Bournemouth, who's never seen the Clarets win for seven years? Well, he's here!' Cue stunned silence from husband.

Then looking past me at Christian, she further enquired, 'And is that your son – the one who hasn't seen them win for 13 years?' 'Yes', I replied, proudly! 'Eric, – he's brought his son – that boy who has never seen the Clarets win ever!' She never spoke to me again. And I was conscious that word spread through the stand that 'the Bournemouth vicar and his son – you know the one who's never seen them win' were present with the claret and blue army.

The result that night was 1–1, and once again the Wiseman curse had struck.

It was the following season, 1995–96, on 14 October, when the curse was lifted. Christian and I saw the Clarets win at Bournemouth 2–0 – the first time in his young life of 14 years and five months that the lad had seen his team win!

THE 'D' TEAM

Dawson

Davis (2)   Docherty

Duff   Davis (1)   Deakin

Devine   Dougall   Dobson   Deary   Djemba-Djemba

Subs: Down, Dixon, Douglas, Diallo and Dyer

THE TWO STEVE DAVII!

In late 1989 Stephen Mark Davis was transferred to Burnley, where he joined Steven Peter Davis. Steven was (1) and Stephen was (2). They played just eight games together, during which time the Burnley fans enjoyed singing 'Two Steve Davii, there's only two Steve Davii....'

JERRY DAWSON
(a Burnley legend who played for the first team for over 20 seasons)
Hello Jerry!
'Dawson, the reserve goalkeeper, who was given a chance in a League match for the first time, had no opportunity of showing what mettle he is made of. He only handled the ball once, and hadn't really a single shot to stop.'
Burnley News, **Burnley v Stockport, 13 April 1907**

Good Old Jerry!
'Five minutes from the end with the score one all, McClean of Burnley gave a penalty. Bowman took the shot and lifted the ball up to the right of Dawson. But Jerry was prepared, and lame though he was (he had been off the field 20 minutes earlier), he jumped for it, and kept the ball out of the net. McClean gave it a kick, and then Ogden got it away altogether. Then some of the Burnley players ran to Dawson and hung round his neck.'
Burnley Gazette, **Burnley v Leeds City, December 1908**

Shoulder High Hero
'When the whistle blew with honours even the Burnley contingent cheered lustily and rushed for Dawson, whom they carried shoulder high off the field.'
Burnley News, **Crystal Palace v Burnley, FA Cup 1909**

He was human after all!
'Dawson picked up the ball and had plenty of time to clear, but instead of throwing away, he waited until two men were close upon him and then attempted to throw the ball over their heads. Apparently, the ball slipped from his hands, struck Hewitt on the head and cannoned off him onto Skinner, who had no difficulty in tapping it through. The nature of this reverse had a depressing effect on the Burnley players.'
Burnley Express, **Bolton v Burnley, October 1910**

Oh, Jerry!
'Dawson missed the train, and Moffat the captain went in goal.'
Burnley Express, **12 September 1910**

What was it Jerry?
'Dawson always rises to great heights when he goes to Barnsley and Saturday was no exception to the rule. He rose to great heights after dinner, when, in a billiards match,

he made a great break. What he broke would better be left to Jerry to tell!'
Burnley Gazette, 1911

Pull your pants up, Jerry!
'Bradshaw took the free-kick at once. So quickly, in fact, that Dawson who was hitching up his pants found the ball entering the net just above his head, before he had time to stretch his hand up.'
Burnley Express, Rovers v Burnley, 1916–17

Jerry the hero!
'Dawson was one of the great heroes of the Blackburn Rovers Cup tie. In many respects, he was the saviour of his side. No one could have done better, and his brilliance in saving what looked like three certain goals was of incalculable value to his side. Dawson is still one of the greatest custodians in this country.'
Burnley Gazette, 1913

'The outstanding figure'
'Dawson cleared in great style…he made a magnificent save under difficulty, and he fielded again most dextrously, especially one in the last minute just under the bar. Dawson was the outstanding figure, his great anticipation and his wonderful agility saving his side when they appeared to be hopelessly beaten.'
Burnley Express, 1921

Bolton v Dawson
For quite a long period, one man alone seemed to be standing between Bolton and victory, and that was Dawson. His was one of the most wonderful exhibitions of goalkeeping ever seen. It was a memorable performance, in which Jerry defied the whole side, beating them by lightning strokes, parrying first from the right and then from the left, leaping out to foil Bolton's every method, diving out with unerring judgement and flicking away high shots.

Nothing came wrong to him. Pepper him as they would, and as they most certainly did, he clearly anticipated their most dangerous efforts, and he aroused the Burnley crowd to frenzied admiration, and the Bolton supporters to wonderstricken ejaculations, the audacity of some of his saves almost taking their breath away.'
Burnley Express, March 1921

'Nay Jerry……..'
Jerry Dawson told me the other day that he does not remember ever hearing a harsh word said to him (in over 20 years) from the crowd behind the goal, even when he has done badly. The worst he has ever heard was 'Nay Jerry, what were ta doing?'
Burnley Express, 1928

He kept 82 others out!
When Jerry eventually stood down from the first team in May 1929 the *Burnley Express* reported that an amazing 82 other goalkeepers had come and gone at Turf Moor in the various Burnley sides since Jerry's debut 22 seasons earlier.

DEATHS

'Football passed away peacefully last Saturday at Turf Moor, so peacefully indeed that long before the end a big section of the crowd stole quietly away, rather than disturb the mourners, by any convulsions at the last. And not a tear was shed – except for the 'bobs' which had been handed in at the turnstiles, prior to the death.'
Burnley Express, **Burnley v Leicester 1–1, the last match of the 1926–27 season**

DEBUTS

When Jimmy McIlroy arrived in Burnley from Northern Ireland in 1950 the club found him digs at a 'marvellous abode' on Stoney Street. It was here that Jimmy Mac would pass the time playing draughts with his landlady. These were competitive games and on one occasion Jimmy was so engrossed with the draught board that he completely overlooked the time and only a quick pre-match sprint along Todmorden Road prevented him from missing the kick-off by minutes. Later, trainer Billy Dougall took McIlroy aside and asked if his late appearance had been intentional, suspicious that this young boy was too big for his boots.

He could not have been further from the truth of course, but Dougall had reason to be aggrieved. The date was 25 October 1950 or, more precisely, it was Jimmy McIlroy's home debut. It would be interesting to hear if Ryan Giggs has a similar account of his Old Trafford debut.'
Burnley's Greatest Goal, **Peter Fyles**

Dazzling debut
Aged just 17 Ian Lawson made his debut in 1957 against Chesterfield in the FA Cup. Everything went well for young Ian as he scored four on his first appearance.

Dodgy debuts (particularly by goalies)
William Smith let in five on his League debut for Burnley in 1888.
Walter Napier let in five on his League debut for Burnley in 1895.
Edwin Towler let in six on his League debut for Burnley in 1903.
Colin McDonald let in five on his League debut for Burnley in 1954.
Billy O'Rourke let in seven on his League debut for Burnley in 1979.
Tony Woodworth let in six on his League debut for Burnley in 1987.

DID THEY REALLY SAY THAT?

⊕ 'Glen Little is feeling his little hammy.' Stan Ternent on Glen Little.

⊕ 'Chris Waddle is off the pitch at the moment – the position where he is most menacing.' Commentator Gerald Sinstadt.

- ✪ 'I have met Charlie George and Leighton James in hotels,' said young tennis star Sue Barker in 1976.

- ✪ 'It's a figure that will never be beaten'. Chairman Bob Lord on the £310,000 fee that Derby County paid for Leighton James in the mid-1970s.

- ✪ 'Life is life, footballers are footballers. Once they've crossed the white line, there's nothing you can do'. Burnley manager, Jimmy Mullen.

- ✪ 'It's a big club in a small village'. Jimmy Mullen during a barren Burnley spell in 1995.

- ✪ 'There's more life in a box of fishcakes'. Manager John Benson in 1985 when Burnley were relegated at the end of the season.

- ✪ 'There's a village somewhere that's missing a fool'. Millwall chairman Theo Paphitis on Stan Ternent after accusations of alleged racism from the Millwall crowd at home to Burnley.

- ✪ 'The referee was booking everyone. I thought he was filling in his lottery numbers.' Ian Wright.

- ✪ 'They will be consistent throughout the season, but the consistency will be up and down.' Manager Steve Cotterill discussing his young players Kyle Lafferty and Chris McCann.

DIRECTORS

- ✪ 'A thought for the Burnley FC shareholders. When the team won the Championship in 1921 the players won it, but now in 1923 that the Championship and the FA Cup are not coming to Burnley the Directors have lost them!' *Burnley News,* **April 1923**

- ✪ In the 1960s Ken Bates once tried to join the Burnley board of directors, but Bob Lord blocked any move and gave him short shrift.

'DIXIE'S COMING!'

Burnley v Everton 3–5, April 1928
'Everybody seemed to have the wind up because Dixie Dean was on the field. One only had to say "Dixie's coming!" and everybody was scared, and even the referee appeared – like the players – to be overwhelmed by the one personality, and to give him the benefit of decisions which were denied to others.

In my opinion not one of Dean's three goals were legitimate. The first came off his elbow, the second Dean knocked the ball down with his hands, and the third was offside.'

'Kestrel', *Burnley Express*

DOING A 'JIMMY MAC'!

In the 1960s Scotsman Jimmy Gabriel of Everton was a hard player and idolised Jimmy McIlroy at a time when there was some rivalry between the two clubs. Gabriel rated McIlroy as one of the most brilliant players he had played against. However, it was in the 1966 FA Cup Final (which Everton won) that Gabriel practised the old McIlroy trick of taking the ball to the corner flag, shielding it and wasting time, as the game neared its end. 'Do what the opposition don't want you to' was Burnley coach Billy Dougall's constant instruction, so McIlroy was one of the first, if not *the* first, to use this ploy to wind down the clock.

Gabriel noticed how McIlroy did this. 'The first time I'd seen someone do that was in the 1960s when I came to England. It was Jimmy McIlroy, and he was playing for Burnley at the time. Towards the end of the game he got the ball and held it, but he didn't just stick his backside out, he did it with such skill. He got the ball and he would turn it, and twist it, and put his foot on it; I was fascinated and so impressed.

So in the Cup Final I thought I should head for goal and try for a fourth, and then it flashed into my mind about Jimmy McIlroy, and I headed off to the corner flag and started messing about. If I'd been a Sheffield Wednesday player, I'd have been booted up in the air, but they didn't attempt to do that to me. I wasn't trying to take the mickey out of them, because they were worthy opponents. I was simply *doing a Jimmy McIlroy*.'

DOUGALL THE DENTIST

Before one game Jimmy McIlroy recalls that Billy Elliot was sitting in the changing room holding his face and clearly in pain. Elliot asked trainer Billy Dougall if he had a file. 'What for?' asked Dougall, to which Elliot replied that his teeth were killing him; some of them were missing and he wore dentures. As blood trickled down the side of his mouth, Elliot took out his dentures and, using the file, he smoothed down one of the teeth that was rubbing into his gums. Elliot looked at them, decided that they were OK, and put them back in his mouth. 'That's better' he announced, and he went out to play as normal. What a tough guy!

Chapter Three

(From Early deaths and Early games to Foreign players and Funerals)

EARLY DEATHS

Quite a number of former Burnley players have died at a comparatively early age. Among these are:

Sandy Lang, who played at Burnley 1885–95, died aged 38 in 1901.
Jimmy Ross, who played at Burnley 1897–99, died aged 36 in 1902.
James Crabtree, who played at Burnley 1888–95, died aged 37 in 1908.
Bernard Donaghy, who played at Burnley 1907, died aged 32 in World War One.
William Pickering, who played at Burnley 1912–14, died aged 23 in World War One.
Alf Lorrimer, who played ay Burnley 1913–14, died aged 23 in World War One.
Teddy Hodgson, who played at Burnley 1911–14, died aged 33 in 1919.
Arthur Bell, who played at Burnley 1902–09, died aged 40 in 1923.
Tommy Willighan, who played at Burnley 1928–34, died aged 33 in 1936.

AN EARLY GAME

30 September 1882
'On Saturday last, both the first and the second teams of Burnley and Brierfield had a trial of strength, and in both cases victory was declared for Burnley; the first team beating Brierfield by two goals to none and the second obtaining a signal victory over Brierfield by 10 goals (five of which were scored by W. Brown and two by A. Sutcliffe) to nil.'
Burnley Express

EDWARDIAN EULOGIES

In January 1907 Burnley met Aston Villa in the FA Cup. Villa were in the middle of a sequence of 13 seasons when they always finished in the top half of Division One:

Champions once, runners-up five times and Cup winners in 1905. They were by far the most successful team in the country and so excitement was high when they came to Turf Moor. Naturally, it brought the best out of our Burnley poets, especially Mr J. Bradshaw of No. 42 Yorkshire Street, Burnley, who was a regular contributor on all things Burnley FC to the local paper.

'What's all this stir and noise?
Why this, the Aston boys
Mean to upset the joys
Of our Burnley team.

Well let them come and try,
Our men will do or die,
Just to pull off this tie
This is our dream.

Aston hath got a name,
Known far and wide its fame.
Our boys we will not blame,
Even if they draw.

But if they chance to win,
There'll be an awful din,
Each face will wear a grin,
All round the show.

Let Green be on his guard,
Dixon and Barron ward
Soft kicks, and even hard,
Kick them away.

Let Moffat, Cawthorne too
Break through the Aston crew,
Let Cretney play up true,
Bold in the fray.

Let Albert Smith and Bell
Do what they do so well,
That centre – Dick 'hissel'
Shall give them praise.

If we can beat these cracks,
We then must face the facts,
Our players won't relax
Till we've won the Cup!

If Burnley score the first,
There'll be a mighty burst.
Some Villain will have curst -
If there's a goal.

We've got another chance
To make the shekels dance.
We've long been in a trance,
For gates we pine.

This gate may ease the bank,
For this our men we thank,
Let all of every rank
Come – wet or fine!'

The game was lost but the attendance (over 16,000) helped to 'ease the bank'.

After the 9–0 defeat of Crystal Palace in the 1909 FA Cup, someone wrote:

Smilingly, readily enter the fray,
Men who really know how to play.
Into the net quickly, finding their way,
They double and dribble, on goal getting bent.
Hurray my lads! You have done what you meant.

The victory over Crystal Palace was a high-water mark for the Burnley club, and it inspired many budding Turf Moor poets.

'In Affectionate Remembrance'

Alas! We never more may roam
As far as London town,
To see the best of football played,
For London has "gone down".
And Burnley has "gone up" – hurrah!
Nine entries with the ball
While Crystal Palace (best of teams)
Failed to secure a goal.

Oh death! Oh death! Where is thy sting?
'Twill sure in London lie,
While Lancashire with victory rings,
For Burnley's won the Tie.
Down, down, within the silent grave
Without a sign of malice,
With nine to nought, we've laid to rest
Poor, poor old Crystal Palace!
G.H.

The FA Cup draw meant that Burnley were at home to Manchester United, and what a draw it was! Poems flooded into the local papers, like this from 12-year-old Edgar Hewitt of Trafalgar Street, Burnley.

'The Palace' and the 'Spurs'
Were laid beneath the earth,
With nine to nought, and three to one,
Were mangled on the Turf.

If United come on Saturday
And suffer same as Spurs,
There will be great rejoicing,
For the Cup will sure be ours.

We then will trim our badges
And paint all green and white,
And Burnley'll roll their sleeves up,
And for the Cup will fight.

It may not be nine-nothing,
Or even three to one,
But let us hope its something,
If only one to none.

Let's hope we get to London,
And in the Final play;
Here's luck to good old Burnley,
We every team will slay.
Edgar Hewitt

Alas! As the history books record, when beating United 1–0 the referee, Mr H. Bamlett, abandoned the match due to the incessant snow; much to the 'annoyance' (or other words!) of the Burnley supporters.

The United hopes were blighted,
One nought was in their crop,
And what is more, they could not score,
Their courage seemed to drop.

But to them stuck a slice of luck
Dropped from the very cloud;
It was a shame to stop the game,
It quite upset the crowd.

Time was too short to end the sport
Of such a glorious fight,
It was just then our gallant men
Had victory in their sight.

We own its true a blizzard blew,
But who had it to bear?
It was just then our fearless men
Had got a double share.

The referee – he may not see
With us just eye to eye,
But yet we claim, stopping the game
Robbed Burnley of the Tie.

In spite of wind. Bear this in mind,
In spite of blinding snow,
We mean to beat the Champions feet.
Defeat our men don't know.

Then go the pace and all things face
Amid the noise and din.
Fight inch by inch, and never flinch.
The Cup – brave boys, you'll win!

This was from the aforementioned John Bradshaw, who seemed to have moved from No. 42 to No. 54 Yorkshire Street, Burnley.

In 1911 Burnley changed their colours to claret and blue, which appears to have inspired the following poem:

Claret and blue, claret and blue,
Out on the Turf once more,
Willow and wicket are stealing away,
For cricket is nearly o'er.

Claret and blue, claret and blue,
We're anxiously watching you start,
Take care of your bodies, look after your limbs,
And above all be plucky at heart.

Claret and blue, claret and blue,
Your battle has only begun,
Let's hope you'll stand in the League much higher,
Than when last season was done.

Claret and blue, claret and blue,
There are cups in prospect to win,
Go in with a will and a mean to do,
And you surely will bring them in.

END OF A CAREER

'Alec Leake is bidding goodbye to football as a player and is seeking a position as a trainer. He has not yet recovered from an injury received by being knocked off the top of a bus at Euston Station after the Fulham match in March, even though he afterwards figured in three first-team matches. He is now carrying on business in Birmingham.'
Burnley Express, 1 October 1910

ENGLAND MANAGER

Not many people get offered the job of being the England manager and probably no one has ever turned it down. But Burnley's Jimmy Adamson did. After Walter Winterbottom stood down as the England team manager Jimmy was approached by the FA and declined the invitation. The FA approached Alf Ramsey as second choice, and the rest is history.

Some years later Ron Greenwood became the England manager. Ron was born in the nearby Burnley village of Worsthorne and one of his earliest experiences in football was when he acted as mascot at the age of seven for the Worsthorne Manufacturing Co. team. He went on to play for Bradford, Brentford, Chelsea and Fulham, but never for his home-town team – Burnley.

ENGLISH TEAM

16 September 2000 was a curious day for the Burnley team – a watershed day in the club's history. On that day (as far can be ascertained) the club fielded the last 'all-English' team to play in Burnley colours in the League.

The team read: Crichton, Cox, Davis, Thomas, Weller, Ball, Cook, Briscoe, Little, Cooke and Payton. There were even three English subs that day – Mullin, Branch and Jepson.

It was goalkeeper Paul Crichton's final game for the club and the following Saturday, having been caught in traffic and missed the Huddersfield away game, he was replaced by a long line of overseas goalkeepers (except for Marlon Beresford), accompanied by countless players who were qualified to play for nations other than England.

These days Burnley has more than double the number of non-English players as compared to English. They are almost back to the 1880s, when they regularly fielded 10 Scottish players and one lone Englishman!

THE 'F' TEAM

Furnell

Fergus   Forrest

Flynn   Farrell   Futcher

Fisher   Fletcher   Freeman   Facey   Francis

FA CUP

Problems, problems, problems!'
'Since the draw was announced to take place at Exeter, the officials have put forth every endeavour to bring their ground measurements up to Cup tie regulation size. It was found that even if the pitch were slanted and both goals put back to their utmost limits it would still be over three yards short. The owner of an adjoining field was approached on the matter, but his terms of selling were not such as the directors found acceptable. The match, therefore, seems likely to be played at Burnley.' (The match was played at Turf Moor and Burnley won 2–0).
Burnley Express, **Exeter v Burnley, January 1911**

Cup tie preparations
'The men stayed about home under the personal supervision of the trainers and directors, the old aversion to foreign conditions and different water met with at seaside and such resorts being again expressed. On Monday, the men tripped over to Whalley, yesterday they walked as far as Keb Cote, while today they are spending at Blackpool, and on Thursday at home. They return home every night, having their usual home conditions, and having their meals under the supervision of the directors.'
Burnley Express, **Burnley v Exeter, January 1911**

The time Burnley won the Cup!
It was April 1914 and Burnley were in the FA Cup Final for the very first time. This was the programme for the team that weekend:
Friday
10.16 Depart from Burnley Bank Top Station. Lunch served on the train.
4.00 Arrive at London Euston Station. Taxis from Euston Station to Charterhouse Hotel.
5.00 Dinner served.
6.10 Attend Palladium Theatre.
Saturday
9.00 Breakfast.
12.30 Lunch.
1.30 Taxis to Crystal Palace.
3.00 Match.

6.00 Taxis to Connaught Rooms for Dinner, by kind invitation of Philip Morrell, MP and Lady Ottoline Morrell (for players and officials only).

7.00 Dinner at Charterhouse Hotel for rest of party.

Sunday

9.00 Breakfast

10.00 Motor drive to Kew Gardens (stay half an hour). Then to Hampton Court and Windsor. Meals en route.

Evening as desired.

Monday

9.00 Breakfast.

10.00 Team leave hotel for Euston Station.

10.30 Depart Euston Station.

3.40 Arrive Burnley Rosegrove Station.

The team will proceed by charabanc from there along Accrington Road. On reaching the Mitre, they will then turn along Trafalgar Street and proceed via Manchester Road to the town hall. There will be a civic reception when the party reaches the town hall, and at the conclusion the team will go to Turf Moor in readiness for the game at 6pm against Bradford City.

The day Burnley won the Cup!…helped by 'speaking strange tongues and wearing caps'.

'The King, fresh from his triumphs in Paris, will this afternoon honour the Cup Final at the Crystal Palace with his presence, and the great English football carnival of the year will get a rare fillip.

His Majesty has not hitherto been present at a Cup Final, and the Royal visit will prove a rare attraction to the tens of thousands of Londoners who would not in all probability have joined the crowd that will visit Sydenham's slopes, and Liverpool and Burnley, the lucky finalists, will in consequence benefit considerably.

His Majesty is assured of an uproarious welcome for not even the Derby draws the public from all parts of the British Isles like the Cup Final. It was officially announced yesterday that bowler hats and short coats will be the proper wear today, and not silk hats.

All through the season in the North of England, football enthusiasts, some call them fanatics, subscribe some few pence a week to clubs, and today every big railway company in the land will be running special trains into the London termini, all full of people speaking strange tongues, and all wearing caps and many of them decked in the colours of the rival clubs.

This year both hail from Lancashire, and Lancashire in consequence will send up the bulk of the great invading army which will descend upon London in the early hours of this morning, and clear out the refreshment rooms in the vicinity of the Euston Road, all of which will do a roaring trade practically from the first glimpse of daylight, for many of the trains started last night.

Practically all the saloon carriages on the Midland (27 specials), London and North Western (47 specials), Great Northern (41 specials), Great Western (40 specials) and Great Central (25 specials) have been booked up weeks in advance, and in some cases the catering has been fearful and wonderful. The officials of the various clubs have laid in eatables and drinkables enough to last them for three days. And the biggest barrel of beer that can be got into the saloon door is usually installed in a place of honour.

Whichever way it goes, Lancashire will hold t' fitba Cup for the year and that is something that those who visit the Palace this afternoon will tell the rest of the world in what will sound a strange and wonderful dialect to the average Cockney. The other provincials, those from Birmingham who relied upon the Villa getting through, those fra Sheffield who pinned their faith on t'United, those from Sunderland who had started to subscribe before their favourites were knocked out, will tell t'Lancashire lads how much better their own particular team would have done, but for the bad luck of being beaten earlier.

At most of the London termini, brakes and motor charabancs will be in attendance to pick up the club parties and take them for a tour of London's sights, before driving them to Sydenham. Among them will be 200 motor omnibuses belonging to the London General Omnibus Company. Music of all kinds from the cornet to the mouth organ will give more or less harmonious renderings of the latest popular songs.

All the tickets were sold weeks ago, and it is safe to say that quite £3,000 is banked before the first turn of the stiles announces that the first shilling has been taken at the gates. For visitors to the Palace, a special boxing show will be staged in the Centre Transept immediately after the football. A 'white hope' competition and an exhibition bout between the two Lonsdale Belt holders Bombardier Billy Wells and Pat O'Keefe will make up a very attractive two hours programme.'
Daily Mirror, 25 April 1914

THE KING SEES BURNLEY WIN THE CUP

'The King wound up the football season of 1913–14, so far as general interest is concerned, when he presented the English Football Cup to T. Boyle, the Burnley captain at the Crystal Palace on Saturday. Burnley had beaten Liverpool by a goal to nothing, and had secured the highest honours of the year.

His Majesty has never had a greater reception. When he arrived the hoarse cheers of the 74,000 people massed around the playing arena were most impressive, and when he was leaving after presenting the Cup and medals the vast assemblage, which seemed to be concentrated in front of the pavilion, once more sang *God save the King* in a manner which testified to their loyalty.

And there was another demonstration of affection and loyalty. Outside the pavilion at the rear of the stands, another great crowd began to assemble just before the end of the match, and when his Majesty came out, he received another ovation from this army of football enthusiasts. That the King was pleased was obvious from his smile, and as the motor car took him away from his first final, he repeatedly raised his hat to the cheering multitudes. There was no mistaking the heartiness of the greeting football gave his Majesty.

Burnley played in their usual club colours of claret and blue, and on the left breast wore the royal coat of arms. In the 1880s, the late Duke of Clarence, the King's elder brother, visited Burnley to open the Victoria Hospital, and in the afternoon saw Burnley play Bolton Wanderers. It was after that match that Burnley received permission to wear the royal coat of arms.

When the teams came out they lined up with the referee and the linesmen and gave three cheers for the King. The captains, Boyle and Ferguson, were presented to his Majesty and the match started.

After the final whistle had proclaimed Burnley's victory, and after Boyle had taken the Cup from the hands of the King, the massed bands of the Irish Guards and the Liverpool Regiment played *God save the King*. One of the most interesting things in the match was the display given by the bands of the King's Liverpool Regiment during the interval. They took up the centre of the ground and marched and countermarched to the delight of the crowd. It was a more brilliant spectacle than the football had been.

By the way, the whole of the regiment was brought to the Palace from Aldershot by special train, and they were allowed to wear the Liverpool club's colours in their caps and on their sticks. There were many distinguished people at the match. The King sat between Lord Derby and Lord Kinnaird. His Majesty wore a dark overcoat and bowler hat.

It was real final tie weather. Somehow or other, the Clerk of the Weather is always friendly towards the match. The crowd was a rather disappointing one, but many people remembering last season's experiences decided to stop in town and do the sights of London, instead of visiting the Palace.

There were the usual scenes in Euston Road, and in the vicinity of the other big termini at night, when the invading army evacuated London. There were to all appearances as many people up from the provinces as ever, but they were not greatly attracted by Burnley and Liverpool. Even on the ground, the crowd was strangely apathetic about the football. The King was the great attraction, and they reserved their heartiest cheers to testify their delight at his Majesty's visit to t'final for t' fitba' coop.'
Daily Mirror, **27 April 1914**

Buy that defence!

In February 1913 Burnley beat Gainsborough 4–1 in an FA Cup tie. More sensational than the result was the fact that immediately after the game Burnley signed on the entire Gainsborough defence: Ron Sewell, Sam Gunton and Cliff Jones. Ron Sewell went on to win a Cup-winners' medal the following season, while Cliff Jones was a regular player in the League Championship-winning team of 1921.

The three of them replaced the regular back three the next Saturday after arriving at Turf Moor, but sadly Sam never played for the club again. Curiously, he never played for any club ever again.

The 'Lancashire' FA Cup

In 1925–26 the first-round draw (equivalent of the third round today) saw eight Lancashire teams drawn at home – four of them against other Lancashire teams. Everton, Preston, Blackburn, Blackpool, Liverpool, Bury, Bolton and Accrington Stanley all had home ties and these included Everton versus Burnley, Preston versus Manchester City, Blackburn versus Oldham and Blackpool versus Barrow.

Perhaps the most interesting feature of these games was the attendances. The aggregate gate for these eight ties was well over 200,000, stretching from the 10,000 who were at Accrington to the 50,400 at Bolton. However, not one of those Lancashire teams managed to reach the Final.

FA Cup bonuses
Up to 1919 the bonuses that clubs were allowed to pay their players for success in the FA Cup were as follows:
Winners £275
Runners-up £220
Defeated semi-finalists £165
Fourth round £110
Third round £55
Second round £22

This meant that when Burnley won the FA Cup in 1913–14 the players collected £275 between them – approximately £23 each. Well done lads!

In 1919 these sums were revised – it appears not always for the better. So it was that players received £2 for winning games in rounds one to six, £1 for a drawn game, £4 for a semi-final win and £8 for a Final win. For example, when Rovers won the Cup in 1928 each player received £8 for 4 wins, £1 for a drawn game, £4 for the semi-final win and £8 for winning the Cup. This gave a total of £21, which was £2 per man less than Burnley players received in 1914.

Cup-winners' medal blunder
After the Burnley versus Charlton Final in 1947, when the winners Charlton got back to the dressing room, their captain, Don Welsh, discovered that the Duchess of Gloucester had given him a loser's medal. 'Well that's a funny thing' he exclaimed, 'this is a runners-up medal! When the Duchess handed it to me she remarked that it had been a very hard game. She must have been more excited than I was!'
Meanwhile, in the loser's dressing room, Reg Attwell, the boy with the wrong medal, grinned, 'At least I've held a winner's medal for a few minutes. Perhaps they thought I'd deserved it!'
Daily Mirror, **April 1947**

FA Cup Final tickets
When Burnley last reached the FA Cup Final in 1962 there was much speculation as to how the Final tickets would be distributed among the fans. The club came up with what seemed a good and fair idea at the time. As we went through the turnstiles on 17 April 1962 we were all handed a voucher with a bold letter of the alphabet printed on it. Over the loudspeakers it was announced that a draw would be made at half-time and letters would be drawn, with holders of successful vouchers being eligible to purchase a Cup Final ticket. On the face of it it appeared to be a good idea.

Unfortunately (had the directors thought it through?), the game was against Blackburn Rovers and there was a good gate that night, some 30,000! This meant that their supporters were given vouchers at the turnstiles too, as there was no segregation of away fans in those days. Thus it was that many hundreds of Rovers' fans were in the Burnley crowd at Wembley.

For the previous few years I had worked for Barclays Bank in Burnley. The football club banked with us. We sold season tickets for the club, Cup tie tickets on Sundays, collected the gate money on Saturday afternoons, counted it on Monday evenings and so on. Bob Lord had promised our manager that whenever Burnley reached Wembley the bank staff would not be forgotten as regards tickets.

Later I entered college to be trained as a Christian minister. One night the college phone rang and it was my young friend Harry from the bank in Burnley. He told me that there had almost been a fight with Bob Lord in the bank. It seems he had come into the bank that day with three tickets to be shared among the entire staff. The bank manager was so offended that he refused to either share them or make a draw for them. Instead, he gave all three to the junior clerk – my pal Harry. And there was my friend on the phone asking if I wanted a first class seat at Wembley! Problem solved.

100 goals

- Walter Place (Senior) was the player who scored Burnley's 100th goal in League and FA Cup competitions. This came in the home game against Wolves on 1 November 1890.

- The 100th League goal came a fortnight later when Claude Lambie scored in the home game against Derby County.

- Bert Freeman was the first Burnley player to score 100 League goals. His 100th goal came in the away game at Derby County on 21 February 1920.

- It was a Burnley player who scored the 100th goal in FA Cup Finals at Wembley. Jimmy Robson achieved this feat when he equalised against Spurs in 1962.

- Andy Lochhead was the last Burnley player to score 100 League goals for the Clarets. His 100th goal came in the last game of the 1967–68 season in the home game against Leeds United.

Stan at Stafford

When Burnley played Stafford Rangers in the Cup in 1990–91, little did they know that one of the Stafford team would go on to fame and fortune – Stan Collymore. Stan distinguished himself in the game by scoring an own-goal, and the Clarets won 3–1.

Albert and Andy

Both Albert Cheesebrough and Andy Lochhead moved from Burnley to Leicester City, and both of them played in Cup Finals for Leicester.

Here and there

When Burnley lost 7–1 at home to Arsenal in the FA Cup in 1937 the record away score remained for nearly 70 years until Birmingham lost at home to Liverpool 7–0 in 2006.

Longest Tie

Burnley's longest Cup tie was against Chelsea in 1955–56. The first game at Turf Moor was drawn 1–1 (scorer: Peter McKay). The following Wednesday the two clubs drew 1–1 at Stamford Bridge after extra-time (Brian Pilkington).

Five days later they drew again, 2–2 after extra-time on the neutral ground of St Andrew's in Birmingham (McKay and McIlroy). One week later Burnley and Chelsea drew again 0–0 after extra-time, this time at Arsenal's ground Highbury. And finally, Chelsea beat Burnley 2–0 in the fourth replay at White Hart Lane, Tottenham. The entire tie lasted nine hours and over 163,000 people watched the five games.

Curiously, after being so well matched, the two teams met a month later in the League and Burnley won 5–0!

FAMILY TIES

⊕ Brothers Jack and William Gair played alongside each other for Burnley in 1883, but David and Jack Walders were the first pair of brothers to appear for the club in a League match (versus West Brom, 1904–05).

⊕ History was repeated in 1979–80 when brothers Vince and Richard Overson played for Burnley against Orient.

⊕ Brian Miller's son David Miller made his League debut for the Clarets on New Year's Day 1983. Brian was the team manager at the time, and he chose to send on his son as substitute. The player who was 'subbed' was Derek Scott, Brian's son-in-law (and David Miller's brother-in-law!).

⊕ In later years, Derek Scotts's sons, Chris and Paul, also made their League debuts for the Clarets.

FANCY THAT!

⊕ Wolves and Burnley are the only two clubs to have won the Championships of all the old Divisions – One, Two, Three and Four.

⊕ In 1994 Peter Shilton was the oldest player to appear for Plymouth Argyle when, as manager, he picked himself to play against Burnley at the age of 44.

⊕ The 0–0 draw in September 1999 between Preston North End and Burnley was the first goalless game between the two clubs for over 100 years.

⊕ As the son of a mill owner, Peter Kippax played as an amateur for Burnley. If a game meant travelling away on a Friday, he sometimes had to miss the game so that he could attend the Manchester Cotton Exchange.

- Striker Andy Payton once called the Radio Lancashire phone-in to deny stories that he was joining Wigan for £55,000. 'Burnley are my club. I love this club', he said.

- When Bob Lord met the Duke of Edinburgh at the 1962 FA Cup Final, he introduced himself as 'Lord of Burnley', to the Duke's great amusement.

- In 1946–47, when the Clarets won promotion, they only played 16 regular players. Another six 'reserves' played 10 games between them.

- In 1959–60, when Burnley won the First Division, they only played 15 regular players. Another three 'reserves' played four games between them.

- And in 1972–73, when the Clarets won promotion, they only played 14 regular players. Three other players made four substitute appearances between them.

- In the 1890s Burnley regularly fielded 10 Scotsmen in their first team. Mind you, they had 64 Scots on their books!

- Burnley captain Wayne Thomas was sent off five times in his first 23 games.

- Burnley player Ray Deakin sometimes drove the team bus in the mid-1980s, partly, it is said, so the club could save money. Others have said that it was to practice for his HGV licence!

- Burnley players clocked up 12 red cards in season 1994–95, which is the club record for a season. The club were also relegated.

- In 1982–83 Burnley scored nine goals in their first two away games (4–1 at Middlesbrough and 5–3 at Bury). What was unusual was that all nine goals were scored by different players – Mike Phelan, Paul McGee, Derek Scott, Andy Wharton, Trevor Steven, Brian Laws, Martin Dobson, Billy Hamilton and Kevin Young.

- The 1920–21 all-conquering Burnley team, champions of Division One with 30 consecutive League games unbeaten, were featured in an advert for OXO at the time, which read 'OXO gives stamina, the power to stay when others fail, the strength to endure – to fight on!'

- In the January transfer window of 2007 Burnley were first off the blocks with the signing of Ade Akinbiyi on 1 January, and then last in the country with the signing of Steve Caldwell at nine minutes to midnight on the last day.

- A bag of McDougall's flour was once thrown at Burnley, at Norwich striker Ted McDougall.

- The 1920–21 Championship-winning team celebrated their success by going to Morecambe for the day.

- Burnley chairman Barry Kilby was also a member of the Burnley youth squad in the early 1970s.

- In 1946–47 Burnley's defence was known as the 'iron curtain'. During one 14-match sequence they conceded just two goals.

- Having once sat behind it, commentator Stuart Hall always referred to Hilda Lord's hat (wife of chairman Bob Lord) as her 'flowerpot' hat!

- By far the largest League gate to watch Burnley, home or away, in the last 30-plus years, was the 51,482 at the Crystal Palace versus Burnley game at the end of 1978–79. Palace needed to win to gain promotion to Division One, and they did it.

- Jimmy Robson is the only Burnley player to hold two Charity Shield medals. One when he played for Burnley versus Wolves in 1960, and another when he appeared for an FA XI when Spurs did the double in 1961.

- Mike Summerbee came to Turf Moor from Manchester City towards the end of his career. To his surprise, his salary was £300 a week, far more than he had received at Maine Road. It was a reward, said Bob Lord, for not mentioning money throughout the transfer negotiations!

- Another Manchester City favourite, Tommy Hutchinson, came to Turf Moor in 1983. He only stayed two seasons but he never missed a match – 106 consecutive games altogether.

- Ex-player and manager Jimmy Adamson, who had not been to watch a game at Turf Moor for 20 years or more, was persuaded to attend the FA Cup game between Burnley and Liverpool in 2005 by his friends Colin Waldron and Paul Fletcher. Due to rain the game was postponed with minutes to go, so Jimmy has still not seen a game at Turf Moor since he left football.

- John Bond, manager at Turf Moor in 1984–85, had to watch a game at Shrewsbury in 1992 disguised as a steward, fearful that Burnley fans would recognise him.

- Nematodes were blamed for Burnley's poor run of form at the end of 2005–06. The little worms ruined the soil, grass and playing surface, and affected play...allegedly.

- Ex-Claret Mike Summerbee is the only Claret ever to make a film and also to play with Pelé! He did both in the film *Escape to Victory*.

- Bob Lord once threatened to burn the BBC TV cameras at Turf Moor before the FA Cup game against Bournemouth, because the fee was so poor and he said it would cut attendance!

- When Ian Wright came to Turf Moor he was given the number-33 shirt – to commemorate the 33 caps he had won for England.

- A Burnley couple broke into Turf Moor on the eve of the Millennium to have sex in the dugout, so that they could conceive a 'special' child.

- When Brian Miller was sacked as club manager in 1982–83, Frank Casper was made caretaker manager. Frank would not use the manager's office, saying he would only do that when he was appointed full-time manager!

FANS

Speechless!
'One Burnley follower who was at the Bolton game was asked to give his version of the affair, but was so disgusted that he said there was only one way of expressing his feelings without the use of strong expletives, and that was as follows, "Of all the feelings I have felt, I never felt a feel like that feel felt!"'
1890s

Crystal Palace v Burnley, FA Cup 1909
'The team were followed to the Metropolis by a good crowd of Burnley folks, calculated to number well over a thousand people – a crowd which made the welkin ring when it gathered in its full force from the four corners of London on Saturday afternoon. Wearing favours of green and white, the Burnley followers paraded the outskirts of the ground bearing aloft a banner inscribed 'SUCCESS TO GOOD OLD BURNLEY!'

At no time did the Palace people rival the good-natured aggressiveness of the Burnley contingent. The Burnley folks early gave way to song and with strong lungs, giving the lie direct to the cry of race degeneracy, drowning the music of a particularly good band. *The Lassie from Lancashire* was a particular favourite.

The cinematograph man was there and he seized the opportunity of an exceptionally robust outburst of cheering a demonstration with the flag to turn the lens on them, and the result will probably be seen in Burnley. The players were also photographed as they turned out.

After the 9–0 victory over Crystal Palace in the FA Cup, 1909, the Burnley players attended the Palace Theatre and the Hippodrome and were given a warm reception by a large crowd.'
Burnley Gazette, **1909**

Bradford City v Burnley, FA Cup March 1911
'Saturday morning came and saw 7,000 people at least transferred to Bradford. There

were some enthusiastic scenes at Manchester Road Station and the club's new colours of every shade of claret and blue were prominent everywhere. A band consisting of drummers and concertinas rattled its way to the station and when it was known that Jerry Dawson was approaching, a plot was laid to chair him to the station. But Jerry's motto is "Don't halloo till you are out of the wood" and by a flanking movement around a tram car, he eluded the vigilant spies and got into the station platform. Here, he was joined by the other Burnley players, and a horse shoe decorated with claret and blue and bearing photos of the players was presented to Mayson. Tall hats, umbrellas in various claret and blue stripes and a host of different favours were sported by the Burnley supporters.'
Burnley Gazette, 1911

Blackburn v Burnley, FA Cup 1912–13
If Blackburn had caught the Cup tie fever, it was simply raging in Burnley. The confidence of Burnley's supporters in the ability of Boyle and his companions to win was everywhere manifest, and the enthusiasm became infectious. It spread from mill to mill, from colliery to colliery, from shop to shop, from office to office.

All classes and conditions of people seemed to be caught up with it. During all last week scarcely anything else was talked of in Burnley except the match and the journey to Blackburn! On Saturday morning, work went by the board. Miners left their work at breakfast-time. Engineering shops were deserted soon after breakfast, and many mills were closed early in the forenoon, either by arrangement or because the weavers had gone.

It is estimated that nearly 20,000 people journeyed to Blackburn – the great bulk by train, but large numbers on foot to Accrington to join the trams there, while big numbers went by motor cars, "taxis", motor charabancs, wagonettes, etc. Never was there such an exodus from Burnley except for the Burnley Fair holidays.'
Burnley News, 1913

'In praise of the Burnley eleven' 1946–47
'By one o'clock on Saturday afternoon we'd emerge from the railway station, run the gauntlet between 11 chip shops and 14 pubs, to arrive by twenty past one at the ground. With an hour and ten minutes to wait. Alone. And dying of exposure.

Looking back on it, the whole of the 1946–47 season seems to have been played on snowbound pitches under leaden skies. It was the first season of the full football programme since Hitler had stopped play back in 1939. We'd been waiting for a long time. So now, each week, an hour and ten minutes was nothing. Especially when you were going to see what we were going to see!

We stood frozen-daft, behind the goals, eating hot torpedoes [Hot torpedoes were an East Lancashire version of Cornish pasties, a now extinct version made of real pastry with real meat inside]. The hour and ten minutes became an hour. The hour became three quarters. Gradually another 20,000–odd worshippers would come shuffling in; sucking warmed air through their scarves, blowing on their mittens, stamping their chilblained clogs. Then the last, endless 15 minutes, memorising every word on the programme, every digit in the League table, even the printer's name.

And then, at last, they appeared. Our unsung, unforgettable heroes, who somehow went unnoticed by the rest of the country. The lads in claret and blue. Our team Burnley. Listen – Strong, Woodruff, Mather, Attwell, Brown, Bray, Chew, Morris, Billingham, Potts and Kippax. Told you, you've never heard of them. But read that team-list again. Read it slowly, savour the syllables – and it's poetry. Say it quickly, roll out that rhythm on your tongue – and it's a magic incantation.'
Jack Rosenthal, *When We Were Young*

The fans on the train
It was the Saturday after Easter, 1960. Burnley were away to Blackpool. They were pushing Spurs and Wolves for the title, but even more than the score (1–1) I recall the journey home on the train.

The trains were packed with fellow fans, still sweating after the very close game, and praising Spurs (who had beaten Wolves away that afternoon). My pal and I sat in the compartment with a short, red-headed lady and her friend, and a large group of 'teddy boys' (for want of a better description). They were in a raucous mood and for some reason they were hyper-critical of my old hero, Tommy Cummings.

Their language was not the best and their criticism of Tommy on a personal level grew in volume. It was impossible to ignore them and I felt quite embarrassed. But the red-haired lady sat and smiled and seemed to agree with most of what the lads were saying. To their accusation that Tommy spent most nights in a pub she replied 'Yes, he does like a drink – but he never gets drunk!' When they suggested that he had a different girlfriend every night, she responded 'OK, he likes female company, but not on the level of…(other first-team players' names were mentioned).

And then, seemingly, she went on the attack. 'Did you know that after the recent Wolves game (lost by Burnley 6–1), some of the Burnley players came off the pitch so dazed that they didn't know the score?' 'How does she know that?' my friend Robert whispered to me. But then, the gang reacted and rose to the bait – how did she know that and anyway, what did she know about the Burnley team or football?

Quietly, she smiled and said to a hushed compartment, 'I'm Joy Cummings. I'm married to the man.' As soon as the train arrived at the first stop – Rosegrove – the gang crept quietly out and presumably moved to another compartment. It was one of the most dramatic journeys of my life, forever remembered for the lady's charm and patience. It was a privilege to travel with Joy Cummings that day. Ah, the pleasures (and the Joy!) of being a Claret.

'The stamp of the old Burnley' – Burnley v Notts Forest, 1–0, November 1972
'There is something special about the relation between the small Lancashire towns and their teams, for though loyalty (in the sense of physical support) and criticism may fluctuate, affection remains. Yesterday, a howling force eight wind and swirling rain cascading down the pitch did not prevent an average 12,000 crowd from turning out to watch the League leaders.

That's good support in a town of Burnley's size. With Leeds, Liverpool and the rest on television almost every other hour, with £1 million's worth of stars having departed from Turf Moor in the past decade, with the ground uninvitingly boarded up along one side, and with the new stand behind one goal providing literally a bird's eye view, not even bangers and chips at half-time makes Jimmy Adamson's young team a 'must' on a wet Saturday afternoon, four weeks before Christmas.

Yet the stamp of the old Burnley still shines through. You could dress Burnley in purple and yellow vertical stripes and black hoods, and for many people they would still be recognisable by their classical style, or at least their attempt at it.

For an hour they were comfortably the better side. The backcloth of glistening smoke-grey slate roofs and empty concrete spaces deadened the appeal, but then Hamlet would be struggling in a disused gravel pit.

The new touchline stand cannot come too soon – it should be worth half a dozen goals a season in improved ambience. I cannot say too much about the goal because it happened at the far end, all of 200 yards away, where events take on the impression of watching another American moon walk.'
Sunday Express, 1972

'Jimmy Mullen's Claret and Blue Army'

'Derby versus Burnley was a match in a time warp. A third-round replay played on fourth round day. But the real blast from the past came from far more distant days, when fans came only to back their beloved team, not fight their opposite numbers. When fences weren't needed and policemen merely smiled in approval. Burnley took 4,000 lads and lasses to the Midlands. And they were sensational.

Soon after goalkeeper Chris Pearce dropped his dreadful clanger, they set up one of the loudest, sustained dins I've ever heard on a football ground anywhere in the world. "Jimmy Mullen's Claret and Blue Army!" was the chant from the terraces and double-decker stand that housed Burnley's admiration society.

Over and over they chanted. Clapping and stamping their feet and drumming the advertising boards in perfect rhythm. On and on for 29 minutes until the end of the match, and another 15 minutes afterwards, until the club chairman urged his manager and players to leave their dressing room, return to the pitch, and wave their appreciation. The bedlam was almost deafening. It was a colourful and spectacular sight.

The bedlam of Burnley was not simply a cry of support for another of the FA Cup's beaten teams. It was a roar of defiance. "Traditions" said Arthur Cox, Derby's manager, whose time in North-East football taught him all there is to know about fanaticism. "You heard the traditions of Burnley's past out there today. A major club of 30 years ago, don't forget." Those who kept up that incessant thunderous clatter were real fans. Genuine football people with a deep love of their club, no matter the result of a single game. They had nothing to do with the executive box brigade and corporate hospitality merchants to whom football is pandering in the modern era. They stood in the rain, sat in the cold, and screamed their allegiance to a game which at the highest level continues to turn its back.

English football has no right to dismiss or take lightly the support of people like those who raised their voices so valiantly at the Baseball Ground. "In all my 23 years in the game, I've never witnessed anything like that", Jimmy Mullen gasped. "It left my players feeling they were prepared to die for those people". It left Arthur Cox thinking out loud, "Burnley have had a reminder of how things could be. It was a demonstration of potential. They now have to try and make sure they get promotion and don't let those people down.'"

And that is a sobering thought.

The Sun, January 1992

MORE FANS

A Burnley fan travelling to all away games in 2006–07 would have travelled a total of 3,831 miles, the nearest game being at Preston (26 miles away) and the longest trip being to Plymouth (319 miles).

Great impartiality
'The game was witnessed by about 300 spectators and throughout – considering a few technical points usually raised at football matches concerning offside in the game – was very orderly and the spectators showed great impartiality.'
Burnley v Kirkham, 1882. So not much change there then!

Better class
'Many of the better class of spectators were loud in their praises!'
Burnley v West Brom, 1893

Naughty!
'There was a large crowd at the Halliwell match and but for the fact that a large number "rushed the gate", the probability is that the receipts would have been considerably in excess of the best on record. The committee estimate that they lost about £25 by the people breaking in.'
Burnley Express, 1886

'Incidents on the way'
A piece of old-style reporting regarding Burnley fans written by 'Kestrel', who wrote for many years for Burnley newspapers in this great style:

'It was probably due to the distance and the cost of the trip, that only a comparatively small handful of Burnley people made the trip south. In fact it was very noticeable that there was more enthusiasm at Accrington, where there was a crowded station for the Friday night journey to Chelsea (Chelsea 7 Accrington Stanley 2). But while the Burnley contingent were quietly confident of their side's ability to pull off the venture, they were not half so sure as were the supporters of the Red and White.

The conditions en route were not so reassuring, for during the night a storm raged, and rain and snow fell, and a gale of wind swept around the train, which to some extent caused delay on the way. Which was to the good; for there is nothing more cheerless than to step out onto the streets of London at 6am on a cold and dark winter's morning. Happily the railway carriages were warm and comforting and the extra hour on the train – nearly eight hours in all – was somewhat of a blessing.

There was something of the old Cup tie fervour seen in the small display of favours. One or two of the party had bedecked themselves in 'fancy' costume, which proclaimed loudly its origin, and that of the wearers. But for the most part, the Burnley supporters were content to conceal themselves as ordinary beings, and to lose their identity in the common crowd. That some of them may have been left behind in London is possible, because just before the return of the excursionists on Sunday morning, one heard the story of the unavailing efforts made by one Burnley individual to persuade three young fellows to leave the tube train on which they had been travelling round and round and round. His protestations were met with the stubborn reply, 'We're not leaving here until we have supped these three bottles of whisky!' He got two of the Burnley men out, but the third was whirled away with only the whisky for company.

It was to a city of strong winds that the visitors made their bow, early on Saturday morning, but the day brightened up, and though the wind remained, there came out a bright warm sun. There was plenty going on to provide interest. Perhaps the most striking thing, by reason of the great contrast between the object of the crowd which arrived (us!) and that of the other crowd that left, took place about 10 o'clock.

This other crowd were the Guards, who during the morning left the city en route for China – a fine lot of ruddy young fellows – the A1's of the nation. To the Fulham versus Burnley game had come a number of Burnley people now living in the South – including Mr G. Lines, formerly in the boot business in Burnley; Mr Airey, formerly of the Burnley Town Clerk's office, and others whom I was pleased to renew acquaintance with. Incidentally, it was of interest to have pointed out from the stand at Craven Cottage, the Ranelagh Club House, and Wimbledon Common further in the distance.

To the game – not an exciting affair. We saw some of the most senseless football imaginable, and Fulham were imbued with the one idea that if the ball were booted hard enough and often enough it would go somewhere. In the last quarter of an hour, the Burnley spider retreated to its lair occasionally for a rest, three goals in credit, and invited the Fulham fly to come out of its parlour, but Fulham were not fly enough to do it.

In other words, in the last 15 minutes, there must have been four or five open goals left for Fulham to shoot at – including a penalty. And Fulham would have none of them. And by way of parting, Burnley went and got another goal.'
Fulham v Burnley 0–4, FA Cup tie, January 1927

The Indian Clarets

All of us need to visit the dentist, and for most it is a local trip of a few miles. Hop in the car, park, in through the door, home in time for lunch. However, for Burnley fanatic Kev it involved a trip to India.

In the UK he was quoted £17,000 for the treatment he needed: four titanium implants and a bone graft. Kev was flabbergasted and just could not afford it. So he turned to the internet and came across a man who could do the work at a fraction of the cost. Dr Virmani was his name and he was able to quote £1,200 to £1,500 for the same job.

So far, Kev has been over there twice and needs one more trip. On his first two trips he left Burnley shirts for the local kids. They wear them proudly and are part of the overseas Claret brigade. He befriended one particular taxi driver – actually it was an Indian taxi in the shape of a rickshaw. That is another new Claret today, thanks to Kev.

Kev was thousands of miles from home and missing his family, but he made so many friends over there, one of them being the hotel security man – another new Claret safely recruited!

Three nuns
Sometime in the 1990s, members of the London Clarets were travelling to a Burnley game they saw three nuns carrying suitcases to the station in London. Immediately, they rushed to carry the cases. Burnley won 3–0; seeing this as a divine sign London Clarets have always looked for nuns carrying suitcases ever since.

Claret Summit
Alastair Campbell is a fanatical BFC supporter. At a Brussels European summit meeting Alastair received text messages from his children about the Burnley score that day.

Too keen!
In 1986–87, to make sure they reached Torquay in time for the 3pm game, Burnley fans left on the supporters' coach at 11.30 the night before. Alas, when they got there they discovered that Torquay had made it an evening kick-off and they had arrived 14 hours too early! The game ended 1–1.

'I'd walk a million miles…'
Burnley fan Durks was serving in the army in Bosnia and had weekend leave and so decided to go home for the Preston versus Burnley game. He made a four-hour drive to Zagreb, was delayed two hours at the airport, took two flights and two train journeys to get home and it all cost him £300. Burnley lost the match 3–5!

Till death us do part…
Stuart Limb, bus driver and Burnley fan, took his family up to Annan in Scotland in the Burnley team coach for his wedding. When he died in 1999 he was buried in his new Burnley shirt and scarf. However, the funeral directors would not allow his coffin to be taken to the crematorium by the team bus.

Dave Timberlake
Dave, who lives in Nottingham, was last year crowned Britain's biggest football fan in a nationwide search conducted by Virgin Media. He owns more than 100 Burnley shirts and countless pieces of memorabilia. He has transformed his house into a shrine to his beloved Burnley and has even painted his windows in claret and blue.

He has spent over £30,000 in the last 40 years on everything from season tickets to Burnley slippers, travelling more than 10,000 miles every season, and never missing a game at Turf Moor. His wife even showed him the red card when he refused to substitute her for the beautiful game. Dave said, 'My friends have nicknamed me "Burnley" for years, and the team really is my life.'

A Damascus Road experience

'God that pie was good and the chips were to die for. And maybe it was just at that moment when I put the plate down on the table, picked up the plastic fork (kind of spoiled it just a little), savoured the moment, that the revelation came to me. This is what it is all about. Travelling up and down the highways with a good bunch of people, bumping into familiar faces, seeing a new ground for the first time, talking to the locals…and a plate of pie and chips lathered with salt, vinegar and tomato sauce.

St Paul must have felt much the same on the road to Damascus.'
Dave Thomas, reflecting on his visit to a pre-season friendly at Partick Thistle.

The Scandinavian Clarets
(English, punctuation, grammar, spelling all untouched!)
'I am sitting up in the snow and is -7 Celsius outside my house. This is a little notice from your neighbour, I [k]now you don't look at us as a neighbour but we are. Then what shall I write about? I will try to tell you about hove [how] we seen it from outside UK.

We are not playing football up here at the moment, as you understand. English football have been on TV since early 1960, that is one reason why all Norwegian are supporting an English club. You can't understand our interest for your national sport. The Scandinavian Clarets have 70 members and Man U have 25,000 members, Liverpool have about 15,000.

I am proud to be a part of the Burnley support, we all [k]now it is not about quantity it's about quality, we are the proper supporters and the others know that's why they do not like us ('who cares'). I have been many places in the UK and other places. One thing is always nice, you always find Burnley people everywhere.

Nearly all people I meet in Burnley are surprised and wonder why we support Burnley, and we are coming faaaaar away from Norway. We have not come from far away, we just have one hour and 45 minutes flight from Torp (Oslo-Ryanair) to Liverpool. If I want to see my Oslo team Valerenga play away in Tromso, it takes three hours on a flight!

Why do we support Burnley? What a question…we saw them on TV and that's it, when you fall in love you can't explain! Looking back on the season so far, we are so proud up here for what our Clarets have run this season. For first time for many years radio and TV have spoken about BFC. I have even got so many emails, text and congratulations. Everybody asks the same question "What's going on in Burnley these days" The answer is easy, for the first time in long time we have a squad. And the second reason is we have got a brilliant manager.

I have been over for three matches this season (Sheff Wed away, PNE home and Southampton home) and have seen Burnley in all TV matches this season. I went to Sheff Wed away in the opener, my Mum of 78 years old was on her first match to see Burnley play…sorry Mum…the support behind the goal was fantastic…sorry mum for taking you there. My mum is never going to Sheffield anymore. But she loves Burnley, everybody does but some few don't know it yet, they will wake up some day!!

I will be back for my match number 30 against Wolves with Burnley. Hope I have to take the train down to London to see Clarets beat Arsenal in the Cup instead. Me and my son are coming back for match nr 31 against Sheff Wed, my Mum tells me to talk to Christian [Kalvenes] and he has the licence to give one Sheffield player a good kick…

I hope you can read this notice and not complain about my English, but read it and have a good laugh. To you lucky Clarets who can go to all the matches, make lots of noise and support the team – I can hear you all on my computer…

Up the Clarets,

Best from **Atle Normann,**
Scandinavian Clarets

Chinese Clarets

'I have lived and worked in China since 2004 and in my spare time I am the head coach of an expat kids' football team. Even though they are only eight and nine-year-olds, they are pretty good; we take them all over Asia and we have an impressive trophy cabinet. I mention them because they give a fascinating insight into the view of the football world from the perspective of a modern day kid living abroad. There are about 20 kids in the squad coming from more than 10 countries with only three or four Brits. All of them claim to 'support' Liverpool, Manchester United, Arsenal or Chelsea. They have heard of Barcelona, Real Madrid, AC Milan, etc, and they occasionally turn up to training wearing their colours, but that is about it.

It is actually quite amusing to see German and Dutch kids running around with Rooney on their shirts while their parents look on in total horror. When I mention 'claret and blue' only a few have ever heard of West Ham or Aston Villa, so what chance do I have to educate them about the mighty Burnley? This season's Cup exploits are written off by them either as "matches that their reserves play in" or "one of those games where you sometimes get knocked out by a non-League team, but it doesn't matter because we will win the Champions League instead."

When I asked one of them once did they know about Burnley, they asked if "this" was something to put on the fire? Next question was "well, who have you got then?" to which I replied "we've got Robbie Blake, and Chris Eagles – he used to play for Manchester United if that helps?" Following a look of total incredulity, the child then sloped away clearly thinking I was totally mad. Even worse, when I tell the adults here that we were once in the European Cup no one believes me although they told me that they would attempt to verify my claim by asking a still living grandparent!

I have an eight-year-old son (who plays in the team above). He knows about my passion for Burnley (to quote him "that other team that nobody knows about!") I have endless debates over beers with other friends on the subject of which team your child should support. Should the child be obliged to follow in Dad's footsteps or have a free choice? Opinion is divided, though it helps if Dad comes from North London! However, given that somebody has to be born in Macclesfield, Aldershot, or dare I say, Burnley, you are potentially consigning the child to a lifetime of frustration and ridicule, while his 'free choice' friends with Arsenal scarves count their trophies. Tough one these days!

My son, he's a good kid – and sensitive to his Dad, but living on the other side of the world I can not exactly take him to Turf Moor, get him a Chris McCann autograph or even a replica shirt (well not easily anyway!) He has not really declared his hand yet and it pains me to say it, but it is going to have to be a free choice…maybe we will do a compromise and he will start to follow Beijing Guo'An. At least I could take him to the matches then…?

Following Burnley from the other side of the world is not easy. Even though we live in the information age – getting access to Burnley news is not easy. First you have the time zone differences. Saturday games kick-off at 11pm here and the evening games are in the middle of our night. So quite often it is a question of waking up and dashing down to log on to the PC. Imagine not knowing you have beaten Chelsea in a penalty shoot-out at Stamford Bridge until you are tucking into your cornflakes the next day! Even the websites with video footage often flash up a "sorry not available in China" message!

We have ESPN and Star Sports here, broadcast from Singapore and Hong Kong, and there is zero coverage of the Championship. On a more positive note, I have managed to find two other Burnley supporters in China – both in other cities though! One of my best mates out here comes from Rochdale – imagine the task he has – we often console ourselves that everyone else in the world is just plain ignorant – though he has been showing a worrying interest in Manchester United lately. Amusingly, he felt duty bound last season to jump on a plane to watch them in the Division Two Play-off Final – which they promptly lost – but money well spent none the less.

Sadly, Burnley do not come to Beijing. Only Real Madrid and Manchester United do that! One day I will get back to the Turf when hopefully we will be hosting them in the Champions League! I would really like to keep in touch, Up the Clarets!
Darrell Barnes

FANZINES

To say that the club have had a number of fanzines would be wrong; the supporters have had a number of fanzines. The club has rarely if ever recognised the fanzines, written, printed and sold by the fans. That fact gives the fanzine a free voice, often irreverent, a little bawdy, humorous at times, always passionate, and as distinct from the club view as printed in the official programme.

There is room at Turf Moor for both, one representing the club and the other the voice of the fans. Fanzines have been on the streets of Burnley for 20 years now.

⊕ It is believed that the first fanzine was called *No Nay Never*. It came out around October 1989 and lasted (as far as is known) until September 1994. Originally it cost 50p, but eventually rose to £1. It described itself quite rightly as 'an alternative view of Burnley Football Club'.

⊕ *Who Ate All the Pies?* came to public attention in 1992 and lasted until 1997. It cost 50p, and began as every quarter but later slipped to every six months. It varied from being published occasionally to infrequently.

⊕ This title was supplemented in 1995 by *The Official Who Ate All the Pies?* This came out monthly and lasted a year.

⊕ The 1990s saw a lot of comings and goings as regards Burnley fanzines. There was the *Longside Loyalist* in 1995, which was published every two months for 50p, and *The Claret Flag*, which first appeared in 1994 and cost 60p.

✪ *Kicker Conspiracy* lasted from 1996 until 1999 and was published by the Huddersfield Clarets. It came out every two months and cost £1. *Bob Lord's Sausage* lasted from 1997 until 2001. Describing itself as 'the meaty Burnley fanzine with only a little gristle', it began as a quarterly production but declined to once every six months.

✪ *For Ever and 9 days* appeared from 1995 until 1996 and cost £1. This title later became *Marlon's Gloves*, starting at £1 but sometimes reduced to 50p.

✪ Currently, there appears to be only one fanzine, *When the Ball Moves*, which is edited by Martin Barnes, a Sheffield Claret. This is by far the longest lasting fanzine and the best value of them all. It usually runs to 60-pages plus and is jam-packed with Clarets' opinions, statistics, articles and verses.

✪ P.S. A few results from the end of season questionnaire from 2008, as conducted by *When the Ball Moves*.
Which part of the ground do you sit? James Hargreaves Upper 48 per cent, Bob Lord 7 per cent.
How do you rate the whole 'match day experience' at Turf Moor? OK, 50 per cent.
What do you think of the general atmosphere at Turf Moor? OK, 48 per cent.
How do you rate the stewarding at Turf Moor? Poor, 41 per cent.
What is your favourite type of pie? Meat and potato, 60 per cent.

'FAST FALLS THE EVENTIDE...'

'Burnley arrived a little before 2 p.m. expecting to commence play at 2.30, but owing to the Haslingden players being totally indifferent as regards punctuality, the game was not commenced until 3.20 p.m. with the Burnley captain losing the spin.'
Burnley Express, 1883

'Kicking off at 3.40 p.m. in December was far too late. The latter part of the game was played in total darkness, a state of affairs which should not be repeated, as spectators who pay their money have a right to witness the game from beginning to end.'
Burnley v Enfield, 1883

A FEW FIRSTS

First competitive match, 14 October 1882
'Today, the Burnley Football Club play their first competition for the Lancashire Challenge Cup at Calder Vale. While wishing them every success in their endeavour to

introduce good football into Burnley, we may say that we think there is the foundation of a good strong team in the town, and if the players will only try to become more acquainted with each other's capabilities, and study more the science of the game, we feel convinced that success will ultimately attend their efforts, and place them in the front ranks of Lancashire football players. May the field be a large one, and may our local football players work shoulder to shoulder and lower the colours of the Astley Bridge team.'
Burnley Express

How did they go on? – 18 October 1882
'On Saturday afternoon last, Burnley and Astley Bridge met on the ground of the former at Calder Vale, to contest in the first round for the Lancashire Challenge Cup. Astley Bridge had it all their own way throughout, and won the game eight goals to none. A large company assembled to watch the match. This is the first year the Burnley club has played Association rules.'
Burnley Express

- Burnley's first win in the League was 4–3 at Bolton Wanderers (September 1888).

- Burnley's first home win at Turf Moor was 4–1, also against Bolton Wanderers (October 1888). Thus, we also have Burnley's first 'double'.

- The first time Burnley ever beat the team destined to be League Champions was against Everton, 3–2 in season 1890–91.

- The first ever substitute for Burnley was Ian Towers, who came on for Willie Irvine in August 1965.

- The first sub with a number 12 on his back was Sammy Todd. He came on for Brian Miller in April 1967.

First Black Player
It is believed that the very first black player registered on Burnley's books was Alf Charles. Alf, born in Trinidad in 1912, came to Lancashire primarily as a cricketer and for many years played for Nelson in the Lancashire League, alongside his great friend Learie Constantine.

Alf arrived at the football side of Turf Moor in November 1933, and though he never appeared in the Burnley first team he went on to play for Nelson, Darwen and Stalybridge Celtic. Playing at inside-left, Alf only made one Football League appearance, which was for Southampton in Division Two in 1936.

The first black player to play in the Burnley first team was Les Lawrence. Though he only played in 24 games and a further 11 as a sub, Les has gone down in Turf Moor history as the club's first first-team black player. He arrived at Burnley in 1984 after a £20,000 transfer from Rochdale, and remained at Turf Moor until the summer of 1986.

FIXTURES

A fact little known outside of Burnley is that for well over half a century the Football League fixtures were arranged by Charles E. Sutcliffe of Burnley. C.E. Sutcliffe had been one of the earliest of Burnley's players in the 1880s. He rose to become a League and an international referee, then a Burnley FC director and eventually president of the Football League.

He was first and foremost a solicitor and it was he who helped formulate many of the laws of the Football League. He worked out the League fixtures from the early days of the League until he died in 1939. His son Harold Sutcliffe then took over the task and he carried on until he died in 1967. It was then the turn of the computers.

FLOODLIGHTS? NOT IN MY LIFETIME!

'It is suggested that football should be played under floodlights in order to compete with the greyhound tracks. There does not seem to be any reasonable basis for such talk nor any reasonable grounds for night football coming into vogue.

The argument is that shopkeepers and shop assistants who do not get to see Saturday matches would have a chance of attending night matches, but it is questionable whether the number is so great that it would make a difference.

Previous floodlit experiments such as Dick Kerr's Ladies versus Bradford Ladies played on the cricket field in 1923 have been but novelties, and however great the attraction might have been for one experience, it is hardly probably that football by electric light will pay as a regular thing'.
'Kestrel' *Burnley News,* **October 1932**
(Incidentally, it was 25 years later, in October 1957, that Burnley first used floodlights to play a First Division game.)

FOLDS ROAD SCHOOL

This is a junior school in Bolton with an incredible reputation for producing schoolboy footballers who later became reputable professional players. Obviously Bolton Wanderers have benefitted over the years, but the Clarets also have cause to be grateful to the school teachers at that school in Bolton.

Among the players who began their education at Folds Road and who went on to play for the Clarets are Tommy Lawton (1935–37), Harold Mather (1939–55), John Marshall (1936–1949), George Knight (1938–49), Jack Knight (1938–48), Len Martindale (1937–51) and Billy Holden (1949–55).

While at Turf Moor they played in 693 first-team games and scored 104 goals between them. Some record! Some school.

FOOD

'The Burnley players like to play at Derby County for one thing – though there are lots of drawbacks – and that one thing is the exceptional good meals that are put on by the host and the hostess of the George Hotel!'
***Burnley Express,* November 1911**

FOOD FOR THE FINAL 1914

✪ 'The task of feeding the thousands of spectators will be in the hands of Messrs J. Lyons & Co. The following items will comprise the Cup Final menu:
75 rumps of beef
25 sirloins of beef
35 ribs of beef
60 loins of mutton
100 shins of mutton
250 fowls
150 hams
A ton and a half of pressed beef
400 heads of lettuce
A ton and a half of potatoes
12,000 sandwiches
2,500 veal and ham pies
25,000 pats of butter
30,000 rolls and butter
75,000 slices of bread and butter
25,000 buns and scones
48,000 slices of cake
6,000 pastries
1,500 gallons of milk
1,500 dozen bottles of minerals
1,000 dozen bottles of beer
2,000 gallons of beer'

✪ During a club tour of Spain in 1949 the Burnley team complained vigorously about the food being cooked in olive oil. It was not until a supply of lard was obtained that harmony was restored in the Lancashire party.

The menu for the **Club's 1962 Celebration Dinner** at the Imperial Hotel, Blackpool, was:

Claret and Blue Melon in Port Wine
****
Ightenhill Clear Vegetable Soup

Padiham Thick Mock Turtle Soup
****

Brun and Calder Rainbow Trout in Butter
****

Escalope of Turf Moor Veal
Read Garden Peas in Butter
Simonstone Berny Potatoes
****

Newchurch Crème de Menthe Sorbet
****

Roast Breast of Gawthorpe Chicken
****

Habergham Imperial Illumnee
****

Bee Hole End Coffee
****

The men had House of Lords cigars!

BEATEN BY A RICE PUDDING

Derby County's goalkeeper Jack Robinson took his dietary regime very seriously. His teammate Jimmy Methven remembered him well in his memoirs, 'Jack's motto was "no pudding, no points!" If he missed his pre-match rice pudding, he seemed unable to stop a shot. We once had a narrow squeak at Burnley when somehow the milky perquisite was omitted from our lunch. So Johnny Goodall set out to scour the town and returned carrying a large dish of what he called "Burnley mixture" – quite what it was no one knows, but my diagnosis would be something like Quaker oats and tripe!

Jack polished off the lot and we beat Burnley 3–2. That day, Jack played the game of his life!'

WHO ATE THE CHICKEN?

Young Burnley players were placed in lodgings with sometimes as many as four of them together in one house. Conditions were not always luxurious, in fact far from it. Some players were barely fed, while others were in attic rooms so cold that ice formed in the winter. In most the toilet was in the back yard and more than one player used a bottle by the bedside to save the trip outside.

Sometimes the landlady was lonely and the young lads were happy to warm her bed for her and keep her company. One landlord was an undertaker, while one landlady was a fortune teller. Willie Irvine remembers one landlord who smoked a pipe and was forever spitting into the coal fire. It made a lovely sizzling noise if it hit the fire, but sometimes, unfortunately, he missed. In short, they were varied places, where sometimes the lads were lucky to find somewhere comfortable and others they could not wait to get out.

Ralph Coates and his fellow apprentices were once in digs where they were hardly fed and were constantly hungry. One night the smell of chicken cooking in the oven drifted upstairs. The lads could not help but notice and decided it would be just the job after a meagre tea. The landlady had gone out so they found the chicken and ate the lot, hiding the carcass and bones afterwards. The landlady was baffled and never did find out who ate the chicken!

FOOTBALLER OF THE YEAR

Jimmy Adamson is the only Burnley player ever to be chosen as Footballer of the Year. This occurred in 1961–62, the season when the club finished runners-up in both the League and FA Cup. The club were so dominant in football at the time that colleague Jimmy McIlroy finished runner-up in the same poll.

How it all began! Bolton v Burnley, February 1951
'The man who earned the bouquets in the Burnley side – apart from Strong – was Adamson; he made a great debut. He got up well to the high ball and his heading out to the wings was indicative of a football brain. Young Jimmy saved a certain goal when Lofthouse manoeuvred clear of a ruck of players, moved inside Cummings, who had watched him throughout like a lynx, and had the goal at his mercy.

Adamson rushed up as the centre-forward was about to shoot, and did the only thing possible – slammed the ball off the England leader's toes for a corner – and not even a muscle of his face slipped!'
Burnley Express

FOREIGN PLAYERS

These days, players from overseas can be seen in every team. But it was not always so.

Burnley created a little bit of history and caused quite a stir when in 1910–11 Max Seeburg turned out for the Turf Moor team. Max was born in Leipzig in Germany and had played just once for Tottenham.

He was a versatile player and in his 18 games for Burnley he played at right-half, right-wing and centre-forward. He is generally accepted as the first foreign player (born outside the UK and Ireland) to play in the Football League. He left Turf Moor at the end of the season when he was transferred to Grimsby Town.

Compare that to the 2008–09 season when Burnley players have come from seven nations outside of the UK including Iceland, Norway, Denmark, Hungary, Albania, Holland and Peru.

FULHAM ROUGHS

'Burnley set out for Fulham yesterday to meet the Fulham roughs. The match is generally looked upon as ranking with that of Grimsby!'
Burnley News, October 1911

FUNERALS

I have shared in a fair proportion of Burnley-related funerals. One of the first and certainly the most moving was of young Gary Woodward in the 1970s. In those days, I taught RE at Singleton Hall, a special school on the Fylde. One of the pupils there was Gary from Accrington who was in his early teens. He was a passionate Burnley fan and always sat in my RE class with his claret and blue scarf round his neck! When he tragically died aged only about 14 I had the difficult task of conducting his funeral. He was buried in his scarf and rosette – a true Claret to the end.

At another funeral in Rochdale the family gave me a splendid claret and blue scarf at the close of the service. It was their much appreciated way of saying 'Thank You.'

I have a good friend called Tony Bradshaw who is also a fellow Claret. In March 1997 Tony's Dad died. He had been a Burnley fan all of his life, rarely missing a game, and was at Maine Road in 1960 like me. After the funeral of his Dad, Tony approached Burnley about scattering the ashes at the Turf. This was arranged for the close season and the ashes were scattered before the 1997–98 season began. Under Chris Waddle the Clarets went their first 10 games without a win, their worst start to a season since 1979! To this day Tony still worries if there was any connection.

In 1982 I appeared on Radio Lancashire along with three other vicars. The year marked the centenary of the club and the four of us were being asked about our faithful following of the Clarets. The interviewer began with me and asked what I had done for the club. 'Oh, I wrote the first history of the club,' I explained. 'And you sir', the interviewer said, turning to the Revd Alan Reid, vicar of Read, 'what have you done regarding Burnley FC?' 'I buried Bob Lord!' came the immediate reply.

Chapter Four

(From amazing Gates and Giant-killers to Humiliation and How are the mighty fallen)

THE 'G' TEAM

Green

Gunton   Gallagher

Gnohere   Gardner (S.)   Gudjonsson

Gray (W.)   Gascoigne   Gayle   Gray (A.)   Grewcock

Sub: Gardner(T.)

AMAZING GATES

⚽ The earliest 'record gate' at Turf Moor was in **1883–84** when the Turfites met their greatest rivals, Padiham. Over 12,000 people turned up to see the game in March 1884.

⚽ This record stood for 10 years until **December 1893** when over 13,000 came to Turf Moor for the Blackburn Rovers League game, which saw record receipts of £339.

⚽ This figure was equalled in February 1896 when 13,000 saw the Stoke City FA Cup tie.

⚽ However, by far the largest attendance of the 19th century for Turf Moor was at the Everton FA Cup tie in **February 1898** when 20,500 paid an unprecedented £794 for admission.

⚽ It was another decade before Turf Moor saw an attendance to beat the Everton game. This came in **February 1909** when an FA Cup replay with Spurs drew a gate of 30,000 to Turf Moor.

⊕ The League record, which had stood for many years, was smashed in **March 1912** for the visit of Derby County. A crowd of 31,000 attended 'among whom were an unprecedented number of ladies' and the receipts were another Turf Moor record of £831. (Both Burnley and Derby were vying for promotion that season.)

⊕ 1913–14 was the first season when gates regularly topped 20,000. On **8 September 1913** the League record was beaten at Turf Moor when 36,000 saw the match against Blackburn, but this was dwarfed in the last match of the season (**27 April 1914**) when over 40,000 attended the last game of the season, against Bradford City. (This was the same night that the team had brought back the FA Cup to the town.)

⊕ That same season also saw the FA Cup record attendance broken when on **21 February 1914** 32,734 people rolled up for the third-round game against Bolton Wanderers, paying a record £2,153 to see the match. Many walked from Bolton, arriving long before 10 in the morning, while nine excursion trains made the trip from Bolton to Burnley. That record was broken again in the next round at home to Sunderland (**11 March 1914**) when 49,737 filled Turf Moor. They paid a record £2,838 in receipts, which was by far the greatest in the club's short history.

⊕ 1913–14 was the first season when the average gate at Turf Moor topped 20,000 (21,820), and season 1920–21 was the only time in the club's history when the average gate exceeded 30,000 (31,535).

⊕ The League record lasted until **15 January 1921** when Burnley entertained Blackburn Rovers; 41,534 saw the game. That record lasted just over a month until **26 March 1921** when Turf Moor welcomed Bolton Wanderers and the record rose to 42,653.

⊕ From those memorable days gates dropped, except for the 1923–24 season when the all-time record attendance came to Turf Moor for the Burnley versus Huddersfield Town third-round FA Cup tie on **23 February 1924**. That day saw the 50,000 figure broken when 54,775 people jammed into Turf Moor. In the 1930s other notable gates were 48,717 (Manchester City 1932–33 FA Cup) and 47,670 (Birmingham 1934–35 FA Cup). The all-time record was almost broken in 1937 when 54,445 fans packed Turf Moor for the Burnley versus Arsenal FA Cup tie.

⊕ However, it was after World War Two in 1946–47 that gates both locally and nationally began to rise again. The Clarets topped 40,000 for the home game against Bury, and the Cup record gate was almost broken when 49,244 saw the Middlesbrough Cup replay. The next season, 1947–48, witnessed Turf Moor break the 40,000 mark six times for League games (versus Derby County, Arsenal, Blackpool, Manchester City, Preston and Blackburn). By far the most outstanding attendance was on **11 October 1947** when 52,869 saw the Burnley versus Blackpool Division One game. That League record gate had stood since 1921 and remains the League record at Turf Moor to this day.

⊕ On several occasions in the next few seasons the Turf Moor gates topped 40,000 – Manchester United and Blackpool (1949–50), Arsenal (1951–52), Manchester United and Preston (1952–53), Blackpool (1953–54), and Blackburn and Manchester United (1958–59).

⊕ The League Championship season 1959–60 saw just one 40,000 gate at Turf Moor, against Manchester United. Everton(1960–61), Spurs (1961–62), (1962–63) and Manchester United (1966–67) also topped the 40,000 mark.

⊕ **The last League game to have a 40,000 plus attendance** at Turf Moor was against Leeds in 1973–74 (40,087).

⊕ **The last League game to have a 30,000 plus attendance** at Turf Moor was against Liverpool in 1974–75 (32,111).

⊕ **The last League game to have a 20,000** plus attendance at Turf Moor was against Blackburn Rovers in 1976–77 (22,189).

⊕ Equally as spectacular as League attendances have been Cup tie gates. Since World War Two, Turf Moor has had 10 FA Cup ties with a gate exceeding 40,000 and a further eight FA Cup ties when the gate exceeded 50,000.

⊕ The 50,000-plus gates for FA Cup ties at Turf Moor since World War Two have been:
1951–52 Liverpool 54,031
1952–53 Sunderland 53,105
1952–53 Arsenal 51,025
1953–54 Manchester United 52,847
1953–54 Newcastle 52,011
1959–60 Bradford City 52,850
1959–60 Blackburn Rovers 51,501
1961–62 Everton 50,514

⊕ When Burnley won the League in 1959–60 they only finished 15th out of the 22 clubs in the 'best average home gate' table (26,869). However, the town's population that year was 80,500, which was by far the smallest of the 22 clubs. At least two clubs, namely Birmingham and Leeds, had populations of over half a million people, while another nine clubs could top a quarter of a million local residents. The attendance that season at Turf Moor amounted to approximately 33 per cent of the total population – twice the average proportion achieved by the other 21 clubs that season.

GIANT-KILLERS!

⊕ The Clarets have often been the subject of giant-killers in Cup competitions. One of the first major upsets was in 1903–04 when Darwen, then in the Lancashire Combination, beat Second Division Burnley 3–0 in the FA Cup.

⊕ Giant-killing seemed to happen every two years. In 1905–06 Southern League Spurs knocked Second Division Burnley out of the Cup, 2–0. Two years later, in 1907–08, Southern League Southampton knocked Burnley (still in Division Two) out of the Cup, 2–1. And that was at home.

⊕ Two years later Southern League Swindon beat Second Division Burnley 2–0 in the FA Cup.

⊕ The biggest shock in the first 39 years of the club's history came in 1920–21 when, halfway through the famous 30 consecutive games without defeat, the Clarets were beaten by Second Division Hull City, 3–0. This is why the consecutive sequence takes into account League games only. Said the *Burnley Express* at the time, 'Hull went into it hammer and tongs; they kicked the ball anywhere, raced about for it, and whenever it came their way, it had to be either man or ball, or both. The Turf Moor side were not only knocked off their game; they were knocked off it with bounce, bustle and speed.'

⊕ It was another eight years before the Clarets were 'killed', this time by Swindon. In 1928–29 the Clarets were beaten 3–2 by Swindon, who then played in the Third Division South. Just after World War Two Swindon Town did it again. The year after Burnley had been beaten at Wembley (1947), Swindon came to Turf Moor for the third round. Burnley were soundly beaten 2–0 by a Swindon team who were in the bottom half of Division Three South. To add to the irony, Swindon were managed at the time by Louis Page, an ex-Claret player.

⊕ Without a doubt, most Burnley supporters of the modern generation recall the day in 1975 when Southern League club Wimbledon came to Burnley for an FA Cup tie. At the time the Clarets were riding high in Division One, but they were brought down to earth by a 1–0 home defeat.

⊕ 'Hang your head in shame after this defeat Burnley,' wrote *Burnley Express* columnist Peter Higgs. 'The match they said was a "free pass" into the next round of the FA Cup provided arguably the most humiliating result in the history of Burnley FC.' Never since the Football League was reorganised in the 1920s had a non-League team visited the home of a First Division club in the FA Cup and won. But Wimbledon did! That day at Turf Moor (4 January 1975) the town noted for tennis and strawberries made its mark in football, and left its mark on Burnley!

⊕ Since then there have been other humiliations: 3–0 at Telford in 1986–87 when Telford were in the Conference; losing on penalties to Scunthorpe in 2000–01 when Scunthorpe were in Division Three and the Clarets in Division One; and sad defeats by Rotherham (0–3) in 1997–98, Darlington (2–3) in 1998–99 and Cheltenham (1–2) in 2000–01, with all the winners playing in divisions well below Burnley.

⊕ In recent years the boot has been on the other foot, and our once-mighty Burnley have been doing the giant-killing. Within the last 10 seasons giant-killing acts performed by the 'no-hopers' from Turf Moor have included:
1999–2000 Derby County (away) 1–0
2002–03 Fulham (home) 3–0
2004–05 Liverpool (home) 1–0

⊕ However, let us not forget Burnley's League Cup giant-killing exploits, of which there have been many. All the teams listed were in the top division at the time, and Burnley were not.
1982–83 Coventry (away) 2–1
1982–83 Birmingham (home) 3–2
1982–83 Tottenham (away) 4–1
2002–03 Tottenham (home) 2–1
2004–05 Aston Villa (home) 3–1
2008–09 Fulham (home) 1–0
2008–09 Chelsea (away) (on penalties)
2008–09 Arsenal(home) 2–0
2008–09 Tottenham (home) 3–2

GOALKEEPERS

'He kept it out 30 times'
'Crystal Palace never had a chance. That is all one can say, except that if Johnson, the Crystal Palace goalkeeper, let the ball through on nine occasions, he kept it out 30!'
Daily Chronicle, **Burnley v Crystal Palace 9–0 FA Cup tie, 1909**

Walking off the pitch – Burnley 7 Aston Villa 1, February 1921
'Sam Hardy, the England goalkeeper, with a look of disgust and weariness, came out of his goal – never bothered to stop Anderson getting his fifth and walked straight off the pitch, leaving the ball in the net.'
Burnley News

Running out of goalkeepers
In the game at Bolton on 27 November 1928 Burnley's goalkeeper George Sommerville broke his collarbone. Captain Jack Hill deputised for the first half, and in the second half Albert Freeman took over 'between the sticks'.

'A god in a green jersey'
'Harry Thomson was a god in a green jersey under a cloudy Mediterranean sky here today. Burnley's little Scot had one of those goalkeeping hours when the impossible seems to have happened not once but frequently. Burnley survived the most one-sided match I have ever seen. And throughout it, Thomson was brave, brilliant and lucky, and as 60,000 Neapolitan fans will confirm, sometimes "fantastico".'
Daily Express, **Naples v Burnley 0–0, February 1967**

A surplus of goalkeepers
When Burnley were Fourth Division Champions in 1992 they used five goalkeepers: Chris Pearce, Andy Marriot, Mark Kendall, Nicky Walker and David Williams. Contrast that with seasons 1946 to 1951 when they had one goalkeeper: Jimmy Strong.

GOALS

The Goal that won the Cup
'From a throw in on the right, Nesbitt banged the ball across to Hodgson, who had to compete with Longworth. It was a great leap that Hodgson made before he reached the ball above the head of Longworth, but he managed to get his head to the ball and directed it across to Freeman. Like a flash, the Burnley centre was on the ball, and he snapped up the opportunity without hesitation. Campbell in the Liverpool goal had no chance of saving, and Freeman was almost overwhelmed by the exuberance of the Burnley team who swarmed around him.'
Burnley Gazette, **Burnley v Liverpool, FA Cup Final, April 1914**

A glimpse of Freeman
'One of Freeman's dribbles with a goal at the end of it is worth going a long way to see, and he trotted one out on Saturday. He ran the ball a third of the length of the field, was challenged by Mitton and Carnpey, eluded them, drew out Cornthwaite, and scored. The shout was almost reminiscent of pre-war days.'
Burnley v Bury, 1917–18

'Hey up!'
'Who can recall Watson's goal, without at the time remembering Watson's action as he thundered down the field with big hefty strides, uttering at the same time his long-drawn out cry of "Hey-up!" It was an action which in a manner hypnotised the whole of the players, and they practically stood still, waiting for him to shoot. Nearly all the players stood transfixed watching the ball go in the net more as an act of curiosity to see what the ball would do, more than anything else.'
Burnley v Manchester United, November 1919

Burnley v West Brom, March 1927
'West Brom had a gift goal in the first minute. Whether it was a goal or not that Davies was credited with will be questioned for a long time. There are those from the

grandstand who have no doubt it was a goal, while hundreds will say that the ball was never within feet of the goal.

When Glidden made his run and shouldered Parkin off, he put the ball across, and though Dougall attempted to tackle Davies, the latter eluded him and got in a shot which Somerville covered, caught, and then allowed to spin away from him. It appeared to swerve goalwards, and the custodian made a sweep back for it, knocked it against the upright, and then turned it round the post.

At which point the referee decided it had been over the line could not be said, but he was nearer the penalty line, and had no hesitation in pointing to the centre of the field, in spite of the protests of Somerville, Hill and company. In my opinion, it was a question of inches either way.'
Burnley Express

The 'goal' that relegated Burnley!

In 1929–30 Burnley travelled to Leicester and lost the game 4–3. But a 'goal' scored by Alex Hutchinson for the Clarets was disallowed by the referee, Mr Mee of Mansfield, because he believed the ball had not crossed the line. However, a photograph taken of the incident by the *Leicester Mail* and reprinted in the Burnley press showed the ball clearly over the goalline. The loss of this goal and an important point disappointed the club greatly. But worse was still to come.

At the end of the season Burnley were relegated on goal average. If the Leicester goal had counted Burnley would have finished fifth from the foot of the League, Sheffield United would have been 'rightly' relegated and the history of the Burnley club might well have been different. And that of Sheffield United too.

Ray Harrison's pivot shot, Burnley v Liverpool 1–0 (FA Cup semi-final replay), April 1947

'34 minutes of the second half had gone when Kippax unmarked, gets possession, and begins one of those scintillating runs on goal. As he approaches the corner of the penalty area, Harley offers a challenge. Peter has him beaten with the ball, but when about to round the back, Harley extends a leg and Kippax still in full flight is unbalanced and eventually goes sprawling headlong into the penalty area.

It is no penalty, but certainly a free-kick. Bray tries his luck. It is a powerful, rising shot, right on the target. With the agility of a cat, Sidlow turns the ball gracefully over the bar for a corner. Billingham's corner kick is a beauty – a high ball which seemed to hover over the Liverpool goal. Several heads bob up to try and reach it, and finally Morris finds himself in possession. In a twinkle, the ball is switched to Harrison, standing with his side to the goal.

Immediately on receiving from Morris, Harrison pivoted round and shot with tremendous power straight into the net. The pace was so great that I doubt if many were able to follow its flight. No goalkeeper in the world would have kept out a shot of this calibre.'
Burnley Express

The goal of a lifetime, Burnley v Newcastle United, January 1952
'As the seconds were ticking out for a draw, Cummings robbed Milburn just outside
the Burnley penalty area and started his great run.

He beat seven players and the Newcastle defenders expected him to pass. He
feinted to do so by veering right in the United territory, then came in for goal. From
about 18 yards, he hit the ball just inside the post past Simpson.

Instantly, all Turf Moor rose in a sustained roar.'
Burnley Express

Comments after the goal:
'Bloody hell Cummings, where the blazes did you get that one from?' Joe Harvey,
Newcastle captain.

'When everything else about this great game is forgotten, there will be talk by those
who saw it, about that wonder goal. What a goal, the like of which Turf Moor fans
have probably never seen before.'
Daily Telegraph

'It made one feel proud to be present – a goal which will be talked about in years to
come as one of the most spectacular ever seen on Turf Moor.'
Burnley Express

'If nothing else were written about the game, I should make no apology. This was an
epic goal.'
Newcastle Sunday Sun

What a goal! Chorley v Burnley 1–1, November 1965
'They'll talk about it for years – that crazy, almost unbelievable, 90-yard goal scored
by Burnley goalkeeper Harry Thomson in the 16th minute of the Lancashire Senior
Cup tie at Victory Park.

It was just like one of those stories out of a schoolboy's annual come true, as
Thomson gathered a Chorley shot, picked up the ball, and with a near gale at his
back, kicked it downfield from the edge of Burnley's penalty area.

It bounced...and what a bounce...about seven yards inside the Chorley box, and
goalkeeper Salisbury, at full stretch, completely misjudged it.

The looks on the faces of the crowd as the ball flew just under the bar were worth
the price of admission money in themselves, and it was amusing to see the Burnley
players looking back in sheer astonishment towards Thomson, who flung up both
arms in a "come and congratulate me" gesture that Willie Irvine would have been
pleased to call his own.'
Burnley Express

'Lovely – here goes!' Burnley v Manchester United 1–0, September 1968
'Looking more cheery than ever before this season, Brian O'Neil gave me his
version of his best-ever goal which came with a 30-yard run and a 25-yard shot. He
said, "I was near the halfway line; Ralph Coates was behind me on the right. He had

the ball and when I shouted for it, he pushed it for me. George Best was alongside I think, but I got past him with no bother. Then Nobby Stiles came in and started jostling a bit.

I increased speed and kind of burst past Stiles, and then everything happened quickly. Fitzpatrick moved in at me and I can't remember whether I dribbled past him or just pushed the ball on and ran. Their defence was expecting me to pass, but when I got about six yards short of their box, the ball bobbled just right, and I thought, 'Lovely – here goes!' I banged it as hard as I could with my right, and then I thought 'Oh, it's too high…' I could see Stepney couldn't get near it, and then it dipped just under the bar into the far corner."

How did it feel then? "All right", he smiled. "I turned round and saw Harry Potts on his feet with his arms in the air. It was great, and then the lads just surrounded me.'"
Burnley Express

LEADING GOALSCORERS (League goals only)

George Beel	178
Ray Pointer	118
Jimmy McIlroy	116
Louis Page	111
Bert Freeman	103
Andy Lochhead	101
Bob Kelly	88
John Connelly	86
Bill Bowes	79
Jimmy Robson	79
Billy Holden	75
Frank Casper	74
Paul Fletcher	71
Dick Smith	71
Gordon Harris	69
Andy Payton	69
Brian Pilkington	67
Leighton James	66
Robbie Blake	59

LEADING GOALSCORERS (League, Cup, Friendlies, etc)

George Beel	187
Ray Pointer	133
Jimmy McIlroy	131
Andy Lochhead	128
Bert Freeman	115

Louis Page	115
John Connelly	105
Jimmy Robson	100
Willie Irvine	97
Bob Kelly	97
Frank Casper	89
Paul Fletcher	86
Bill Bowes	84
Gordon Harris	81
Leighton James	81
Andy Payton	81
Peter Noble	80
Billy Holden	79
Billy Hamilton	77
Brian Pilkington	77
Dick Smith	76
Robbie Blake	70 (up to last season)

YOUNGEST GOALSCORERS

⊕ Tommy Lawton scored two against Swansea Town on 4 April 1936 in Division Two. He was 16 years and 181 days old.

⊕ Eric Probert scored against Spurs on 29 March 1969 in Division One. He was 17 years and 40 days old.

⊕ Ian Lawson scored four goals against Chesterfield in the FA Cup on 5 January 1957. He was 17 years and 287 days old, which gives him the youngest hat-trick as well!

OLDEST GOALSCORER

As far as can be ascertained the oldest scorers of a goal for the Clarets have been:

⊕ Graham Alexander – he scored a penalty against Reading on 9 May 2009 when he was 37 years and 211 days old.

⊕ Ian Wright – he scored against Brentford on 24 April 2000 when he was 36 years and 172 days old.

⊕ Keith Newton - he scored against Charlton on 26 April 1977. He was 35 years and 307 days old.

MOST GOALS IN CONSECUTIVE LEAGUE GAMES

In one game
9 v Darwen, Division One 1891–92
9 v Loughborough, Division Two 1897–98
In two games
13 v Notts Forest (5) and Reading (8) in 1930–31
In three games
15 v West Brom (3), Birmingham (6) and Leicester (6) in 1961–62
In four games
20 v Notts Forest (5), Reading (8), Notts Forest (3) and Wolves (4) in 1930–31
20 v Fulham (5), Blackburn (4), Manchester United (5) and Chelsea (6) in 1960–61
In five games
23 v Notts Forest (5), Reading (8), Notts Forest (3), Wolves (4) and Bradford (3) in 1930–31
In six games
24 v Sheff United (6), Sheff United (1), Preston (3), Blackburn (4), Blackburn (3) and Aston Villa (7) in 1920–21
24 v Notts Forest (5), Reading (8), Notts Forest (3), Wolves (4), Bradford (3) and Stoke (1) in 1930–31
24 v Leicester (2), West Brom (3), Birmingham (6), Leicester (6), Everton (2) and Fulham (5) in 1961–62
In seven games
27 v Manchester City (3), Leicester (2), West Brom (3), Birmingham (6), Leicester (6), Everton (2) and Fulham (5) in 1961–62
In eight games
31 v Wolves (5), Bolton (5), Spurs (4), Leicester (3), Arsenal (5), Everton (1), Everton (3) and Newcastle (5) in 1960–61

MOST INDIVIDUAL GOALS IN CONSECUTIVE LEAGUE GAMES

In one game
6 by Louis Page (v Birmingham) 1925–26
In two games
7 by Claude Lambie (v Aston Villa, Derby) 1890–91
7 by Louis Page (v Birmingham, Bury) 1925–26
In three games
8 by Claude Lambie (v Wolves, Aston Villa and Derby) 1890–91
8 by Louis Page (v Birmingham, Bury and Sheff United) 1925–26
In four games
8 by Claude Lambie (v Wolves, Aston Villa, Derby and Blackburn) 1890–91
8 by Bert Freeman (v Barnsley, Bradford, Wolves and Leicester) 1912–13
8 by Louis Page (v Birmingham, Bury, Sheff United and Spurs) 1925–26

8 by Ray Pointer (v West Brom, Birmingham, Leicester and Everton) 1961–62
In five games
10 by Bert Freeman (v Fulham, Barnsley, Bradford, Wolves and Leicester) 1912–13
In six games
11 by Bert Freeman (v Fulham, Barnsley, Bradford, Wolves, Leicester and Stockport) 1912–13
In seven games
13 by Joe Anderson (v Preston, (twice) Sheff United(twice), Blackburn (twice) and Aston Villa) 1920–21
In eight games
13 by Joe Anderson (v Preston (twice), Sheff United (twice), Blackburn (twice) and Aston Villa) 1920–21

GET THE GRASS CUT!

'Since last season, the ground has been levelled and it is now covered with turf, and though this to some extent could not help but militate against play, still it was considered inadvisable to cut it short at the commencement.'
1888

THE GREATEST TEAM THAT EVER WAS

The end of the 30 consecutive League games without defeat, March 1921
'And so an end has been put to Burnley's record breaking run. But do we mind? Not a bit of it! We have been partners with the greatest team that ever was. We know full well that never in our time will such a thing be accomplished again, and we like to think that we live in an age that will be remembered when we personally are forgotten.'
'Kestrel' *Burnley News*

GOOD OLD DAYS?

'Last Saturday, the referee had to stop the reserve match at Turf Moor in order to speak to one of the spectators for having used bad language to one of the players. It is generally these dirty mouthed members who are the severest critics, men who never did a day's training in their lives, and who could not run a hundred yards if they wanted. Obscene barracking of this kind, which is becoming common, must be stopped at all costs.'
Burnley Gazette, **1908**

'There used to be a time in the history of the club when to mention that one was connected with it was to be instantly tabooed; a time when Burnley was spoken of as being outside the pale of civilisation, owing to the conduct of its football supporters and some of its players.

However, during recent seasons the use of foul language and undesirable epithets on the part of the crowd, and the use of dirty tactics by the team, seem to have gone. But I was at Turf Moor last Saturday. And what a change! What did one hear called out, not from the sixpenny crowd alone, but from the better paid seats in the grandstand? "Kick his...... legs off!" and "Send the ...... off!"

One is bound to ask if it is the old spirit cropping up again, now that the younger generation has gone off to the war. For the offenders as far as I could see were not the youngest members of the crowd, but those over whose heads too many summers have passed to make them of any value for military purposes.'

Burnley Express

GOODBYE BERT!

'Bert Freeman is to leave Burnley! That announcement will be received with a pang of regret, for "Gentleman Bert" as he is widely known, has been totally beloved by Burnley football supporters. No player has been more faithful to the club, nor has the Burnley club ever been better served by any player, and though "Bert" has not been much in the limelight during this season, he is still affectionately remembered by the Burnley public. Truly, as one Burnley man said the other day, Freeman owes Burnley nothing.

He came to Burnley, just as the fortunes of the club were beginning to rise, and he did as much as any man, and more than most, to place them at their present high level. None who saw him in his prime, will ever forget his inimitable style, his lightning darts and his twinkling feet, as he hung over the ball, controlling it wonderfully. All his work bore the stamp of inborn artistry. And though this last news has been expected, it is none the less regretted.

There never was a more gentlemanly player, and truly it can be said that Bert Freeman was a pattern to all who step on to a football field. He rarely if ever did a dirty action on the field, and if he did forget himself, it was usually when some other member of the team had been knocked about. Rather, did he take buffetings calmly and without protest, and seldom did he protest against the decisions of the referee. He was of a type rarely to be met with, and his name will live in football so long as the game continues, because he was one of those who elevated the game by his participation in it. There have been occasions when spectators have complained that he did not bustle into the opposition sufficiently – but Freeman was of the true sporting type, who believed in playing the game to the letter and in the spirit.'

Burnley News, 30 April 1921

THE 'H' TEAM

		Hillman			
	Hird		Hayes		
	Halley	Hill	Harrison (G.)		
Hornby	Hamilton	Holden	Hankin	Harris	

Subs: Hansbury, Hubbick, Harrison (R.), Hutchinson and Hays

HAIR STYLES – ONE IN PARTICULAR

No one will ever forget Ralph Coates's hairstyle. If Bobby Charlton had the most famous ever comb-over style to hide his emerging dome, then Ralph Coates was not far behind. On 11 March 2006 BBC Red Nose Day viewers voted for the Top 10 all-time worst sporting haircuts and Ralph Coates came a very creditable ninth. Considering that the competition consisted of Charlton in first place, Carlos Valderama, with the style of a mop, in second, Jason Lee of the nineties and the pineapple top in sixth, Coates can be very proud to be in the Top 10 worst sporting haircuts of all time. Today, as Ralph approaches the end of middle age, his hair is *au naturel.*

HAT-TRICKS

- Not many players score a hat-trick and end up on the losing side. However, Gareth Taylor did just that and finished up on the wrong side of a 4–7 defeat at home to Watford in 2002–03.

- Willie Irvine had the same experience in the FA Cup tie at Tottenham in 1965–66. He scored three times, but ended up losing 3–4.

- Peter Noble scored four goals for the Clarets in the home game against Norwich City in 1975–66. But the Clarets could only draw 4–4.

HEAVY DEFEATS

A miserable display, Liverpool v Burnley 8–0, December 1928
'There was no fluke about the win, and in no sense does the score flatter Liverpool, for besides netting eight legitimate goals, the Anfielders netted three offside shots, and missed a penalty.

There was the slightest excuse; it was the most miserable failure of a side that it has been one's lot to see in a number of years, for Burnley had hardly a redeeming feature, and were beaten in every department. Out-paced, out-manoeuvred, out-pointed, out-everythinged, and without a scintilla of grace, the side was KO'd in the easiest fashion, and never showed a glimpse of response after the first 20 minutes.'
Burnley Express

And again, three weeks later! Sheffield United v Burnley 10–0, January 1929
'Rarely have I seen a side so pounded and pulverised as Burnley were as the time went on. One heard sympathisers say that they did not like to see a team pile on goals like that, nor did they like to see a game so one-sided. I only wished I could have seen Burnley do it! They would have had my hearty congratulations!

It was all hugely humorous to the Sheffield crowd, especially to the boys. It was a gala day for them, one they will remember when they are tottering around with sticks, and when they will be able to say, "What did the United do in 1929?"'
Burnley Express

THE HERO HAS GONE

Local hero Jimmy Ross was transferred in 1899
'Burnley's first visit to Bristol was remarkable for being the last appearance of Ross in the Turf Moor team. I suppose that now Ross has severed his connection as a player, that Burnley must make up their minds to lose every match. Does any body wish to know why? Well, simply because it will be impossible for them to notch up another League point without the Master Mind to guide the men. Whoever can follow him as skipper?'
Burnley News, March 1899

HILLMAN

Jack Hillman was one of the great characters in Burnley and English football in the Victorian era. These are just a few of the hundreds of incidents in which he was involved.

His first mistake
'Hillman had an easy task, but by some means the shot took effect, the ball shooting as it were, owing to the sand. This mistake, the first of the season by Hillman, caused considerable laughter.' **November 1891**
(And later)...'Because it was his first mistake of the season, Hillman has been forgiven. The committee do not think that the mistake is likely to be repeated.'

Making gestures
'On the players retiring to the dressing room, Hillman had to be protected by the police and other officials, the crowd believing that the Burnley custodian had deliberately struck Davey. But the affair was accidental and done in the act of clearing the ball. Hillman was guilty of making gestures after the incident at the crowd, who became exasperated and made for him at the close of the match.'
Aston Villa v Burnley, December 1891

A pack of cards
Reporting on the incident of Jack Hillman being left at Stockport railway station on the way to the West Brom versus Burnley game in January 1893, the *Burnley Express* said, 'It appears that at Stockport station, Hillman asked to be supplied with a pack of playing cards. He was told that the Burnley committee did not supply them, and so he sent a lad for a pack. Because those in charge of the team would not pay for

them, he said he would not go a stop further, and got out of the train, smashing a window into scores of pieces as he banged the door to. He walked up and down the platform, and was told by Mr King not to be a fool. By and by the train moved on and Hillman made an attempt to get into one of the last compartments, but was pulled away by the railway officials. Hillman has been suspended indefinitely for his behaviour.' (He missed the first half of the game, and Burnley lost 7–1.)

Mussels for tea!
'On Saturday morning, rumours were afloat respecting Hillman's inability to take charge of the sticks, and these proved to be well founded. It transpired that the burly one had been seized with illness during the night, the cause being attributed to his eating mussels for tea.' **Burnley v Sheffield Wednesday, November 1894**

A very offensive expression
'Hillman delayed the start a few minutes and on coming on to the field, made use of a very offensive expression in reply to a spectator, and this has been much commented on. Such conduct can have only one result, that of alienating a great number of honest admirers of his prowess. I am sorry that Hillman so far forgot himself.'
Burnley v Bury, 1893–94

Private Hillman
'The other night, a rumour spread around the town like wildfire that Hillman had gone and enlisted – the report having arisen owing to a little lark on the part of the Burnley custodian. It appears that he had met a friend of his, the wearer of Her Majesty's uniform, and for the fun of it, Hillman donned the soldier's overcoat, and as he was seen by several people who recognised him, it can readily be imagined that the little incident was greatly magnified. Nobody stopped to inquire about the probability, or even possibility of the truth of the statement, for recruits of a day or two do not usually don the uniform so early.'
Burnley Express, **January 1894**

'Some unpleasantness!'
'It was reported that the authorities at Burnley FC and Hillman had had some disagreement. That there had been some unpleasantness, there is no reason to doubt, but from the fact that Hillman appeared in goal, it would appear that the differences had been healed.'
Burnley v Liverpool, FA Cup, January 1895

'The old love'
'A great deal of interest was centered on the first meeting this season of Burnley and Everton, mainly originating from the fact that Hillman would appear against his old comrades and this would afford people an opportunity of comparing the old love with the new.'
Burnley Express, **1895**

'An open air lecture!'
'Hillman received the ball from a long shot, and Beats endeavoured by charging at the ball as much as the man, to effectively dislodge the sphere from the custodian's grasp. Hillman, resenting this, collared the Wolverhampton player and flung him onto the turf. Hillman's action led to the belief that he had been kicked. The referee delivered an open air lecture to both delinquents.'
Burnley v Wolverhampton, April 1900

Allegation
'With reference to the League match, Notts Forest v Burnley, played at Nottingham on Saturday, serious rumours are current locally as to the action of one of the principal players on the visiting side. Having in view their possible relegation to the Second Division, the allegation is that before the game started, he offered to guarantee the Forest players £2 each if they would let Burnley win. This was indignantly declined, but when the Forest led by two goals to nil, the offer was raised to £5 per man, with the same result. Burnley lost by four goals.'
Nottingham Evening Post, **May 1900**

'Look here…'
'At the match between Nottingham Forest and Burnley last Saturday, when the players had entered the field, Hillman said to McPherson, "Look here, take this match easy today, and we stand you £2 a man." McPherson replied, "No, it is more than I dare do, and we are paid to play and go straight." To which Hillman responded, "All right, I will see you at half-time."

During the interval Hillman said to McPherson, "Look here, we will make that £5 each." And McPherson replied, "No, if you want to do anything of that sort, you had better see our committee".'
Nottingham Forest report to the FA

'The charge against Hillman'
'The charges made by Notts Forest against the Burnley captain, of attempted bribery, came before the League committee. The chief witness for the plaintiffs was McPherson, and for the defendants, Hillman. The Burnley goalkeeper went so far as to admit that the text of the accusation was true, and he did make use of such a term as implied, but the spirit of it, i.e. that he did knowingly and with intent offer the Forest team through their captain £5 each to be 'easy on' or words to that effect, so that Burnley might collect two badly needed points, he denied. According to his statement, it was all chaff. McPherson, however, took the matter in all seriousness, or he would not have reported it. The Football Association held a commission at Manchester on Monday.'
Burnley Express, **May 1900**

Hillman suspended
'We find that Hillman did approach McPherson and offered a bribe with a view to affect the result of the match, and consider that in doing so, he committed one of the most serious offences in football; and suspend him until the end of the 1900–01 season. But

for his previous good conduct, we should have been prepared to recommend that he be not allowed to take any part in football again. We are satisfied that the Burnley club had no knowledge of, nor are they responsible for, Hillman's action.'
Football Association Commission Report, May 1900

Jack Hillman, back in town
'Big Jack Hillman always was an attraction for Burnley folks and now that he is once more operating with Burnley, there is a feeling that every match in which he is playing will be worth watching.'
1909

MAKING OF HISTORY

One of the most brilliant achievements
'In the history of Burnley Football Club, it will be recorded that one of the most brilliant achievements was the victory over Sunderland, which paved the way to the semi-final for the second season in succession.'
Burnley Express, **Sunderland v Burnley 1–2, FA Cup, March 1914**

One of the best
'It was a great triumph for Burnley – one of the best in the club's history, looked at from whatever point of view one likes. They were a great side, fore and aft. Admirably captained by that great centre half-back, Tommy Boyle, they had not a weak spot. There was nothing better in the match than the wing play of new international Mosscrop – easily the best forward on view.'
Daily News, **Sunderland v Burnley 1– 2, FA Cup, March 1914**

HOBBIES

❀ Club legend Jimmy McIlroy, now in his 70s, is a supremely talented artist and painter.

❀ Brenda Thomas, wife of Dave Thomas, is a skilled horsewoman, painter and artist.

❀ Burnley's right-winger during the late 1950s, Doug Newlands, became a top-class crown green bowler after he left football.

HONOURS

The players who have won most honours while playing for Burnley are:
1. Billy Watson   League Title   Cup Winner   3 caps, 5 Football League games
2. Jerry Dawson   League Title   Cup Winner   2 caps, 4 Football League games
3 Eddie Mosscrop League Title   Cup Winner   2 caps, 1 Football League game

4.	Tommy Boyle	League Title	Cup Winner	1 cap, 3 Football League games
5.=	Billy Nesbitt	League Title	Cup Winner	
5.=	George Halley	League Title	Cup Winner	
7.	Jimmy McIlroy	League Title	Cup Finalist	51 caps, 2 Football League games
8.	Alex Elder	League Title	Cup Finalist	34 caps
9.	John Connelly	League Title	Cup Finalist	10 caps, 7 Football League games
10.=	Brian Miller	League Title	Cup Finalist	1 cap, 2 Football League games
10.=	Ray Pointer	League Title	Cup Finalist	1 cap, 2 Football League games

This table is based on the order of priority – League Championship, FA Cup winner, international caps and Football League appearances.

HOW TO BUILD A STAND

When the club's offices were moved from St James Row to a brick structure underneath the Brunshaw Road Stand director Dick Wadge organised the work, goalkeeper Jack Hillman, a bricklayer, did the brickwork, while other players like defender Fred Barron and goalkeeper Billy Green did the labouring. Another director, Jimmy Harrison, who was a builder by trade, helped with the erection of the new stand.

GOALS

- Louis Page still holds the club record for his six goals in one game, against Birmingham in April 1926. (What is not often recognised is that this was an away game.)

- Burnley's club record for the highest number of League goals scored in a season was 102 in 1960–61. It was only achieved 14 times after the war, and Burnley did it twice. However, it did not help Burnley win the title – they finished second.

- Nathan Peel only ever scored twice for the club and both goals were in the same game when he came on as sub against Plymouth. Between the sticks for Plymouth was Peter Shilton – not a bad 'keeper to score your only goals against!

- In 1982, in two consecutive games, Burnley scored nine goals. All of them were scored by different players – Phelan, McGee, Scott, Wharton, Stevens, Laws, Dobson, Hamilton and Young.

GOALKEEPERS

- Burnley used three goalkeepers in one match in 1982. In the home game against Leicester Alan Stevenson was sent off and forward Paul McGee went in goal for a spell. Later full-back Brian Laws took over. Curiously, both McGee and Laws missed penalties during the game as well. Not surprisingly the Clarets lost 4–2.

⊕ In the 3–3 draw at Oldham in 1998 the combined age of the two goalkeepers was 78. Chris Woods playing for Burnley was 38, while Oldham's Bruce Grobbelaar was 40!

⊕ In the Burnley versus Sheffield Wednesday game at the end of 2002–03, all four goalkeepers were used, Burnley's players being Beresford and Nichopoulos.

⊕ Goalkeeper Jimmy Strong played 203 consecutive games for Burnley when League football resumed in 1946 after World War Two. That was nearly five seasons without missing a match, and he averaged less than a goal conceded per game.

⊕ Ouch! Manchester City goalkeeper Harry Dowd conceded six goals in a 6–3 defeat at Turf Moor when he deputised for Bert Trautmann in 1962. When Trautman returned the next week Harry played for the City reserves against Burnley reserves and let in another seven.

⊕ Goalkeeper Tony Woodworth made just one appearance for the Clarets, which was never to be forgotten. It was 24 January 1987 and it proved to be Burnley's record home defeat, 6–0 to Hereford. Tony never played for the first team again.

⊕ In the first season of the Football League Burnley lost 7–1 to Blackburn Rovers. This was hardly surprising, since their regular goalkeeper Robert Kay had emigrated to Australia just a few days before the game and centre-forward Fred Poland went in goal. Poland was never picked again.

⊕ 'The Burnley goalkeeper did not handle the ball once during the entire match.' **Burnley 3 Irwell Springs 0, 1884.**

HOW ARE THE MIGHTY FALLEN

'Burnley went over to Rotherham on Saturday to initiate the benighted beings of that town into some of the secrets of high-class football; but after an uninteresting game, they returned beaten by one goal to none.'
April 1891

'Hush! Touch wood! Four matches in succession without defeat! If ever a crowd were fearful of breaking the spell, it is now! We are not accustomed to such things, and glad as we are, we can scarcely believe our good fortune.'
September 1932 (The next game, against the bottom team in Division Two, Charlton, Burnley lost 1–0)

HUMILIATION

'One thing I should not like the Burnley players to do is the humiliation that the Bristol City players must have suffered on Saturday by seeing a sheet carried round the field – even when they were on it – bearing the inscription "FUND FOR NEW PLAYERS!"'

After Burnley were beaten 10–0 by Aston Villa in 1925, a Villa reporter suggested that 'Burnley might do better in the second innings!', while a local cartoon in the *Burnley News* showed a Burnley player looking towards a flag marked 'The League Championship'. Meanwhile an old sailor suggested, 'You'll need a good telescope to see it properly!'

Chapter Five

I–J

(From In my dream and Injuries to Job centre and Jokes)

'IN MY DREAM – IT'S OUR CUP!'

A Wembley final counterfoil.
Now creased and worn by time,
Which brings to mind the glory days
Of Burnley in their prime.

For over two and thirty years
I've carried it around:
A token of our game with Spurs
At soccer's premier ground.

The five bob ticket it denotes
Cost me a full week's pay.
I did not care…I would be there
To watch my heroes play.

'The two best teams in all the land!'
…That's how the match was billed.
I never doubted I would see
My greatest dream fulfilled.

…The Clarets 'vintage '62',
A feast of football, crown,
By taking back the FA Cup,
In triumph to our town…

But fate decreed it would not be,
No plaudits, only pity,

No wild elation like the night,
We won the League at City.

No rapturous journey home; the coach
Was like a funeral car:
Within two years, great joy, then tears,
So near and yet so far;

League runners-up, then in the Cup,
Another second prize.
That we had finished up with 'nowt'.
'Twas hard to realise.

Though sadness filled my heart that day,
I still recall with pride,
The complementing attributes
Of a classic Burnley side.

The strength of Blacklaw keeping goal;
Cool Angus at the back;
The elegance of Adamson;
The skills of Jimmy Mac.

Connelly's speed and Elder's poise;
Brave Pointer, e'er a thriller;
Cultured Cummings's calm command;
Sharp Harris, stalwart Miller.

The 100th Wembley Final goal,
Earned 'poacher' Robson fame.
… I see the faded counterfoil
And oft replay the game.

…But each time, on that hallowed turf,
In my imagination,
The Clarets win!…The Cup is ours!
I join the celebration…

That torn and tattered ticket stub
Still conjures up the dream
A kid had, many years ago,
When Burnley were supreme.

(Mervyn Hadfield, Lenton Terrace, London)

INJURIES

⊕ Between his penultimate and his final League goal for Burnley Frank Casper had to wait 18 months due to injury.

⊕ They all broke legs: Bill Holden 1952, Colin McDonald 1959, Albert Cheesebrough 1965, Willie Irvine 1967, Martin Dobson 1970, Ashley Hoskin 1985 and Wayne Dowell 1994.

⊕ Brian Miller, a player in the 1950s and 1960s who later became club manager, was a tough old boot. Even with the heavyweight, stiff football boots of the 1950s that came up to the ankle to give great protection, as well as enabling a player to kick down a barn door, Brian still managed to break a toe. But there was no spell on the sidelines for Brian. He was so keen to play that he simply cut a hole in his boot so that his strapped up toe would fit in and then played on as normal. This was the age when a sponge and a bucket of water was the cure for most injuries. Scans and oxygen tanks – what were they to players like Brian Miller, in an era when they had never heard of metatarsals?

INTERNATIONALS

Three international teams:
Pre-war

			Dawson			
		McCluggage		Waterfield		
	Bowsher		Boyle		Watson	
Bruton	Kelly		Freeman		Crabtree	Mosscrop

Reserves: Hill, Emerson, Page

Post-war

			McDonald			
		Angus		Elder		
	Dobson		Miller		Flynn	
Connelly	McIlroy		Pointer		Coates	Pilkington

Reserves : Cochrane

Or, if you prefer

			Blacklaw			
		Aird		Elliott		
	Cassidy		Todd		Harris	
Morgan	Morris		Irvine		Hamilton	James

And more recently

Coyne

Alexander	Duff	Cox	Caldwell
Jones	Hyde	McCann	Gudjonsson
	Lafferty	Taylor	

Reserves: Gray, Michopoulos, Papadopoulos

- Burnley's first international player was left-winger Jack Yates, who was chosen for England to play against Ireland in 1889. He is one of the very few players to score on his international debut, and he belongs to an even rarer collection who have scored a hat-trick on that debut. Jack scored three in a 6–1 victory that memorable day, but he was never selected again.

- In the years following World War One Burnley could regularly play six full English internationals in their team – Jerry Dawson, Tommy Boyle, Billy Watson, Bert Freeman, Bob Kelly and Eddie Mosscrop. No wonder they won the League title.

- In the early 1960s Burnley could field a team of eight international players, including Adam Blacklaw (Scotland), Brian Miller (England), John Angus (England), Alex Elder (N. Ireland), John Connelly (England), Jimmy McIlroy (N. Ireland), Ray Pointer (England) and Brian Pilkington (England).

- In January 2006 Burnley could field a team of 11 international players – Djemba Djemba (Cameroon), Duff, Lafferty and Jones (N. Ireland), Mahon (Eire), Gray and Caldwell (Scotland), Akinbiyi (Nigeria), Coyne (Wales), Sinclair (Jamaica) and Gudjonnson (Iceland).

- In the 1920s, clubs were allowed to refuse permission for their players to play in international matches if games clashed with club fixtures. However, this only applied to Irish, Scottish and Welsh players, not English! Billy Emerson and Andy McCluggage (both Irish) were two of Burnley's earliest victims to have to turn down caps.

- The only full international match ever played at Turf Moor took place in November 1927 when England played Wales. Wales won the game 2–1.

- The *Burnley News* took the opportunity to compare England unfavourably with the Burnley team. 'And this is England! If this is the best that England can produce, then we are poverty stricken indeed! Burnley and England captain Jack Hill spent his time trying to help out a defence that McCluggage and Waterfield could have swallowed. "Dixie" Dean – the name has been dinned into our ears so often that big things were expected – but he was just a wandering spirit. With some of his opportunities, Beel would have done much better.'

    In brief, Burnley provided two of the England team, Jack Hill and Louis Page, with Hill as the captain. The team were managed by Burnley chairman, Charles E.

Sutcliffe, and the trainer was Burnley's own Charlie Bates. Jack Hill distinguished himself by putting through an own-goal! (A first for an England captain?)

'J'

'J' is for unlucky Jack Yates
Whose career seemed rather grand,
Not only playing for Burnley,
But – selected for England.

The game was one against Ireland,
In March, eighteen eighty nine,
At Goodison Park, where Jack Yates
Apparently did just fine.

England won by six goals to one,
A display assured and slick,
And surely no one bettered Jack,
Who scored half with his hat-trick.

Alas, he was not picked again,
Much to the selectors' shame,
Though Jack still has the best average,
Having scored three goals per game!

Dave Alton
A tribute to Burnley's first international player, Jack Yates.

THE 'J' TEAM

Jensen
Joyce   Jones (C.)
Johnson   Jepson   Joyce
Johnrose   Jakub   Jones (T.)   Jenkins   James
Sub: Jones (R.)

JANUARY WOES

When Burnley beat Charlton Athletic 2–1 in the last minute of injury time on 31 January 2009 it was the club's 32nd January League game of 10 seasons. Of these, the club have won only seven times! No wonder Clarets always dread the new year. (Incidentally, three of those seven were all in one season, 2007–08, which makes it even worse!)

JIMMY GREAVES'S *BOOK OF LISTS*

In 1983 Jimmy Greaves compiled his *Book of Lists*. Included in it were the following:
Best full-backs 1960s to 1980s – Alex Elder.
Best midfield maestros 1940s to 1950s – Jimmy McIlroy.
Best wing wizards 1960s to 1980s – John Connelly.
Irish international with most influence on English football – Jimmy McIlroy.
10 greatest British international teams – the 1958 Northern Ireland team, which included Jimmy McIlroy.
10 great players 1940s to 1950s without a single cap – Jimmy Adamson.
Select Welsh team from 1960s to 1980s – Leighton James.
Select Irish team from 1940s to 1950s – Jimmy McIlroy.
Select Irish team from 1960s to 1980s – Alex Elder.
Best-ever Burnley team – Colin McDonald, John Angus, Alex Elder, Martin Dobson, Tommy Cummings, Jimmy Adamson, Willie Morgan, Ralph Coates, Ray Pointer, Jimmy McIlroy, John Connelly. Sub: Leighton James.
If Greaves were to produce a book of lists from the 1980s to the current decade, it is highly unlikely that any Burnley player would appear in any lists of 'the best'!

JOB CENTRE

Pick your own team from these 'odd jobs' who have played at Turf Moor. There has been a Baker (Steve), Bishop (Charlie), Chippendale (Brian), Cook (Paul), Dyer (Nathan), Miller (Brian), Noble (Peter), Painter (Robbie), Smiths (too numerous!) an Abbot (Walter) and a couple of Knights (Jack and George)! There has even been a Waiters (Tony)!

JOKES (aimed at Ewood!)

- FOR SALE! Blackburn Rovers' tablecloths. Suitable for any occasion, but tend to slip down the table after a short time!

- FOR SALE! Rovers' videos. All the highlights from the last 40 years of action. This 30-minute video including repeats is a must for every Rovers fan!

- FOR SALE! Rovers' joke book. This 900-page book is full of all the best jokes about the club and includes the one about having lots of fans pre-Walker!

Chapter Six

K–L

(From Keen as… and Kelly to Lucky flowers and Lucky horseshoes)

KEEN AS…

Perhaps the player with the most unusual name was Jack Mustard. Jack came from Preston in 1933 and played 15 games for Burnley. He played in three positions – both wings and centre-forward – and scored four goals. In 1934 he left Turf Moor for Southend United.

KELLY!

Although the aim of this humble volume is to portray the 'queer, quaint and quirky' stories of Burnley FC, it is important to 'keep our feet on the ground' by recalling one or two of the truly remarkable footballers who have played for the Clarets. To educate the uninformed and to thrill again the Burnley fans, here are a few memories of the immortal Bob Kelly.

'Kelly's little lot' Burnley v Stoke City 4–1, October 1916
'Fifteen minutes to go, Stoke winning 1–0, and then came Kelly's little lot. The whole forward line sprang into life as if by a wave of a magician's wand, and bang! Four goals in six minutes!'
Burnley News

'An inspiration to see' Burnley v Oldham 7–1, November 1920
'The play of the Burnley side was too staggering for words. Kelly was surely an inspiration to see, swaying like a reed in the wind, deceiving, feinting, then slipping through the defence on his own, or co-operating with Nesbitt in a manner which brought the pair cheer after cheer. Theirs was surely the acme of scientific skill.'
Burnley News

'The Magic of Kelly' Manchester United 0–3 v Burnley, March 1921
'And so Kelly took matters into his own hands, and thrilled the crowd by his stupendous individualism. Swerving, writhing, wriggling through obstacles, jumping over extended

feet, and carrying the ball with him all the time, he electrified the crowd by some of the most magnificent runs it has ever been their lot to see. Not once or twice, but a host of times, he broke away like a fox with the hounds streaming in full cry behind him, and the crowd hugged themselves in ecstasy, and the cry of "He's off again!" could be clearly heard.

Wildly fascinated, the crowd waited for these exciting runs. They commenced towards the close of the first half. Just a minute was wanted till half-time, and then Kelly set off again. He worked right away from his own position to the left, dodging and dribbling cleverly, and avoiding the defence till he was well within the penalty area, and an almost certain scorer. And then Silcock kicked his legs from under him. Referee! Spot! BOYLE! Goal!!!'
Burnley News

'The greatness of Kelly' England v Scotland 5–4, April 1920
'England's strength was in attack, all five players were first-class, with Kelly touching greatness. The Burnley man has a turn of speed, an elusive swerve, and perfect ball control, and England has not had a better inside-forward since Steve Bloomer at his best.'
Sunday Chronicle

'He's got it again!' Derby v Burnley 0–2, 1920
'Kelly was always to the forefront and it was really Kelly's day out. He was very difficult to hold, though he was unfortunate with two lightning drives which just whizzed past the post.

He shot whenever he came within range, and as the half-back could not hold him, he was a formidable force. He "put the wind up" the home spectators, whose gasping "he's got it again" told how they were taking matters.'

'An electric spark' Leicester v Burnley 3–7, 1921
There were stars among the Burnley team – Kelly was one of the brightest of them all, in fact he could best be described as an electric spark, flashing here and there. One never knew where he was going to strike, and his stroke was so swift and certain that it hardly could be followed.

He seemed to have the ball tied to his toe, and once when he waltzed around the opposing half-back in a minute circle, keeping the ball under control all the while, that the City man tried in vain to get near it, the Leicester crowd were compelled to see fun in such delightful jugglery.'

'Head and shoulders above the lot' Burnley v Blackburn Rovers 3–1, January 1921
'The next moment, without warning of his intention, Kelly would be away, either combining in graceful swift onslaughts along with the ever ready Nesbitt, or opening out the game with a long swinging pass right, to the left, from where attention had been diverted; or again trailing the opposing defence along with him in a will-o'-the-wisp dance. Kelly was without doubt the moving spirit of the Burnley front line. Indeed one never knew what he was going to do next.

His goal was a picture. Halley took a free-kick and dropped the ball into a mass of players. And above them all rose Kelly. To what a height he seemed to jump! He towered, so it seemed, head and shoulders above the lot, and meeting the ball with his head, he had it into the net before Sewell was aware.'

'A blinder!' Burnley v Sunderland 2–2, May 1921
'Rarely have Kelly and Nesbitt operated better than on Saturday. Nesbitt had the Sunderland defence in a hopeless tangle, and seemed able to do just as he liked, while Kelly let himself go thoroughly, and played what is known in football parlance as a "blinder". He dragged the Sunderland defence over half the field with him on many occasions.'
Burnley News

'Kelly, the wizard' Spurs v Burnley 2–1 FA Charity Shield, May 1921
'Kelly of course. There was not another like him. He was a gay spark, full of humour, and often his way of running around the ball, side-stepping and dodging, aroused great peals of laughter and cheers.'
Burnley News

A cartoon caption, August 1924
'There are few changes in the Burnley team – Kelly still wears the longest trousers – and Hill the longest legs!'
Burnley Express

The departure of Bob Kelly, December 1925
'To those who saw him, the memory of his brilliant play will remain for life, the sinuous moves, his deceptive body swerve, his speed off the mark, the spectacular shot, his ball jugglery, all in all – a football wizard. We part with him with regret, fearing that we may never see his like again.'
Burnley News

'KIPPERBANG!'

Acclaimed author Jack Rosenthal lived in Colne for several years, having been evacuated to the area from Manchester in World War Two. He became a great fan of Burnley in those years, and he was devoted to the great team of 1946–47. One of the members of that team was left-winger Peter Kippax, whom Rosenthal and his pals at the Grammar School idolised. They devised a nickname for him which eventually became 'P'Tang Yang Kipperbang', and was also their secret password. This became the name of one of Rosenthal's TV plays many years later.

LADIES' DAY

One of the latest additions to the Turf Moor calendar is 'Ladies' Day', usually held one Saturday each autumn. The club states: 'It's time to dig out the glad rags and indulge in pampering and elegance.' Sponsored by Harvey Nichols, the day includes pink champagne, balloons and floral hats. Whatever would Tommy Boyle and Jack Hillman have said?

THE LANCASHIRE CUP

The Lancashire Cup is one of the oldest competitions in the country. Since the Cup began in 1879–80, Burnley have played in the third highest number of competitions, 104 in total. Only Bolton (108) and Blackburn (106) have competed in more Lancashire Cup games. (This, incidentally, is out of over 220 Lancashire clubs).

Burnley are the second most successful club in the history of the competition, having won it 12 times and been runners-up on a further 11 occasions. Only Blackburn Rovers have won it more times – 17, with 15 seasons when they were runners-up.

✪ **1.** On the first occasion that Burnley won the Lancashire Cup in 1889–90 they beat Blackburn 2–0 in the Final at Accrington. The attendance was 15,000 – a Cup record.

✪ **2.** Burnley were beaten in four Finals – 1899–90, 1900–01, 1901–02 and 1910–11. Fred Barron was a member of all four teams!

✪ **3.** The biggest Lancashire Cup attendance at Turf Moor was 16,898 for the Final in 1950 between Burnley and Liverpool and the Clarets won 3–0.

✪ **4.** When Chester beat Burnley 1–0 in the 1956 Final it was the first time that a non-Lancashire team had won the Cup!

✪ **5.** Burnley were only the second team in football history to win the Lancashire Cup three seasons running – 1959–60, 1960–61 and 1961–62. Five players played in all three winning Finals; Andy Lochhead, Fred Smith and John Talbut had been winners three times and had yet to taste defeat in a Final, while Ron Fenton and Trevor Meredith had both played in four Lancashire Cup Finals, having been in the runners-up team of 1956–57.

✪ **6.** When the Clarets won the Lancashire Cup in 1966 it was for the fifth time in seven seasons: a Lancashire Cup record. Fred Smith played in all five winning teams, which equalled the record for an individual set by Fergie Suter in the 1880s. John Talbut played in four of the winning teams.

✪ **7.** In 1968, when Burnley were beaten in the final by Morecambe, Fred Smith made his sixth appearance in a Lancashire Cup Final, thus equalling the previous all-time record of six Final appearances by Fergie Suter and Jimmy Brown in the 1880s. It was the first time that Freddie had tasted defeat in a Lancashire Cup Final.

✪ **8.** Burnley won the Lancashire Cup seven times within 13 seasons, from 1960 to 1972.

✪ **9.** The club's worst defeat in the Lancashire Cup was 8–0 at home to Astley Bridge in 1882–83.

✪ **10.** The club's best victory in the Lancashire Cup was 15–0 at home to Haydock in 1889–90.

LANGUAGE (bad!)

During the 1–1 draw at Ipswich on 2 December 2006 play stopped and the lull allowed the crowd to clearly hear Burnley captain Wayne Thomas giving instructions to a colleague with some very poor language. Thomas realised that the crowd – which included children – had heard his expletives and went over to the barrier to apologise. 'I'm really sorry, my language was out of order', he said to the spectators, and held up his hand in acknowledgement. He was applauded by the nearby Ipswich fans.

LAUGHTER

Winger Ralph Coates teased the Blackburn defenders by actually sitting on the ball in a game at Ewood Park, daring them to come and get it off him!

LIMERICKS

In the 1970s there was a craze for Claret and Blue limericks. Here is one of the best:

> To John Angus
> Burnley had a full-back called John,
> Whose footballing days are now gone.
> An example to young 'uns
> He was one of the good 'uns
> And his memory at Turf Moor will live on.

More recently we have had a few 'Longside limericks', which include the following:

> After nineteen games without winning,
> Our attendance numbers were thinning.
> The remainder were bored,
> Because we never scored.
> And wanted our manager binning.
> **(Cheshire Exile)**

> 'There is a small team from Turf Moor,
> They love to go forward and score,
> But sometimes our defence,
> Has us nervous and tense,
> But the football is never a bore.
> **(Burnleybeerandchips)**

Turf Moor is where legends are born,
But the Rovers just look on with scorn,
We're off to Spurs in the Cup,
Because we're on the up,
And the Rovers look tattered and torn.
(Burnleybeerandchips)

These proud players in claret and blue,
Will show the League what we can do.
In defence and attack,
From the front to the back,
And our manager goes 'och ay the noo!'
(Jabberwocky)

A young female Claret called Rhona,
Was known as a bit of a moaner,
Her boyfriend said 'Lass,
You're a pain in the ass,
It's Burnley not Barcelona!'
(Nutsinmay)

Our lads play in claret and blue,
But Villa and Scunny do too,
This isn't a jest,
We're simply the best,
All the world now knows this is true!
(Burnleybeerandchips)

I spied on my way to the Turf,
A fan of considerable girth,
He ate pies to order,
His dad – a Bob Lorder,
Had reared him on Hollands from birth!
(Nutsinmay)

LOCAL LADS

Among the 'local yokels' who have played for Burnley are: Brian Miller, Mike Phelan, Martin Dobson, Albert Cheesebrough, Richard Chaplow, Colin Blant, Andy Wharton, David Walker, Alan Shackleton, Andy Payton and Jay Rodriguez. (Quite a few games, goals and internationals there!)

THE LONE RANGER

It was Liverpool versus Burnley at Anfield in the 1970s. Liverpool were at their best, beating everybody in sight, while Burnley were not doing very well. Manager Jimmy Adamson was scratching his head, wondering how to get a point, let alone a win.

In the team talk the day before the match he looked at each and every Burnley player and gave detailed instructions to them individually. 'Stevo in goal, I want you to keep everything out, you need to play the game of your life…the full-backs, I want you to defend everything, and even try to attack…midfield, you need to be everywhere, in attack, in defence, and snuff out every Liverpool move…forwards, you must track back and help midfield AND attack, and put pressure on at every chance.'

He looked at every player bar centre-forward Paul Fletcher and told them that this was a great Liverpool team and they would have to defend with their lives.

'And you…', he looked at Fletcher, 'YOU are going to be on your own all night up front.' Adamson paused for effect. 'YOU…are going to be the Lone Ranger.'

At Anfield there was a telegram waiting for Fletcher before the game. It had been sent by Peter Noble and contained just three simple words, 'Good luck, Tonto.'

The team talk worked, and so did the tactics. Stevo kept everything out and full-back Ian Brennan scored a peach of a goal from some 30 yards out. That night the points went to Burnley.

THE LONGSIDE

Over the years the Clarets have had numerous favourite areas for the supporters. Long before there were stands named after well-known figures there was the Bee Hole End and the 'Scrattin' Shed'(Cricket Field End), but as famous as any was the 'Longside'. This had grown in popularity from the 1920s and 1930s when it was simply a mound of grass, to the 1940s when it became terraced. In 1954 it was covered by a stand, but it was really in the 1970s, 1980s and early 1990s that it blossomed.

Curiously, these were the years when there were not vast numbers on the Longside, such as there had been in the 1940s, 1950s and 1960s. But the atmosphere created by the Burnley fans always made up for the lack of numbers. Eventually, the Longside became segregated for home and away fans, and on 16 September 1995 the fans bid an emotional farewell to their beloved terracing in the game against Hull City. It was demolished so that the entire Turf Moor stadium could be made into the all-seated arena it is today. However, the Longside will long be remembered, for it had witnessed chants and cheers, riots and protests, laughter and near tragedy over the years.

'A LOOK OF INTENT'

Many Burnley players have been sent off over the years, but the one incident that Burnley supporters still talk about over 50 years after it happened was at Maine Road, Manchester, during the City versus Burnley game in March 1952. Billy Elliott, the Burnley left-winger, was sent off – not for a bad tackle, not for breaking someone's leg, not for abusive language, not for retaliating – but for 'a look!' Added to this is the fact that he was the victim of a deliberate foul, which went unpunished. The *Burnley Express* reporter relates the story:

'Three minutes before the final whistle, Elliott raced away down the wing. Westwood dashed across from the left-back position, and with Revie, closed in on Elliott. Westwood whipped away both Elliott's legs from under him for as obvious and deliberate a foul as one could regretfully wish to see. Elliott went sprawling, the referee blew, and waved the player to approach.

Most people thought that Westwood was in for a lecture. But the official, Mr Thurman, beckoned Elliott, and sent him off. It was the worst decision I have ever seen – and I can recall a few. Burnley officials saw the referee after the game, and were told that he had sent the player off for 'a look of intent'.

As one who regularly watched and admired Billy Elliott, I can well believe the sort of glare that he gave Westwood. He was as tough a player as ever played for Burnley, but on this occasion there was no retaliation. Over half a century later, Burnley fans still remember the name of Mr Thurman!

LOST CHANCES

⊕ In 1896–97 Burnley only won twice in their last 13 games. As a result they finished bottom of the League, but only by four points.

⊕ In 1899–00 Burnley won just once in their last four games. They were relegated, finishing just one point behind Preston. Preston were one of the three teams to beat Burnley in those final matches; if it had been the other way round, Preston would have gone down instead.

⊕ In 1911–12 Burnley only won once in the last five games. They had been in the top two places of Division Two all season, but by losing three and drawing one of their final five games they finished third and missed promotion by two points.

⊕ In 1929–30 Burnley won only twice in their last six games. They were relegated due to goal average.

⊕ Similarly, in 1961–62, after topping the table for most of the season, the Clarets only won one game in the final 10 (drawing five and losing four) to finish runners-up to Ipswich Town.

⊕ In 1975–76 Burnley lost their last two games and were relegated by two points.

⊕ In 1979–80 the Clarets played their last 16 games without a win. And they were still relegated by just two points.

- In 1982–83 Burnley drew and lost their last two games to go down by a single point.

- In 2001–02 the Clarets missed getting into the Play-offs in Division One by a single goal. (The difference between Norwich City and Burnley's goal difference at the end of the season.)

LAST CHANCES

- In 1889–90, when they were bottom of the League, Burnley won four and drew once in their last five games to escape the foot of the League. (Incidentally, they scored 18 goals in those last five games, just half of what they scored in the entire season. In bottom place were Stoke, who went out of the League.)

- In 1925–26 Burnley were bottom of Division One with just two games to go. The Clarets won them both and escaped relegation by a single point.

- In 1931–32 Burnley won their final game and escaped relegation from the Second Division by just two points.

- They did exactly the same thing in 1932–33. Phew!

- Burnley won the last match of the season in 1986–87 to finish a point above Lincoln City, who lost their place in the Football League.

- In the final game of 1997–98 Burnley played Plymouth at Turf Moor, with the winning team staying up. The Clarets won 2–1 and Plymouth were relegated.

LUCKY FLOWERS

'Before leaving Cheltenham for the match, Mr Tom Grey again provided the team with buttonholes of claret and blue flowers, and as the team won – a thing they have done every time they have sported the club's colours in flowers, the superstitious may be inclined to consider whether the flowers are lucky or not.'
Bristol City v Burnley, March 1912

LUCKY HORSESHOE!

'The team entrained on Friday afternoon at 12.30, a horse shoe being thrown into the carriage, but fortunately it did not strike anyone!'
Burnley Gazette, **February 1909**

Chapter Seven

M–N

(From McIlroy and Magical month to Northern and proud of it and No such player)

THE 'M' TEAM

Mellor

Marshall   Mather

Miller   Merrington   Moffat

Morgan   Morris   Moore   Morley   Mosscrop

Subs: Morrison, Meredith and Murray

VERSUS

THE 'MAC' TEAM

McDonald

McCluggage   McLintock

McFettridge   McGreal   McCann

McDonald (K.)   McGee   McKay   McIlroy   McMinn

Subs: McFarlane and McGregor

McILROY! Arguably the best Claret of them all?

He may be the answer
'Today, 18-year-old Jimmy McIlroy receives his big chance. If he is successful, as we all hope he will be, he may be the answer.'
***Burnley Express,* October 1950**

Debut Sunderland v Burnley, October 1950

'Young Jimmy McIlroy came in for rough treatment, and his debut could be described as a baptism by the boot. But Burnley's spasms of attacking brilliance owed much to the trickery of the young Irishman. McIlroy combined the craft of the veteran with the enthusiasm of the youngster. His passing was accurate, particularly his through ball and the diagonal pass; he thought fast, moved quickly with the genius of anticipation and helped to make the line "go". His inclusion in the side was a bold move, but it was justified, and on this display the youngster can be classified as a "discovery".'
Burnley Express

McIlroy Magic – Manchester United v Burnley, November 1958

'Connelly broke away and was upended by Greaves. The referee examined the place of the foul and pointed to the penalty spot.

Then came a touch of Irish magic. Gregg craftily tried to steal a few inches, but was ordered back to his goalline. McIlroy had stationed himself as the nearest player to the ball, but he had such a disinterested air that one had second thoughts as to whether he intended taking the penalty. With his back to goal, as if to pass the time of day with Adamson. Then he casually turned around and "looked" at the ball which suddenly "materialised" in the back of the net.

Gregg had not even moved. Everyone except the excited Burnley contingent was dumbfounded. Gregg included. This was the first goal Burnley had scored at Old Trafford for four years, and their first goal in the last four games.'
Burnley Express

The Master Magician – Manchester City v Burnley, December 1958

'McIlroy illuminated the murk of Manchester with one of his star performances. He was the mentor, the master magician whose sorcery conjured the ball around, through, between heavier bodies and left them sprawling. They tackled him in pairs, they crowded him in threes; he showed them the ball, flicked it away from them, worked it on with little skips and feints and shuffles, while the crowd gazed on in silent wonder.

He was so baffling that one received the impression that had the Laws of Football allowed it, he would have waved one of his magic feet over the ball three times, and produced it reduced in size from the referee's pocket! Once, Hannah, no mean artiste as a ball player, chased McIlroy almost to a corner flag as if trying to find out how he achieved this uncanny mastery.'
Burnley Express

With one hand behind his back – Burnley v West Brom, September 1959

'Jimmy McIlroy had one of his greatest afternoons, for he showed that his Irish heart was far from daunted by a shoulder injury which kept him off the field for 13 minutes. He returned in pain, bandaged about the body, and virtually beat the Albion with one arm tied, if not behind his back, at least fastened firmly to his side.

Yet despite this handicap, McIlroy inspired and schemed from the right-wing position, where he was anything but a passenger. He demonstrated the use of the open space, how to create one, how to use it, and in addition, how to cross a ball with accuracy and dispatch.

McIlroy used his one good arm and both clever feet to excellent purpose, signalling with the former, and stroking the ball into suitable positions with the latter, for the launching of an attack, and chipping across centres into the goalmouth.'
Burnley Express

On one leg – Arsenal v Burnley, December 1959
'The injured McIlroy did enough on one leg to make observers wonder to what depths of humiliation Arsenal would have sunk if he had been able to bewilder them on two!'
Burnley Express

A cartoon caption, *Burnley Express*, March 1963
'What a shock! It's unbelievable! My eyes are deceiving me! I never thought it could happen! What was it? Had the Kierby fallen down? Was the Town Hall up for sale? Has Burnley Cricket Club signed up Morecambe and Wise as joint professionals for the 1963 season? Or had Ena Sharples joined Mrs Dale in retirement?
WHY – BURNLEY HAD PUT JIMMY McILROY ON THE TRANSFER LIST!!!'

Tribute
'He was an outstanding player and one of the greatest of that era. He was a very skilful player and a great passer of the ball. McIlroy always stood out in my mind as the outstanding player in a very good Burnley side. It is probably a controversial thing to say, but I often wonder what players like McIlroy would have achieved if there had been a Great Britain side rather than him playing for Northern Ireland, where he was never going to be in the top flight of international football.'
Tom Finney

MAGICAL MONTH

September 1961
Seven games and the Clarets won them all.

Manchester City	(a)	3–1
Leicester City	(h)	2–0
West Brom Albion	(h)	3–1
Birmingham	(a)	6–2
Leicester City	(a)	6–2
Everton	(h)	2–1
Fulham	(a)	5–3

✪ This record has never been beaten by Burnley and rarely equalled by any club – ever. However, in 1912–13 Burnley won all five games in December, and in 1991–92 they won all four games in October and followed it up by winning all five in November. Incidentally, these were Jimmy Mullen's first nine League games. But seven in a month!

✪ While on the subject, the Clarets drew all five games in November 1946.

MANAGERS

'In the early 1950s when Frank Hill was Burnley's manager, before an FA Cup tie every player would be allocated two complimentary tickets. Selling them on was common practice. After one particular Cup tie, several team members were rebuked by the club for selling Cup tickets for private profit. At the same time, Frank Hill entered the dressing room wearing a new pair of fashionable ankle length boots, boasting that they had only cost him one Cup ticket.'
Burnley's Greatest Goal, **Peter Fyles**

'When Alan Brown came as manager he experimented, playing football right from the goalkeeper instead of the normal big kick down the field. In training, much to the consternation of some of the team, he made them practice passing and attacking the goal without any opposition. The meaning behind this madness was that if you couldn't pass and score efficiently against a ghost XI, then you were certainly going to struggle against real life opponents. Big Bill Holden summed up Brown's style, "He would often growl, 'If I tell you to do something and its wrong, you still do it!'"'
Burnley's Greatest Goal, **Peter Fyles**

- Bill Shankly, who in his early years at Liverpool used to ring up Burnley manager Harry Potts at all hours of the night 'for a wee chat', once referred to Burnley as 'that village team!'

- When John Bond arrived at Turf Moor for the board meeting where he was to learn that he was being sacked he found the door to the club locked.

- Manager Stan Ternent sprinkled holy water from Lourdes on to the Burnley pitch to get rid of the bad spirits his wife felt there were – and he vowed to drink a sherry glass of Lourdes water before every game. All of this came after a run of very poor results. The next 11 games were all unbeaten.

- When manager Stan Ternent was banned from the touchline, and Burnley were struggling for money because of the collapse of ITV Digital, Stan thought of a good way to raise money. His seat in the dugout was auctioned to a fan for £561 and the fan spent the game sitting in the hallowed position.

- Shortest spell? Martin Buchan lasted just four months in charge at Burnley in 1985.

- Billy Dougall's service to Burnley covered an amazing five decades, beginning in 1926 as a player, becoming trainer, coach, manager and physiotherapist in the 1960s.

- Manager Brian Miller was replaced by Frank Casper in January 1983. On the same day, in the Second Division and soon to be relegated, Burnley went to

Tottenham with new man Frank Casper in charge and won 4–1. It was one of the biggest-ever footballing upsets.

⚽ Just two managers – Harry Potts and Brian Miller – have both played and managed at Wembley for Burnley.

⚽ Jimmy Mullen began his managerial reign at Burnley with an astonishing nine consecutive victories.

MANCHESTER UNITED

Much could be written about the rivalry between Burnley and Manchester United. It began in 1902, after United had taken over from Newton Heath (who had gone bankrupt). United's first manager, Ernest Mangnall, had previously been at Turf Moor as manager for three seasons.

It may be 100 years ago, but the FA Cup tie in 1909, abandoned when Burnley were leading 1–0, is still recalled in the town. 'Stop the game – it's snowing!' was a regular taunt heard at Burnley–United games for decades afterwards.

Burnley have played United over 100 times in the League, and United lead 47–39 in victories, though the Clarets lead 3–2 in FA Cup ties played.

The best Burnley sequence was in seasons 1952–53 and 1953–54 when the clubs met five times in the League and Cup, and the Clarets won all five games.

In the six seasons between 1958 and 1963 the Clarets recorded victories of 4–2, 5–3, 4–1, 5–2 and 6–1 against United. (Curiously, the only season of the six that Burnley did not beat United resoundingly was when the Clarets won the League in 1959–60.)

In 1963–64 Andy Lochhead scored five goals in the two Burnley–United League games (within three days). Surely a record?

The last time the clubs met in the League was in 1976, and the Clarets have not beaten United in a League game since 14 September 1968. (However, Burnley did not get a chance to beat them in 1974–75, because they were in the First Division and United were in the Second.) I just had to mention that fact.

MASCOTS

The perfect tackle was made not by a Burnley player on the opposition, which happened to be Preston North End at Turf Moor in 2000, but by Burnley's mascot, Bertie Bee.

With Burnley leading 2–0, a male streaker raced on to the pitch to the Preston end, and turned his buttocks towards the Preston fans. On one cheek was a '2' and on the other a '0'. He almost had time to run back to the Bee Hole End and vanish into the crowd, as this was one occasion when stewards and the police seemed mesmerised by the antics and made no reaction. Not so mascot Bertie Bee!

In full costume, with a huge, bright yellow bee's head fixed to his shoulders, Bertie bided his time, stepped on to the pitch and rugby tackled the intruder, tossing him right over his shoulder. The moment was captured live on Sky television and the fan was banned for life. But Bertie's fame was assured forever.

MISSED – AND SCORED!

'I was feeling awful, the week in bed was telling on my stamina, when suddenly the ball was flicked on by Martin Dobson and bounced up high between Norman Hunter and myself. I launched myself into an overhead kick, thinking either the ball or Hunter's head, would go flying into the net. In mid-air I felt my foot come into perfect contact with a round, muddy, empty object – and for a moment thought I'd kicked Hunter in the head!

But as I landed, I saw the ball crash into the net and the ground erupted. I was later to learn this was voted "The Goal of the Decade", but only winning the game, and getting off that pitch seemed to matter at that moment!'

Paul Fletcher on how he missed Norman Hunter's head and hit the ball instead. From *BFC And Me!*

MONEY IS RUINING FOOTBALL

'Let's take a step into a parallel universe for a minute, where Burnley are the richest club in the world. Kaka, while admitting he was very tempted, has chosen to stay with Milan, and the £108 million we earmarked for him is floating around waiting to be put to some kind of use. What might we do with it?

Well, for a start, we get the wheels moving again on the proposed ground developments. First of all, we buy the flipping place back! The current plans for the Cricket Field End would involve a cost of around £30 million, a drop in the ocean compared to the cash we've just saved on the little Brazilian. Hell, we can even renovate the Bob Lord, what's six or seven million quid when you're the richest club in the world? Anything's worth it to stop people getting splinters in their arses! The decision is taken to stop short at splashing out on a brand new ground. Turf Moor is our spiritual home and within easy walking distance of the pub.

While we're being sensible, we give Gawthorpe a new lick of paint and invest in an academy. We were producing pretty good young lads already, but with a bit more funding, we're firing out Beckhams and Rooneys before you know it. It sets us back about £3 million, but it's well worth it.

So we have some of the best facilities about and our youth policy looks set to see us take over the world within a couple of years. We're offered a load of useless players at hugely inflated prices, but we're not interested in over-hyped journeymen like Craig Bellamy or Keith Andrews. It's time to give something back to the fans. Free season tickets for everyone for a whole year! A new look Turf Moor is crammed every week, watching a team of home-developed stars winning games. But as the genius Alan Hansen once said, you can't win anything with kids. They're going to need a helping hand.

Investment begins in the first team squad, with Coyle bringing in young, hungry players to complement his squad. Yes, Coyle is still in charge, rumours that Burnley were going to dispose of his services in spite of doing so well, and replacing him with a "big name" prove to be wide of the mark. A few experienced international players are needed to help nurture the kids and further excite the already feverish fans. We get Patrick Viera on loan so we can give Alexander a rest now and again. We buy the whole Albanian team in the hope of unearthing "the next Bes". We hear rumours about that lot down the road, who are apparently heading for relegation and administration, and so we throw them a bone by taking Santa Cruz off their hands for £15 million. The Paraguayan immediately declares his delight at signing for "a really big club".

After all this, we've still spent only £62 million. Debate rages about what to do next. Should we buy up a handful of Championship clubs and turn them into Burnley feeder clubs? Do we offer to help Preston with paying Jon Parkin's restaurant bills? All these potential plans are scrapped. Barry Kilby puts his foot down and orders the remaining money be given to charity and invested in the local community. A banner is unfurled outside the plush new Turf Moor which reads "MONEY IS RUINING FOOTBALL!'"

Tom Jackson *When the Ball Moves,* **2009**

THE 'MOSES' OF THE FOOTBALL LEAGUE

Charles E. Sutcliffe was a Burnley man, born and bred. As a young man he had played rugby for Burnley Rovers before trying his hand, or rather his feet, at football. He later became a Football League referee and a Burnley FC director. Indeed, for four seasons he refereed every international match in which England did not take part. When he was a League referee he once disallowed six goals in a Blackburn versus Liverpool game in 1896, and in a memorable Sunderland versus Small Heath match he escaped from the ground after the game disguised as a policeman.

In 1896 he became a member of the Lancashire FA Council and received his Long Service medal in 1918. He was elected President of the Lancashire FA in 1926.

He was elected on to the committee of the Football League in 1898 and became a regular member of the England international team selection committee. He was the unfailing defender of the rights of the Football League and was described as 'the brains of football'.

He was noted for the way he travelled around with his pockets bulging with documents, and he became known throughout the country as 'The Moses of the Football League'. Most of the League's book of intricate rules and regulations was his work, and for over 75 years he and his firm compiled the Football League and Central League fixtures.

Sutcliffe brought about the abolition of 'Test Matches'. He was also the man behind referee and linesmen appointments and Football League compensation cases.

In many ways, he was a man ahead of his time, as witnessed in 1905, when at the annual League meeting he proposed the idea of there being 'three up and three down' in the League.

One of his schemes that failed abysmally was the 'Stop the Pools' movement. He thought that the pools were becoming too powerful and were developing into a menace to the game. In 1936, he gained the agreement of the League management committee, and then of the clubs, to a scheme to withhold publication of the League's list of Saturday matches until it was too late in the week for the pools coupons to reach and be returned by the public. It was a nine-day wonder, however. Clubs found that this secrecy involving fixtures affected attendances, and the plan was withdrawn.

Sutcliffe was a partner in the writing of the official history of the Football League in 1938, and in the League's jubilee year (1938) he became President of the Football League. At the celebrations he received life membership and a presentation of silver plate from the League, while, as a permanent memorial, a £100,000 Jubilee Benevolent Fund was launched to assist needy players. He died during his second year in the role as President of the Football League in 1939.

MOST GAMES IN A SEASON

⊕ The most games the club have played in one season was 69 and this was achieved twice, in 1884–85 and 1890–91. In the 1884–85 season most games were friendlies as this was in the days before the Football League. Incidentally, the season began on 1 August and finished on 29 June, while 40 of the 69 games were played at home.

⊕ In 1890–91 the season (between 1 September and 30 May) was made up of:
22 Football League games
2 FA Cup ties
1 Hospital Cup tie
1 Lancashire Cup game
2 East Lancashire Charity Cup games
1 charity match (for Burnley hospitals)
40 friendly games (These were against teams as local as Nelson and as distant as Belfast and Glasgow!)

⊕ In 1960–61 the club played 68 first team fixtures (between 13 August and 27 May):
42 Division One games
7 FA Cup ties
8 League Cup ties
4 European Cup games
4 Lancashire Cup games
1 Charity Shield game
2 post-season friendlies in Portugal

- Other 'busy' seasons have been 1973–74 and 1990–91, when 66 games were played.

- Incidentally, the season when least games were played was the club's first season (1882–83) when only 34 games were played – one game about every nine days.

MUD-SLINGING

'I regret that some blackguard or other had the unmanliness to throw a handful of mud into McFetteridge's face as he left the field. Such conduct cannot be too severely reprobated. The man who cannot bear to see his team lose after a fair and honest game is not fit to witness a football match. However, I expect it was merely some exasperated rough who had dropped his coin on the match and thought to revenge himself by mud-throwing.'
1888

MY SON

When we moved to Bournemouth in 1988 our son Christian was just six years of age. One day in his new Bournemouth school the teacher asked the class who their favourite footballers were. Christian at once replied, 'Please sir, Jimmy McIlroy!' 'Don't you mean Sammy McIlroy?' asked the teacher, who was obviously well versed in all things Old Trafford.

'No sir – Jimmy McIlroy of Burnley!' proudly replied my lad. Until then, Christian had never seen him play nor ever met the man. But I had taught him well! Once a Claret, always a Claret!

NEAR THINGS

Over the years Burnley have been involved in some 'near things'! These are just a few of the many occasions when they did not escape.
By two points
Burnley missed out on promotion from Division Two in 1911–12.
The club were relegated to Division Two in 1975–76.
The club were relegated to Division Three in 1979–80.
By one point
Burnley were relegated to Division Two in 1899–1900.
The club missed out on second place in Division One in 1962–63.
The club were relegated to Division Three in 1982–83.
The club were relegated to Division Four in 1984–85.

By one place in the League table

The club missed out on reaching the Play-off Finals in 2000–01.

By a disallowed goal

Burnley were relegated to Division Two in 1929–30. Earlier in the season the Clarets had lost 4–3 at Leicester, a game which saw Burnley have a goal disallowed because the referee thought that the ball had not gone over the goalline. Photos taken by the Leicester newspaper and which can be seen in Burnley library to this day show the ball several inches over the line. Because of that disallowed 'goal' and that 'lost' point Burnley were relegated.

By one goal

Burnley missed out on getting to the Play-off Finals in 1990–91 when they lost 2–1 to Torquay.

The club missed out on getting to the Play-off Finals in 2001–02.

The club lost in the Football League Cup semi-final in 1968–69, 3–2 to Swindon.

By a per cent of a goal (goal average)

Burnley finished at the bottom of Division Two in 1902–03 (Burnley 0.38 against Stockport County 0.52).

Burnley were relegated from Division One in 1929–30 (Burnley 0.81 against Sheffield United 0.94).

The club missed out on the runners-up spot in Division One in 1947–48 (Burnley 1.30 against Manchester United 1.68).

The club missed out on the runners-up spot in Division One in 1965–66 (Burnley 1.68 against Leeds United 2.07).

By seven minutes

Just seven minutes from the end of extra-time Chris Duffy scored the winner for Charlton Athletic versus Burnley in the 1947 FA Cup Final.

By two minutes

With just two minutes to go, Tottenham scored the winner against Burnley in the League Cup semi-final 2008–09.

And there have been others:

By an own-goal

In the last home game of 1965–66 Alex Elder put the ball in his own goal to give Leeds a 1–0 win. Two points or even one would have given the Clarets a runners-up place in the League.

By a penalty

At the same end (Bee Hole) and with the same player (Alex Elder) Burnley were leading Blackburn Rovers 3–0 in 1959–60 until the referee judged Alex to have 'handled' the ball. Rovers scored the penalty, drew the match 3–3 and won the replay.

By a goalkeeper's two saves

The last game of the season in 2001–02: Paul Gascoigne had to score a free-kick in the last minute to put the Clarets into the Play-offs. He failed but Burnley were awarded another free-kick from the same spot 30 seconds later. Amazingly, Coventry goalkeeper Magnus Hedman miraculously saved both attempts.

NEWSPAPERS

- In 1967 goalkeeper Harry Thomson was called 'A God in a green jersey' by the *Daily Express*, after a stunning display against Naples in the Inter Cities Fairs Cup.

- Thirty-four years later in 2001, former goalkeeper Harry Thomson was described in the club programme as 'A Cod in a green jersey'. A spelling mistake, it is presumed?

- Inside-forward Billy Ingham was given the soubriquet 'the Ginger Pelé' by one national newspaper, on the strength of one game in 1977 and a stunning goal against Chelsea.

NICKNAMES

- Over the years Burnley have had numerous nicknames. The first was 'the Hornets' because they wore amber and black shirts. When the club moved to Turf Moor they were often called 'the Turfites' and 'the Moorites'. In 1911 the club changed their colours and so Burnley FC became 'the Clarets'.

- In 1920–21 a Burnley supporter presented Joe Anderson with a pet monkey. For several games that season it would come on in Burnley's colours before the game and at half-time, climbing the goal post and swinging from the crossbar. After a few weeks the monkey disappeared. Why?

- The club began to realise that several opposing supporters were beginning to call Burnley 'the Monkeys', rather like other teams were called 'the Tigers', 'the Wolves' and 'the Magpies'. And so, in an attempt to remove the nickname, the club removed the monkey.

- Gary Parkinson was nicknamed 'big boy', allegedly on account of his liking for chocolate.

- Jackie Chew was known to the fans as 'Cowboy'. This was mainly because of his bandy legs, but he also packed a shot!

- Burnley cult figure Ted McMinn was never actually christened Ted, or even Edward. His real name is Kevin Clifton McMinn; however, when he was a lad his pals teased him and said he ran like he had a teddy bear under his arm. So they called him Teddy, and then Ted. The name has stuck and is even on his driving licence and bank statements!

NO ONE LIKES US – WE DO NOT CARE!

In the December 2003 online fans' survey of club rivalries, Burnley were surprisingly the country's second club with the most rivals, after Manchester United. The table was topped by the team from Old Trafford; then came Burnley, Leeds, Chelsea and Sheffield Wednesday. Forty-five per cent of fans saw history and tradition as the reason, and 35 per cent quoted geographical reasons.

Is there a close correlation with rivalry and dislike? That is less clear, as the two are not necessarily the same. In some cases, the rivalry is healthy and there can be a grudging respect, while in others it is pure dislike.

Fans were asked to name the team they considered their main rival, and also their second and third. Teams were then ranked by weighted average of the number of fans registering these choices.

Burnley were first choice rivals at Blackburn and Halifax (then a League club) and Stockport (beat them in the Wembley Play-offs in 1994). They were second choice rivals at Blackpool, Preston and Rochdale, and third choice rivals at Bradford City, Bury and Plymouth.

At first sight, the latter club seems a strange one due to the distance apart, but three games provide the origin for this. In 1994 the two Play-off games for the Final at Wembley provided two intensely physical meetings. The first was a brutal 0–0 draw at Turf Moor when Plymouth were clearly instructed to kick Burnley off the field, with Ted McMinn being the number one target. Following the 0–0 draw Plymouth fans clearly thought the job was done and that the game at Plymouth was a mere formality. Coaches and hotels were booked in preparation for the trip to London. Unfortunately, life does not always oblige.

Burnley won the second leg at Plymouth, in spite of severe provocation, with Johnny Francis being subjected to appalling racial abuse from the home fans. Johnny calmly slotted home two great goals. Since then, this game has always been included in any list of legendary Burnley FC games.

In another game between the two clubs, in the very final fixture of season 1997–98 at Turf Moor, Burnley won and consigned Plymouth to relegation. Had Burnley lost, then the Clarets would have been relegated.

Another element of rivalry involves the standing of the clubs involved. Burnley once counted among their main rivals Manchester United, Manchester City, Liverpool and Everton. Though of course, that was only when they were in the same division.

At other times, when divisions differed, rivalries cooled down. From 1951 until 1954 Everton were in the Second Division, from 1954 until 1962 Liverpool were in the Second Division, in 1950–51 and 1963 until 1966 Manchester City were in the Second Division and in 1974–75 Manchester United were in the Second Division.

Things changed radically in the 1970s when the Clarets went down and stayed down for over 30 years. They then renewed their rivalry with 'lesser' clubs such as Bolton, Blackpool, Oldham and Rovers. In 1980, when they sank still further, they learnt to find new rivals, like Huddersfield. In 1985, when they plumbed the depths of Division Four, they discovered rivals which they had never played for years, if ever

– Stockport, Rochdale and Halifax. Gone now were the days when the Liverpools and Uniteds of this world trembled at the name of Burnley. Now they laughed, and not even Stockport, Rochdale or Halifax trembled.

NORTHERN AND PROUD OF IT

'Burnley played Acton on Saturday, who hail from somewhere in the atmosphere of Cockneydom!'
Burnley Express, 1886

NO SUCH PLAYER

In October 1901 Burnley played Burton United in Division Two. The 'Turfites' included their new winger for the first time, 23-year-old William Lambie, a junior Scottish international signed from Hamilton. The result was 0–0 and William Lambie had an appalling game. So bad in fact that the directors enquired into his background.

It was discovered that the club had been misled about William Lambie and that he was indeed an imposter, and not a professional footballer at all! He was never seen again.

Chapter Eight

O–P

(From Oddfellows and Olden days to Punching above their weight and Pundits)

THE 'O' TEAM

O'Rourke

O'Dowd   O'Kane

O'Neil   O'Connor (G.)   Overson (V.)   Overson (R.)

O'Connor (J.)   Oghani   O'Connell   Oster

Subs: Orr and Ogden

AN ODDFELLOW?

'We wonder if Stewart has joined the Oddfellows? He certainly looked like one by half-time on Saturday.'
Burnley Express, November 1891

OLDEN DAYS?

'Immediately after the match George Utley the Sheffield United captain visited the Burnley players dressing room, shook hands with Boyle and Freeman and expressed the hope that the Turf Moor side would win the Cup.'
Burnley News, 1914. After Burnley had beaten Sheffield United in the FA Cup semi-final.

OLD-TIMERS!

⚽ Jerry Dawson was 40 years old when he made his final appearance for Burnley on Christmas Day, 1928. Jack Hillman played for the first team aged 47 in 1917–18, though only in wartime games. His last recorded appearance for the club was in a charity match in 1920–21 when he was 50 years old.

⊕ Ray Pointer was 51 when he scored the winning goal at Wembley in 1988. This was in the pre-match friendly between ex-Burnley and ex-Wolves players, played before the Sherpa Van Final.

'One of Burnley's most ardent supporters is a former captain – the club's first! He is Mr Tom Midgeley of Brunlea, Newton Road, Rhos on Sea, a retired schoolmaster who went to North Wales in 1926. Mr Midgeley captained the Burnley Rovers Rugby Club before they turned to Association rules, and served on the Burnley Football Club board of directors for a time. He will be 100 years of age in March.'
Burnley Express, January 1956

ONE-CLUB CLARETS

The following players have only played for one club in the Football League – BURNLEY! (They may have played in Scotland or English non-League, but that is it.)

	club appearances
Jerry Dawson	569
John Angus	520
Jimmy Adamson	486
Brian Miller	455
Fred Barron	423
Joe Taylor	352
Harold Mather	329
Billy Bowes	295
George Bray	259
Benny Cross	255
Tom McLintock	254
Bobby Seith	238
Billy Morris	230
Colin McDonald	201

ONE-GAME WONDERS (in post-war seasons)

The following players managed just a single first-team League appearance during their time at Turf Moor. The dates refer to their time at Burnley.
Jim Appleby (1953–58)
Tony Chilton (1985)
Paddy Corr (1951–53)
Ian Duerden (1996–98)
Neil Edwards (1985–86)

Bobby Flavell (1973–76)
Marco Gentile (1997)
Lee Grant (1995)
Douglas Hodgson (1996)
Richard Holden (1986)
Stuart Hooper (1988–89)
Neil Howarth (1990–94)
Frank Kval (1998–2000)
Des Lancaster (1954–58)
James McEveley (2003–04)
Jimmy Milner (1952–57)
Ian Muir (1982)
Billy O'Neill (1949–1951)
Bradley Orr (2004)
Leigh Palin (1992)
Amadou Samokho (2004–05)
Michael Southern (1986–87)
Ryan Townsend (2003–04)
Michael Wardrobe (1980–81)
Ronnie Welch (1969–1973)
Anthony Woodworth (1986–87)
William Wright (1981–83)

Some of these went on to play many games for other clubs: Bobby Flavell played over 100 games for Halifax, Chesterfield, and Barnsley, while Rick Holden (one subs appearance at Turf Moor) played over 350 times for Halifax, Watford, Oldham, Manchester City and Blackpool.

Of these players, the distinction of having the shortest League career of any Burnley player in the club's history belongs to Neil Edwards. He came on as substitute after 85 minutes in 1985–86 in the game against Cambridge. He never appeared in the League side again and thus had a Turf Moor career of just five minutes!

ONE-SIDED?

Burnley v Irwell Springs 3–0, February 1884
'The Burnley goalkeeper did not handle the ball once during the entire match.'
Burnley News

THE OPPOSITION

✪ Burnley's most regular League opponents over the years have been: West Brom (120 games), Preston (118), Wolves (112), Bolton (110), Blackpool (106), Manchester United (102) and Sheffield United (102).

- Burnley are unbeaten at Turf Moor by Barnet (2 games), Bournemouth (9), Chester City (4), Hartlepool (8), Macclesfield (1), Tranmere (7), and Wycombe (5) in just League games.

- The most home victories achieved have been against: Preston (32 wins), Blackpool (31), Sheffield United (30), Bolton (29), Fulham (29), Aston Villa (28), Newcastle United (27), West Brom (27) and Manchester United (26).

- Burnley's best away record is against: Blackpool (17 wins), West Brom (16), Chelsea (15), Newcastle United (14) and Manchester United (13).
- The clubs they have beaten the most are: Blackpool (48 victories), Preston (44), West Brom (43), Bolton (42), Newcastle (41), Manchester United (39), Fulham (37), Leicester (37) and Chelsea (36).

- The clubs who have beaten us the most are: Wolves (59 times), West Brom (51), Preston (48), Manchester United (47), Sheffield United (43), Everton (41), Villa (39), Derby (39), Bolton (39) and Sunderland (39).

- The clubs that Burnley have beaten more than been beaten by are: Birmingham City, Blackpool, Bolton, Chelsea, Fulham, Huddersfield, Leicester, Newcastle, Sheffield Wednesday and Spurs.

OTHER CLUBS

The club which has shared most Clarets' players since the war is Bury. Altogether 51 players have played for both clubs in the last 62 seasons, of whom a list now follows: Gordon Armstrong, Paul Barnes, Marlon Beresford, Charlie Bishop, Graham Branch, Chris Brass, John Connelly, Lee Dixon, Martin Dobson, Roger Eli, Tony Ellis, Wayne Entwistle, Brian Flynn, Garry France, Steve Gardner, Andy Gray, Jack Hays, Bill Holden, David Holt, Jamie Hoyland, Joe Jakub, Leighton James, Ronnie Jepson, Lenny Johnrose, David Johnson, David Jones, Andy Kilner, Andy Marriott, Steve Morgan, John Murray, John O'Kane, Terry Pashley, Brian Pilkington, Ray Pointer, Eric Potts, Adrian Randall, Andy Robinson, Liam Robinson, Jimmy Robson, Peter Simpson, Malcolm Smith, Nigel Smith, Danny Sonner, Peter Swan, Alan Taylor, Ian Towers, Colin Waldron, John Walton, Dean West, Winston White, Kevin Young.

DEAR DEPARTED

The teams that Burnley have played in the Football League, who have since dropped into the lower regions – and as a matter of interest, the number of times they met in the League.
Accrington (10)
Bradford Park Avenue (36)

Burton Swifts (2)
Burton United (14)
Cambridge United (22)
Darwen (6)
Exeter City (20)
Gainsborough Trinity (26)
Glossop North End (28)
Halifax Town (14)
Loughborough Town (2)
Maidstone United (6)
Mansfield Town (8)
New Brighton (2)
Newport County (12)
Oxford United (14)
Scarborough (10)
Torquay United (12)
Wrexham (30)
York City (20)

THE ORIGINAL COMMITTEE

When the club was founded in 1882 the original 10 members of the committee were R.H. Wadge, W. Hearne, R.W. Thornton, H. Smith, R. Murray, E. Whitehead, C.E. Sutcliffe, J. Calvert, J. Crook and S. Thomas. The officials in 1883 at the time of moving from Calder Vale to Turf Moor were: chairman A. Jobling, secretary G.C. Waddington and treasurer W. Brown. George Waddington was often described as 'the father of Association Football in this district'.

Other men who helped to make the club in its early days were men like Tom Midgeley, T. Heaton, Walter Curl and A.E. Sutcliffe. These men not only picked the teams and organised the games, but also put a great deal of time and money into furthering the football cause in East Lancashire.

In 1897 the club issued 4,000 £1 shares, and the original board of directors consisted of T.A. Ashworth (joiner), T.A. Bramald (baths proprietor), A.H. Coppock (yeast merchant), J.K. Grimshaw (brewer), E. Whitehead (cotton manufacturer), C.E. Sutcliffe (solicitor), H. Spencer (clothlooker), C.H. Ratcliffe (mineral water manufacturer) and R.H. Wadge (paviour and contractor). The club secretary was Harry Bradshaw.

Harry Bradshaw left Burnley in 1899 for Arsenal and was succeeded by Mr E. Mangnall. Together with Messrs Wadge, Sutcliffe, Whitehead and Thornton, Mangnall bore the whole financial responsibility of the club during the early years of the 20th century, a time when the club was in great financial difficulties. He went four months without salary, and over a period of four years he spent just £10 on transfers (for James Lindsay, who later went to Bury for £200). Without the help and support of these five men, the club could never have survived.

OUCH!

'It was unfortunate for Burnley, that owing to Charlie Bates having worn extra tight pants last Saturday, his legs were too badly chafed to allow him to play on Monday!'
Burnley News, March 1911

OVERCOATS

After a fairly average start to the 1912–13 season a local overcoat specialist made the unique offer of providing a new overcoat to any Burnley player who scored two or more goals in a home match, and also a coat to any spectator of that player's choice. Suddenly, the goals started to flow like never before!

A total of eight overcoats were eventually presented to Burnley players, with another eight going to their friends. Bert Freeman, who scored 36 goals that season, collected five overcoats for himself! He politely declined a sixth coat for his third and fourth goals against Leicester Fosse. If the offer had been made at the start of the season and had covered all matches, 34 overcoats would have been given away – 20 of them to Bert Freeman or his friends.

At the end of the season Burnley had won promotion. This was thanks to a very good team, and maybe an offer of free overcoats?

THE 'P' TEAM

Peyton

Pashley   Parkinson

Phelan   Place   Pender

Price   Pointer   Payton   Potts   Pilkington

Subs: Parton, Pearce, Papadopoulos, Page and Philliskirk

PADIHAM

Burnley v Padiham 2–4, April 1884
'Long before the appointed time for kicking off, the scene in the vicinity of the football field presented an animated appearance. Buses and wagonettes drove up in rapid succession, while crowds of foot passengers both male and female, young and old, thronged towards the field. The Grand Stand was quickly filled with enthusiasts, although the price of admission was raised to 1/-. The spectators conducted themselves in a very orderly manner all over the field.

Nothing added more to the cheerfulness of the scene than the presence of a numerous body of ladies who preponderated greatly in the stand. Half an hour before the time, at least 6,000 spectators were assembled on the field, while Brunshaw Road was thronged with enthusiasts. Vast crowds found there were from

Nelson, Brierfield, Padiham and all the surrounding districts. Admirers of the dribbling code journeyed from Accrington, Blackburn, and even Preston, to watch the great event, while individuals who had never seen a football match in their lives were hurried along by enthusiastic friends, on the ground, in the enclosure, and into the grandstand, with an utter disregard for the expense before they well knew where they were.

There couldn't have been less than 10,000 on the field by now, and the cry was "still they come". A burst of good humour was occasioned by the climbing of the opposite goal posts in the field beyond, by two or three individuals who were determined to see at all hazards evidently. **Burnley Express**

THE PALACE

My Grandad Wiseman always talked about going to the Palace. During my infancy and childhood I listened to his tales of how he had travelled from Burnley to London to go to the Palace in 1914 and how he had seen the King. I never quite understood how or why Grandad had been called to Buckingham Palace but as a small child I was always mightily impressed. It was not until I was a teenager that it dawned on me that Grandad had been one of the several thousands who had travelled down to London from Burnley to see the 1914 FA Cup Final. It was Crystal Palace, not Buckingham Palace!

That story has a touching ending. Ten years after Grandad died, the Clarets reached the Cup Final where they were due to play Spurs in 1962. The day before the Final I went to see Grandma to share some of my hopes and dreams for the Wembley adventure. She got out of her chair and went to her drawer where she got out a brown silk scarf. 'Your grandad bought this when he went to Crystal Palace in 1914. Wear it tomorrow – it might bring you luck!'

And so I did, but it did not bring the team luck! We lost 3–1 of course. But I was the only Burnley supporter in the crowd that day wearing an old brown silk scarf from my grandad who had been to the Palace!

PARSONS, PREACHERS AND PRIESTS

'The Roman Catholic Church challenged Jimmy Hogan to live his life within its strictest rules of behaviour. At the same time, he had to mix with a breed of men with little regard for his dogmatic ethics. Few who worked with him found it easy to follow the guidelines that were, to him, essential to the way he wanted to live. He embraced the principles with such complete assurance that they shaped his lifestyle, his personality, and for better or worse, his relationships with everyone with whom he associated, from fellow professionals to his own family.

Not without good reason would some of the players he coached nickname him "The Parson". Swearing – presumed then as now endemic in the game – was virtually unknown in his company, and those players who joined him at Mass were probably more likely to be forgiven their trespasses on the field and in training than those who did not.

There is little doubt that his father, James, would have preferred to see his son go into the priesthood rather than live a wandering life in football. And briefly, in the natural ferment of teenage years, Jimmy was slightly torn between a career among crude-talking professional footballers and the Church.'

The Jimmy Hogan Story by Norman Fox

'On the Sunday evening, as usual, Jimmy Hogan went to church. In the middle of the service, he felt a tap on his back. He looked round. A stranger whispered that he would like to speak to him and that there was another gentleman outside. Hogan said they would both have to wait until after the service was over. Once the service was over, the men introduced themselves as representing Bolton Wanderers.

Mr Tate of Bolton remarked, "You know Mr Hogan, I've signed players at home in bed, under a street lamp and in pubs, but this is the first time I've signed anyone at church!"'

The Jimmy Hogan Story by Norman Fox

Many is the time that Burnley Football Club has been a part of a church service conducted by myself – just ask any of my congregations. However, the congregations have not always known.

On 6 May 2000 I was conducting three weddings – one o'clock, three o'clock and 4.30pm. Burnley were away at Scunthorpe in a vital game they had to win to secure promotion, and after the 3 o'clock wedding I managed to grab the half-time score – so far so good.

However, when the full-time whistle blew at Scunthorpe I was still conducting the third wedding. To be accurate, I had just pronounced the couple 'husband and wife'. Right then at the rear of the church (seen only by me of course) there appeared my son, dancing up and down like a lunatic! We had won!

Without batting an eyelid I said, 'Let us now sing the hymn *Praise God, from whom all blessings flow!*'

PARACHUTES

The only connection that football has with parachutes is concerned with the system of parachute payments, the infamous system whereby teams relegated from the Premiership receive 'compensation' of many millions of pounds to help them get by in the Championship. Burnley are one of the minority of clubs not receiving this substantial windfall, due to the fact that they have never been relegated from the Premiership. So much then for the famous 'level playing field'! So, if the Clarets want to be associated with parachutes, for say, the contents of this book, they have to take a different approach to parachuting!

The date was 16 August 2008 and Burnley were due to play Ipswich Town. It was the first home game of the season and optimism was high among the home fans at Turf Moor. Add to this excitement the fact that the club had arranged for members of the Red Devils parachute team to free fall and parachute into the stadium. Indeed, the target was the centre circle and the centre spot was highlighted with a big white cross for them all to land upon.

2.40pm and they began to arrive from the sky, one by one. Everyone of them – much to our amusement – sailed way past the centre circle target. At last we awaited the 10th man who was also bringing the match ball with him. A colleague was on top of the James Hargreaves Stand with a red flare to show the parachutists where the stadium was. Speaking personally, I have never had much trouble in finding it, without the help of a red flare!

2.50pm and here he came. But for some reason, unlike his teammates, he did not overshoot the centre circle. Indeed, he never even reached the pitch! After a very bumpy landing, he finished up on the roof of the Cricket Field Stand. The crowd cheered, and after gathering up his 'chute he waved back at us all. However, it was announced that due to 'health and safety' issues, the kick-off would be delayed for 30 minutes. Optimism and amusement changed to annoyance and frustration.

People were making arrangements, mobile phones were being kept busy. A man nearby went to the exit to tell his wife patiently sat outside the ground that he would be late home. But he returned minutes later after being told that if he left the stadium, he would have to pay to get back in. It was now after three and we realised that the game at Turf Moor was going to be different from other games that day which had already kicked off. 3.30pm and a fire engine passed by, unaware that 11,312 pairs of eyes were following its progress, hoping and wishing for a rescue ladder. 3.45pm and half-time whistles were sounding elsewhere.

Four o'clock came and the man was still on the roof, but the players started to appear on the pitch. The ref was ready to start and the whistle blew. The man was still on the roof – what about the earlier 'health and safety' issues? Twelve months later and we still await an explanation on that one. Eventually, to ironic cheers, the rooftop parachutist was rescued, accompanied by songs from the watching crowd of *You aren't very good* and *Going down, you're going down…*

It was nearly seven o'clock that night when I got home from Burnley. What about the London Clarets who missed their return train home? And what about the man we had been told was on the Hargreaves Stand with the flare? Wasn't he a 'health and safety' issue as well?

Eventually the Burnley good humour prevailed and it was suggested that the referee had booked the parachutist for descent ('dissent'). As for me, I would have preferred it if the club had been offered the parachute money in the first place!

P.S. One Claret poet was moved to describe the day:
Paratroopers come swooping down,
Bringing the match ball as planned
Then the game is delayed by the
Para left perched on the stand.
Dave Alton

PASSION

'One Saturday teatime when the slide was on, I remember Dad pushing his jibes too far and my teenage heart suddenly collapsing. As tears flowed down my face,

I passed through a multitude of contradictory emotions. Hatred of Dad, sympathy for Adamson, self-pity and that great hole of sadness that every Claret heart must have passed through when a dream so near abruptly disintegrated into nothing.' **Peter Fyles**

⊕ '"Inchy", I once shouted at him towards the end of a typically sterling performance, "I love you", and I probably meant it. He must have heard me, because when he scored half a minute later, he turned round and blew me a kiss. I didn't stop grinning all weekend.' **Stephen Cummings**

⊕ '2000 was a special year for me. I turned 16, I left school, I passed my GCSEs, but the really special thing for me was 6 May 2000 at Glanford Park.' **Jonny Smith**

PENALTIES

The first
'Hill was fouled near the West Bromwich goal by Horton, who held the left-winger round the neck and then added to the offence by kicking him. Mr Chaplain the referee awarded Burnley a penalty-kick which was the first in a match of first rate importance at Turf Moor, and therefore the proceedings were watched with great interest. Of course, Reeder the Albion custodian was the only player between the kicker and the goal and then the custodian advanced halfway towards Lang, who was entrusted with the kick. The latter made no mistake.'
Burnley v West Brom, November 1891

Three missed!
In the Burnley versus Grimsby Town League game in February 1909, the Grimsby goalkeeper saved three penalties – from Dick Smith and Walter Abbott (two). Despite these failures, Burnley still managed to win the game 2–0, helped very much by another penalty, successfully scored by Walter Abbott. Third time lucky?

'With their toes on the line'
In 1923 players of the opposing team often lined up on the edge of the penalty area to impede a player when he was taking a penalty-kick. 'The first occasion when this took place in a Burnley match was when the Sheffield United team all lined up with their toes on the penalty area line. Many people were inclined to argue that this was not sportsmanlike.'
Burnley News, 1923

Who scored most penalties?
Four players spring to mind when thinking about the number one penalty taker at Turf Moor. In the early part of the century there was only one player who took penalties for Burnley and that was Tommy Boyle. He was an attacking centre-half and amazingly for a 100 per cent midfielder, he scored 43 goals in 235 games. Compare that with Brian Miller

(another attacking half-back) who scored 33 goals in 429 League and Cup games. There is no comparison really. Boyle was famed for his shooting and his powerful heading, and those attributes must have accounted for many of his goals. At a guess, three-quarters of his goals could count as coming from penalties – around 30 out of the 43?

The next penalty taker of note was full-back Andy McCluggage, who scored 24 goals in his 213 games. Full-backs rarely scored in those days, and it would not be exaggerating to suggest that all 24 of Andy's goals came from penalties.

In more modern times, Jimmy 'Mac' was famed for his penalty taking and the manner in which he would 'ghost' the ball into the back of the net. He scored many from the spot, but nothing like the numbers from Boyle and McCluggage.

The player who immediately springs to mind with regards to penalty kicks is Peter Noble. The popular belief at Burnley is that Peter Noble scored 28 times from the spot. One fact we know is that he never missed one! So, though Tommy Boyle may well have scored more penalties, for consistency and accuracy it surely has to be Peter Noble. You cannot beat a 100 per cent record!

PHEW!

October 1946
'Jack Chew came in for some gentle leg-pulling after the Sheffield match. The programme had him down in the team as "Phew". Probably that was what the spectators at the Spion Kop End said when he crashed in the lightning drive, which opened the scoring after nine minutes.'
Burnley Express

PHOTOGRAPHS

When the *Burnley News* began printing photographs for the first time in 1921 of the Burnley players, they patted themselves on the back (and no doubt rewarded the players!) by publishing numerous photographs and letters from the players:

Dear Editor,
Those photographs you took of me were splendid, and I was surprised to see how well they looked in your paper, the *Burnley News*. It is no wonder the *News* has built such a reputation for the football reports are good and the photos are excellent. For a local paper, it is the best I have ever seen.
Thos W. Boyle,
68 Rectory Road
Burnley   (22 March 1921)

Dear Editor,
Allow me to congratulate you on the excellence of the photograph you recently took of me, reproduced in the *Burnley News*. My friends speak of them in the highest terms.

Do you mind finishing a few off for me, as I have so many requests for copies?

Sincerely yours,

Bob Kelly,

14 Clevelands Road,

Burnley   (17 February 1921)

Dear Sir,

I should like to express my appreciation of the splendid football reports which you publish in your excellent newspaper. I certainly think 'Kestrel' is a capital writer, who knows the game from A to Z.

As regards the photograph you published, I am sure I have never seen any picture so good in any paper. Those you printed of me were excellent.

Good wishes,

Joe Anderson

10 Hamer Street,

Burnley   (March 1921)

Dear Sir,

What an attractive paper, the *Burnley News* has become. I look forward to each issue to read the Football Notes by 'Kestrel', whom I consider one of the best writers on the sport that I have ever read.

The photographs are always good. I thought the series of Joe Anderson, our centre, were the best I have ever seen in any newspaper. Wishing my favourite newspaper every success

Yours faithfully,

Jerry Dawson

63 Clifton Terrace,

Cliviger   (March 1921)

'PIES, PIES, AND MORE PIES!'

In 1922 Turf Moor was chosen as the neutral venue for the FA Cup semi-final between Huddersfield Town and Notts County (the only occasion this has happened in over 125 years). A crowd of 46,323 attended the game, and the event was reported in the local paper.

'One wonders what the visiting crowd thought of Burnley! Anyone coming to the town must have thought that it was built upon meat pies and sandwiches! Everybody seemed to have been prepared to give the visitors a hearty welcome – at a price – and to provide them with something to eat of the handiest description.

It is said that great minds think alike. There must have been a lot of great minds in Burnley on Saturday! Wherever a corner could be got, or a cottage or a shop window could be opened, there were to be found, pies, pies and more pies. The visitors must have gone home to dream of mountains of pies with crests of sandwiches!'

Burnley News, March 1922

● Burnley are currently sponsored by Hollands Pies. Hollands serve four different pies at Turf Moor on a match day – Big Eat Meat and Potato, Chicken Balti, Cheese and Onion and Steak and Kidney. All pies have an exclusive Hollands and Burnley FC label.

● Last season, over 70,000 pies were supplied to the club by Hollands.

● It is estimated that 22 per cent of the Turf Moor crowd eat a pie at a game.

● The most popular pie by a long way at Turf Moor is the Big Eat Meat and Potato.

PIE AND CHIPS

At half-time, different groups of Burnley supporters endeavour to 'chip' the ball into a large inflated 'pie'. Teams which have competed include Water Village Clarets, Todmorden Clarets, North Manchester Clarets and Jimmy Mac All Stars.

PITY THE POOR GOALKEEPER!

Goalkeepers who have let in the most goals in one game have been:
1.= Jerry Dawson, 10 goals in the 0–10 Aston Villa game, 1925–26
1.= George Sommerville, 10 goals in the 0–10 Sheff United game, 1928–29
3. Bill Cox, nine goals in the 1–9 Wolves game, 1888–89
4.= Tommy Hampson, eight goals in the 1–8 Bury game, 1925–26
4.= Jerry Dawson, eight goals in the 3–8 Manchester City game, 1925–26
4.= George Sommerville, eight goals in the 0–8 Liverpool game, 1928–29
4.= George Sommerville, eight goals in the 3–8 Blackburn Rovers game, 1929–30
4.= George Sommerville, eight goals in the 1–8 Spurs game, 1930–31
4.= Harry Thomson, eight goals in the 1–8 West Brom game, 1967–68

PLAYERS

'Just fancy – Duckworth being penalised for a foul against a man big enough to eat him!'
Burnley News, **Burnley v Glasgow Celtic, 1889**

'Captain Green led his men out with a rather anxious air'
Burnley News, **Burnley v Barnsley, 1911**

Long servants – little played! (League games only)
James Appleby (1953–58)   5 years 1 game
Jim Furnell (1954–62)   8 years 2 games
Ellis Hargreaves (1892–97)   5 years 1 game
Tom Henderson (1945–49)   4 years 2 games

Des Lancaster (1954–58)	4 years 1 game
James McConnell (1886–90)	4 years 1 game
Jimmy Milner (1952–57)	5 years 1 game
James Scott (1951–61)	10 years 3 games
Peter Simpson (1957–63)	6 years 3 games
Ronnie Welch (1969–73)	4 years 1 game
Neil Howarth (1990–94)	4 years 1 sub appearance

PLYMOUTH – CAN WE PLAY YOU EVERY WEEK?

⊕ The last game of the season 1997–98 saw Burnley in the bottom four teams in Division Two and heading for relegation. So were Plymouth. The two clubs had to play each other in the last game of the season. Winners stay up, losers go down! By far the largest crowd of the season gathered at Turf Moor to see Andy Cooke's two goals save the day. And the club. Sorry Plymouth!

⊕ It was history almost repeating itself. In the Play-off semi-finals of 1993–94 Burnley had met Plymouth. After drawing at Turf Moor Burnley went down to Devon and won 3–1 to go to Wembley. Sorry Plymouth!

⊕ In 2005–06 Burnley ended a bad run of six games without a win by beating Plymouth 1–0. Sorry Plymouth!

⊕ The following season, 2006–07, Burnley went 19 consecutive games without a win, from November until April. This was until Plymouth came to Turf Moor and lost 4–0. Sorry Plymouth!

⊕ In 2007–08, again the Clarets had gone six consecutive games without a win – until Plymouth came to Turf Moor and lost 1–0. Sorry Plymouth! It was also Owen Coyle's first home win at Turf Moor since he had arrived as manager.

⊕ It is now well over 30 seasons since Plymouth Argyle last won at Turf Moor. Good old Argyle – can we play you every week?

POET'S CORNER

The following was taken from the Everton FC programme in November 1913, two years after they had transferred their goalscoring centre-forward Bert Freeman to Burnley.

We once had a centre named Bert,
Who was constantly on the alert;
When a back mulled the ball,
Play the 'Dead March from Saul'.
It's a goal! That's an absolute cert!

In later years, Burnley printed poems by supporters in the club programme. Here are a selection:

Sheer toil and sweat on the part of all,
To be ready and willing to answer each call;
For that little bit extra, strength to pull out
No matter how tired at the end of the bout.
A word of encouragement given to all.
Or you know in your heart they'll never fall;
They work for the club every hour,
Selfishness and thoughtlessness have no power.
Just like a jigsaw the pieces fit,
Each person doing above their bit;
The fact that no matter how big or small,
Whether you sit at a desk or shoot for goal.
They work as a team, no link divided,
One thought in mind, each has decided
That the job they are doing is worth doing right,
This is the target they all keep in sight.
They are proud of the fact that they are part of the crew
Who work under the flag of the claret and blue.

Anon

The Wombles of Wimbledon came into town,
On a hiding to nothing they said.
But at twenty to five on a cold winter's day,
They left with a few faces red.

The moral to learn from non-leaguers again
Is not to treat them with ease;
But to bring these part-timers, less fit as they are.
Down to the ground on their knees.

It's not only skill at the end of the day,
But fitness and courage as well,
So here's to the next time…a lesson's been learnt?
Of this only time will tell!

Revd Fred A. Noden

Every Saturday, rain or shine,
He's off again – that man of mine,
To watch the Clarets play a game.
I wonder 'Will his smile remain?'

I sit at home – results to see,
So I will know what his mood will be.

They lose! His scarf goes on the chair,
He looks at me and gives a glare.

When they've won, then it is alright,
We'll both enjoy our Saturday night!
So 'Come on Clarets! Step in my shoes',
'Cos if you did, you'd never lose!
Mrs Binns

If they held an election in football,
To find the most promising team,
My vote would be given to Burnley,
In adversity they are supreme.

When they're facing a stiff opposition,
Neither Harold nor Ted could subdue,
The outcome's a foregone conclusion,
That Burnley will come smiling through.

Forget about roaring inflation,
Unemployment and all of the rest,
Their policy's good entertainment;
For this they will give of their best.

So wear your rosettes every Saturday,
In colours of claret and blue,
And come to Turf Moor in your thousands,
Where they'll do their darndest for you.
Mrs H.Walton

Last season's memories are still quite clear,
But we'll do even better, so don't you fear.
With Lady Luck, last year would have brought
Those coveted cups for which the lads worthily fought.

The Long Side will be full for one simple reason,
That today – Aug 17th – is the start of the season.
The opposition Wolves will put up a fight,
But we'll get two points, if we play our cards right.

So cheer them on Burnley supporters all,
Cheer the skilful, classy, attacking football.
The last times are devoted to Jimmy no less,
He deserves as manager, much more success.
Kevin Wolski

C must be 'Come on you Clarets…',
The singers and the chanters,
All those who lead with the larynx,
Rowdy ravers and ranters

And its…'No nay never no more…'
Along…'the Longside, Burnley',
Or, as the choir will have it sung,
'Burn-er-lee…' that should be.

And no one likes them, so they say,
Being from the North, loud and proud
Though not quite the Kop in number,
They're just like the Kop, unbowed.

There's surely no need for musak
When a goal's scored? By choice,
The acclamation's better led
By the Longside in full voice!
Dave Alton

POLICE

The Chief Constable
Mr A.E. Edwards used to be the Chief Constable for Burnley during Word War Two, but by 1947 he had been transferred to become Chief Constable of Middlesbrough. He was naturally in charge of the policing arrangements at the big sixth-round FA Cup tie that took place at Ayresome Park in March 1947 between Middlesbrough and Burnley.

Conditions were atrocious and yet thousands of Burnley fans made the journey by road and rail in Arctic conditions, only to find themselves locked out of the ground, which was filled by a record crowd of 53,025. It was then that Chief Constable Edwards became the hero of the hour. Climbing on to the wall surrounding the ground, he gave a running commentary to the thousands of fans locked out of the ground. His act for the fans became as famous in Burnley as the draw which earned the replay at Turf Moor.

HARRY POTTS

P for Potts, Harry. Player.
Of course, for the Clarets who,
Like many, wore the shirt proudly,
But what else could the man do?

Success in all sport is timing;
The well struck volley, crosses,
A flying save, last ditch tackles,
Even how a coin tosses.

So, a second goal was timely,
Celebrated with reason,
As Burnley went top of the League
For the first time that season.

A marvellous time to do so,
That moment of Claret fame,
For no one could beat Burnley then,
Being the season's final game.

No other team, before or since
Went top on the final day
For the first time in the season;
Such is the Harry Potts Way.

(Explanation for non-Clarets: in 1960 when Harry was manager, Burnley won the last game of the season to go top and be champions. Brunshaw Road, Burnley, which runs outside of Turf Moor, has since been renamed 'Harry Potts Way'.)
Dave Alton

PRIDE COMES BEFORE A FALL

10 March 1928
'Today, Burnley make a farewell visit to Hillsborough and Sheffield Wednesday.' So said the football reporter in the *Burnley Express*. At that time, Wednesday were bottom of Division One and facing almost certain relegation. The game ended Sheffield Wednesday 5 Burnley 1, which caused the same reporter to headline his article the following week: 'FIVE GOAL DEFEAT BY LEAGUE WOODEN SPOONISTS!'

Then followed a change in fortune for both clubs. In the end, Burnley finished just one point off relegation, and Sheffield Wednesday were five places above them!

Burnley are back!
'Burnley are back!' was the proud motto that was boldly emblazoned an average of 46 times in every match-day programme for the entire season of 1994–95. They had been promoted in 1994 from the old Division Two. However, that season they were relegated and so in 1995–96 'Burnley were back' – in the old Division Two.

PRIME MINISTERS AND POLITICIANS

⊕ In 1974, the former Prime Minister Edward Heath came to Turf Moor to officially open the new Bob Lord Stand. Prior to the game, both teams were presented to Mr Heath, and captain Colin Waldron introduced Peter Noble, Paul Fletcher and Doug Collins as Albert Hungerdunger, Jimmy Slimsack and Herbert Portgornie. Colin said afterwards, 'Ted never batted an eyelid!'

⊕ Alastair Campbell tells of the politicians he has worked with and his Clarets influence: 'Remember the Play-off semis against Plymouth – John Francis's greatest night? Michael Foot was there.'

⊕ 'Neil Kinnock has been to half a dozen games with me, including the Play-off Final when we beat Stockport, and so far as I can recall, he has never seen us lose.'

⊕ 'As for Tony Blair, his record is not so impressive. He came to Hartlepool away, and we lost 4–1, and John Pender and Adrian Heath were sent off. In my nine years with Tony Blair, he has had to live with our ups and downs, and their impact on my Monday morning mood and performance.'

THE PRINCE AT TURF MOOR

Probably the most outstanding occasion in 1886, not only for the football club, but also for the whole of Burnley, was the visit of Prince Albert, son of Queen Victoria, who came to the town to open the new Victoria Hospital in October. Events like the Hospital Cup had helped raise significant amounts for the new hospital.

And so it was fitting that when Prince Albert came to Burnley, part of his programme was a visit to Turf Moor to watch the Burnley versus Bolton Wanderers game that afternoon. All the proceeds of the game were to go towards the Victoria Hospital. Special prices were in force that day – entrance to the ground was sixpence, the grandstand was the unbelievable sum of five shillings, and if you wanted a seat next to the Royal party they were available at a guinea each. Despite these new prices, a great crowd of over 10,000 packed into Turf Moor that afternoon.

The *Burnley Express* reported, 'When the Prince stepped onto the grandstand in sight of the 10,000 persons assembled, the cheering which had accompanied him all day, culminated in a deafening outburst. Royal permission had been given for the use of the Royal Arms, and the club will have the privilege of using the Royal Arms in future. The grandstand was entirely covered with crimson cloth and the Royal party were accommodated with mahogany chairs, upholstered with leather.

It had originally been intended that the Prince should leave after witnessing the play for about 20 minutes, but so interested were the party that they remained until half-time, being on the field exactly 50 minutes. Both teams appeared in new jerseys, and the home team of Burnley had new caps to match their blue and white jerseys. As they entered, the players gave His Royal Highness a pleasing salute.'

The final result was 4–3 for Bolton. It is believed that this was the first recorded occasion on which any member of the Royal family graced a football match, and for many years later Burnley were nicknamed 'The Royalites'. Incidentally, the 10,000 people paid £215, and after expenses had been deducted (and accusations and suspicions of 'fiddling the books' had been made in the local press!), £62 was given by the club towards the new hospital.

PROMOTION

Since this book was put together, the Clarets have accomplished the impossible, surprised the nation, beaten all odds, and made their fans' widest dreams come true. They have been promoted!

Of course, teams have been promoted before – even to the Premiership. But at the start of the season 2008–09, after four games, Burnley were at the bottom of the Championship. Now less than nine months later, they are back in the top tier of English football since 1976.

This has been achieved with a very small squad (perhaps the smallest ever to win promotion?), no multi-millionaires (in the role of Messrs Walker and Whelan) and all of based in possibly the smallest town ever to be in the Premiership (just 70,000).

And taking the longer view, less than 25 years ago, in May 1987, the club, situated at the foot of Division Four, were within 90 minutes of closing.

After a lifetime of shouting 'Up the Clarets!', the Clarets are up.

PUNCHING ABOVE THEIR WEIGHT

A fact often overlooked by soccer experts (and those who should know better) is that Burnley as a town is in population way below the size of other towns which host professional football clubs. These days, population affects the attendances, which reflect support and weekly income. The following is a list designed to show where Burnley, with a population of 70,000, fits in with those teams competing against them.

Teams in the same League:
Blackpool 142,000, Preston 184,000, Derby 229,000, Southampton 234,000, Nottingham 249,000, Coventry 303,000, Leicester 330,000, Bristol 420,000, Sheffield 439,000 thats until Burnley left them behind on their promotion in 2009.

Teams in lower Leagues:
Colchester 100,000, Brighton 134,000, Huddersfield 146,000, Swindon 155,000, Bournemouth 167,000, Northampton 189,000, Bradford 293,000, Leeds 443,000.

Teams in much lower Leagues:
Sutton Coldfield 105,000, Eastbourne 106,000, Gloucester 123,000, Slough 126,000, York 137,000, Telford 138,000, Oxford 143,000, Poole 144,000, Luton 185,000, Dudley 194,000.

PUNDITS

There is surely no other Football League club which has more TV pundits among its ex-players than Burnley! It is very rare to go through a Saturday or a weeknight without listening to one or other of our ex-heroes. Lee Dixon probably heads the list, but over the years everyone in the nation has disagreed with Ian Wright, Trevor Steven and Chris Waddle. A few years ago there was Paul Gascoigne and only recently there have been Steve Cotterill and Stan Ternent. They all talk a good game!

Chapter Nine

Q–R

(From Quaint and Quantum mechanics to Rochdale rivals and Rough play)

QUAINT

'It is not very often that a Burnley player registers three goals in a game, nor was the feat accomplished last Saturday, for the goals were divided between Morrison and Hogan.'
Burnley Express, March 1902

QUANTUM MECHANICS

Q is for Quantum Mechanics,
All seemingly odd, but true.
What counts as success for Clarets
Depends on their point of view.

Who to support is relative,
Not which team is in fashion,
But where mam and dad make a stand
And their quanta of passion.

Matchday particles are excited
Whenever the Clarets score,
Then there's the virtual stasis
Brought on by a Niels – Niels Bohr.

For those who do not understand
To whom football makes no sense,
It's just a waste of energy, not
The basis of existence.
Dave Alton

QUEER

For my birthday, my grandsons bought me a new Burnley claret and blue scarf (bought in a Wigan shop!). I noticed that the scarf was made in China. A few years ago, as personal thanks after a funeral I had conducted, a member of my church in Rochdale gave me another lovely woollen Clarets scarf – purchased in Rochdale and made in China! Last year in Burnley, my son bought his girlfriend a lovely pair of Claret woollen gloves – made in China!

Is there a vast woollen mill in China working non-stop on Burnley scarves and gloves? 'Hey you – can you work through the night? Have you finished that batch of 2,000 Burnley scarves that Blackburn wanted? There's another thousand wanted in Oldham for next week!'

Note to publisher: this book could be a best-seller in the woollen mills of China. If only we could find a translator in to Mandarin!

QUICK PROGRESS

On 23 October 1993, John Mullin scored twice for the Burnley B team against Manchester City B in the Lancashire League. The following week he scored for the A team against Tranmere A. A fortnight later, on 10 November, John scored twice for Burnley reserves against Middlesbrough reserves. And in December he scored the equaliser for Burnley in their 1–1 draw at Port Vale in Division Two – 55 days from the Lancashire League to the Football League!

That season, 1993–94, John scored three for the B team, 21 for the A team, 11 for the reserves and one for the first team!

QUIRKY

Early in 1932–33 Burnley became the first team in the country to have had 1,000 goals scored against them since World War One. It happened during the game at Preston when the Clarets were beaten 6–1. Ironically, the man who scored the 1,000th goal was none other than ex-Burnley hero Bob Kelly, then playing for Preston.

QUIZ (just for fun)

1. Which Burnley player had the curious Christian name of 'Clewley'?
2. Which colleague of the above had the Christian name of 'Wilkinson'?
3. Which Burnley player, also connected with Blackburn, had the Christian name of 'Gilmore'?
4. What name is easier to say than 'Yanek'?
5. Which goalkeeper has the unusual Christian name of 'Agnew'?
6. Only two 'Freds' have played for Burnley since the last war. Which?
7. Two players in the last 30 years share the honour of having the longest surname?

8. Change one letter in their surname and you have the surname of another Claret. I can think of at least two such couples since the war. Can you?

9. Name at least three post-war players with only three letters in their surname.

10. Which Burnley player died just five years after playing in the FA Cup Final?

11. What is the highest number of League goals scored by the Clarets in a post-war season?

12. And the lowest?

13. How many seasons did Billy Hamilton top the Burnley goalscorers?

14. What is the highest number of League goals scored in one season by a Claret player since the war?

15. How many seasons were the Clarets in Division Four?

(Answers on page 224)

QUOTES BY THE PLAYERS

⊛ 'I will score six and stop at that.' (**Louis Page** before the game at Birmingham, where he played out of position and scored six.)

⊛ 'I have often wondered what took me into the business of association football.' (**Jimmy McIlroy**)

⊛ 'We should have realised that the referee would be biased when he came on the pitch wearing a beret and a string of onions around his neck!' (**John Connelly** recalling the Rheims European Cup tie.)

⊛ 'If you can't get the man, make sure you get the ball!' (**Brian O'Neil**)

⊛ 'I used to be called "the second Gordon Banks". I always wondered if this meant that I played like him…or played like a man with one eye!' (**Alan Stevenson**)

⊛ 'I cannot tell you how I felt for the first 10 to 15 seconds after it hit the net, because it was just pure joy. I remember running towards the Burnley fans and jumping over a little rail, but I'd have jumped over a 30 foot wall to get to the Burnley fans that day!' (**Gary Parkinson** on his Wembley winning goal of 1994.)

⊛ 'Touch wood, I've never scored an own-goal in 10 years of being a professional.' (Ex-Burnley player **David Miller** before a game between Stockport and Derby County. He went on to score the injury time own-goal that gave the game to Derby 2–1.)

⊛ 'I've lost count of the number of times I've played in that fixture, but everyone was a memorable occasion.' (**Trevor Steven**)

⊛ 'For the first time ever at a football match, I felt my eyes moist.' (**Jimmy McIlroy** at the 'Orient game', 1987.)

QUOTES BY THE MANAGER

- 'This could be the team of the 1970s!' (**Jimmy Adamson** in 1970 before Burnley were relegated the same season.)

- 'When Don Revie, Bill Shankly and Joe Harvey claim they have the best team in the land, they are wrong. I've got it.' (**Jimmy Adamson**, 1974.)

- 'What amazes me is how simple the solution is – to get better players. Once I have got that team together, I will take full responsibility for what happens.' (**John Bond**, June 1983.)

- 'If I had £300,000 to spend, it would have been spent by now.' (**Steve Cotterill**)

- 'I just thought that God shone down on us.' (**Steve Cotterill** after Burnley beat Preston 3–2 with a last-minute goal at Turf Moor.)

- 'The people of Burnley live and die for their football and what we have hopefully done is put a few smiles on their faces. There will probably be a bit more productivity on Monday morning.' (**Steve Cotterill** after a win.)

- 'Managers always worry about the next game, and we have Saturday at Sheffield Wednesday. We've got rid of two headaches and we've got 44 more to go.' (**Steve Cotterill**)

- 'There is no remedy for success.' (**Chris Waddle**)

- 'I promise results not promises.' (**John Bond**)

- 'The centre-halves I'd been lumbered with could be outjumped by little Jimmy Krankie!' (**Stan Ternent** on taking over from Chris Waddle.)

- 'If you kick one player, the whole team should limp.' (**Stan Ternent**)

- Speaking of the players he had inherited from previous manager Chris Waddle, **Stan Ternent** described them as 'sausages in shorts'!

- **Stan Ternent** would often chat to his wife about the club and events. She began to suspect that there were evil spirits at the ground after a run of poor results. 'There's something uneasy down at the club,' she told him. 'Yes, it's probably the back four!' replied Stan.

- 'I bear grudges as determinedly as David O'Leary bears his suntan.' (**Stan Ternent**)

- 'David Pleat can talk underwater!' (**Stan Ternent**)

QUOTES BY THE BOARD (OR CHAIRMAN)

☻ 'We don't recognise any supporters' organisations. I never go to supporters' dinners. It only costs a fiver or so, but then they think they own you. I never accept money from supporters' organisations. They hand you a couple of cheques for a few thousand and the next thing you know, they are demanding a seat on the board. My ambition is for the club to function completely without any money coming in through the turnstiles at all. That is the road to Utopia.' (**Bob Lord**, 1974.)

☻ 'When Burnley Football Club issue statements, that is it. They are not to be questioned. The sooner you learn that the better. Good morning!' (**Bob Lord** speaking to *Burnley Express* reporter Peter Higgs for the first time.)

☻ 'These players are among the best paid in the Second Division and they are simply not doing their job!' (**Bob Lord** speaking during the relegation season of 1979–80.)

☻ 'I'll never sack you, Jimmy.' (**Bob Lord** speaking to manager Jimmy Adamson a week before he sacked him.)

☻ 'Some day England will restore prestige by winning the World Cup. Here's hoping the day arrives at Wembley in 1966!' (**Bob Lord** writing in 1963.)

☻ 'I've rattled the tin, and there's not much in it.' (**Barry Kilby**)

QUOTES BY THE FANS

☻ 'I've been praying all week we would stay up. I believe in God now.' (**A young fan** after the 'Orient game'.)

☻ 'Therein lies the problem with Ade. Much as we love him, he has about as much control as a 16-year-old lad at a lap dance club.' (**The Older View**)

☻ 'Stop whingeing – start chanting!' (**The Older View**)

☻ 'When did footballers become upper class twits? Why does a bloke who kicks a lump of leather for a living think himself superior to the people that are paying to watch him?' (**Andrew Lupton**)

☻ 'We have seen extremes at the Turf this season. I certainly did not think that we could see a worse refereeing display than the 10 or so shockers we have already had. I did not think that we could see a team who tried to play less "football" than Stoke, and sadly I never thought that I would see Ade set himself a new standard for missing sitters, but all three were surpassed in the game with Watford!' (**Aidy's best mate**)

QUOTES ABOUT THE PLAYERS

- 'The most remarkable coach produced by any country in the history of the game.' (**Brian Glanville** speaking about Burnley boy Jimmy Hogan, who became an international football coach.)

- 'Ageless Jimmy Hogan is the greatest coach that football has ever known.' (**Len Shackleton**)

- 'Your pace is deceptive son, you're even slower than you look!' (**Tommy Docherty** about ex-Burnley favourite Leighton James when he met him at Derby.)

- 'He has the speed of a racehorse, the strength of a carthorse, and the brains of a rocking horse!' (**Stuart Hall** speaking, maybe a little unkindly, of Steve Kindon.)

- 'TIN MAN IS WIZARD OF AUS!' was a newspaper headline when Ted McMinn signed for Australian club Joondalup in Sydney.

- 'He had moved so little, he was paying ground rent.' (**Stan Ternent** talking about Peter Swan after a match at Hull.)

- 'For defenders, Chris Waddle running at you is the worst sight in football.' (**Alan Hansen** talking about Burnley's player-manager.)

- 'It's not personal, it's business. Steve Blatherwick, Lee Howey, Mark Winstanley, and to a lesser degree Michael Williams, because he will never win the crowd over, will not play for Burnley Football Club again. They are not right for Burnley and they are not coming from where I am coming from. They are on the transfer list – they can go on a free transfer.' (**Stan Ternent** speaking on Radio Lancashire after the York home defeat, August 1999.)

- 'I'm less enamoured of Blake's tendency to appeal to the ref while play is still going on, mind.' (**Ria Hopkinson**)

- 'The first thing I noticed from the press coverage over the signing of Chris Eagles was the depth of his tan and the hairband, neither of which strike me as the most obvious signifiers of resilience and combativeness.' (**London Clarets**)

QUOTES ABOUT THE SPURS SEMI-FINAL

- 'Even as a Spurs fan, there's a huge part of me that wants Burnley to go through. They are better than us, and I don't want to rob a team with such heart of going to Wembley.' (**Damien,** Morden.)

⚛ 'That was a magnificent game of football that had absolutely everything. It's extremely unfortunate for Burnley because they were so close. Burnley won tonight, whatever the final result. They are the winners.' (**Mark Lawrenson,** Radio 5 Live.)

⚛ 'For those of you who missed the match, the highlights will be shown on "Crimewatch" later!' (**Chris,** Brighton.)

QUOTES ABOUT THE MANAGER

⚛ 'Alan Brown was the best manager the club has ever had. He did more for the club both as a player and manager then any other individual.' (**Jimmy Adamson**)

⚛ 'A lot of teams beat us, do a lap of honour and don't stop running. They live too long on one good result. I remember Jimmy Adamson crowing after Burnley beat us, that his players were in a different League. At the end of the season, they were.' (**Bob Paisley**, Liverpool manager.)

⚛ 'Not only is he the first "Owen" I can remember at the football club, but he is the only one with a space shuttle as his middle name!' (*WTBM* editor **Martin Barnes** talking about the Burnley manager, Owen Columba Coyle.)

QUOTES ABOUT THE BOARD

⚛ 'Bob Lord used to miss the start of the game at home games because he was still in his office counting the money. He used to have his own turnstile.' (**An Ipswich director.**)

⚛ 'Lord's personal ambition and dictatorial rule began to destroy the empire he had built. He finally pulled the rug from under the club's feet by sacking Adamson.' (**Colin Waldron**)

⚛ 'Bob Lord. Turf Moor was his personal temple. Gruff, uncultured, maybe uncouth. His manner was a cross of rottweiler with Margaret Thatcher. A total despot. A ruthless manipulator, yet a benefactor. He typified the local dignitary who ruled the town. Built like a pampas bull, deaf as a post – unless you uttered something derogatory. Then you were banned!' (**Stuart Hall**)

QUOTES ABOUT THE CLUB

⚛ 'How the blazes do you live in a place like this?' (**Danny Blanchflower** to Jimmy McIlroy, 1950s.)

⚛ 'I've not been in the north like this. I've only seen it on the telly. It's like going back in time.' (**Ian Wright** on seeing Burnley from the car.)

⊕ 'I went to Burnley on Saturday and saw the Albion fighting with the wild beasts at Ephesus. Burnley is a despised place, anathema to men.' (**West Brom reporter** in 1908.) ['Wild beasts at Ephesus' is a quote taken from St Paul in his First Letter to the Corinthians, chapter 15, verse 32.]

⊕ 'Do we want a successful side or the best ground in the Fourth Division?' (***Burnley Express***, August 1975 – on the sale of Martin Dobson to Everton.)

⊕ 'At Burnley, no moustaches, no sideburns, long hair discouraged. But when I was with Chelsea, I could go through the menu, wine and all, phone home for hours, entertain friends, all on the club. If I run up a 2p phone call with Burnley, I get the bill. It keeps your feet on the ground I'm telling you.' (**Colin Waldron**)

⊕ 'I shall never determine who won the match, the Burnley team or the crowd.' (Reporter **Ian Wooldridge** after the 'Orient game'.)

⊕ 'They have the potential to be a sleeping giant.'(**Chris Waddle**, 1997.)

⊕ 'There's only one team look like scoring – Scunthorpe have had all the play. Burnley look very tired – hang on – Burnley have scored!' (**Alan Mullery,** radio commentary, 2001.)

⊕ 'I was very heartened to read that the players had apologised to Steve Cotterill after the match…well that's alright then. Where was the bloody apology to the supporters? Never mind the manager, he gets paid to watch. We have to pay.' (**Whitto**, London Clarets.)

⊕ 'If you could have bottled some of the games, you could have sold them to the NHS as general anaesthetic!' (A **supporter** sat next to Dave Thomas.)

⊕ 'For Burnley to win, they are going to have to score'. (TV commentator **Chris Kamara.**)

QUOTES ABOUT THE OPPONENTS

⊕ 'Always do what the opposition don't want you to do!' (**Billy Dougall**)

⊕ 'First mention must go to the sadistic Home Park soundman, who presides over the loudest tannoy in the Championship – and that's no mean feat. Plymouth play fairground music, wartime music, and atrocious contemporary film-score music, all so loud that you have to shout to make yourself heard. And the rather unfortunate shade of dark green the Pilgrims sport makes the place look as if it's made of garden furniture.' (**Ria Hopkinson**)

⊕ 'The Blackpool ground? Apparently it's much improved from the days when it used to be the worst ground in the world, which was what it was like when I stopped going to Blackpool. Then it was seemingly held together by rust, which at least went with the club colours. Various parts of the ground were condemned as hazardous and the away end was actually below pitch level, meaning that you spent the game trying to see play through a forest of legs of bellicose stewards.' (**Firmo**)

⊕ 'God, that pie was good and the chips were to die for.' (**Dave Thomas** after a pre-season friendly at Partick Thistle.)

⊕ 'Had we lost this game, my headline would of course have been: "Super Caley Go Ballistic, Burnley Are Atrocious!"' (**Pauline Pratley** after Burnley v Inverness Caledonian Thistle 2–1.)

'R'

R should Really be for Rsenal
And two tRemendous goals scored,
The Beast being in such fine fettle,
The team that got its Reward

R is the Realisation
Injury time has begun,
So, even had they scored
The game was as good as won.

R is the Row and the Rapture,
The noise when the whistle blew,
Because Rsenal just could not score
Whilst the Clarets had netted two.

R now has to be the next Round,
A semi-final no less,
Think of the Ramifications
Should Burnley, once more, impress.

R then would have to be (w)Riters,
Columns of copy they'd (w)Rite
About a proud Championship club
Who R just champion on the night.

R is the Reason for playing
The Reason for being a fan,

Winning may contradict Reason,
But, they can, the Clarets can!
Dave Alton
(Inspired by Burnley's 2–0 victory over the Gunners in the League Cup, 2008.)

REPORTERS REPORTING

⊕ 'My football notes this week must be brief and to the point as my space is somewhat curtailed owing to the approaching elections!' (**November 1885**)

⊕ 'There seemed to be a screw loose with Friel as he did nothing right while Shorrocks was like an old woman in clogs!'(**1885**)

⊕ 'The goalkeeper was truly an "A1 at Lloyds" – he stopped any number of hot 'uns!' (**1885**)

⊕ 'There was a rich mistake in a Saturday evening football paper which credited the Burnley team with "nine" goals. It should have read "none"!' (**1888**)

⊕ Concerning the Burnley versus Blackpool game in 1885, there was merely a four-line report in the local paper as follows, 'There was not one redeeming feature about the match and I think that the least said is the soonest mended. Therefore I leave Saturday's performance – if it can be put under that category – to speak for itself.'

⊕ 'Glorious inconsistency – thy name is Burnley!' (**1898**)

⊕ 'Burnley did not fare any better at the Bolton new ground than they had done at the old one. It was generally expected that Burnley would go down at Burnden – and down they went!' (**Bolton v Burnley, 1895**)

⊕ 'Burnley went to Barnsley on Thursday, and were beaten by five goals to nothing. Burnley took a weak team – a regular end of season XI, not one of them whom seemed to care a jot whether they won or not. Ogden could not get off his work, and the Burnley trainer had to play on the right wing.' (**April 1907**)

⊕ 'The Yorkshire amateur who may be seen in the Burnley ranks, has I hear played frequently for a good club in the Broadacreshire. I am not at liberty to divulge his name yet, but many years ago Burnley possessed a good comic singer of the same patronymic, and there is a place not far from Burnley bearing his name. I leave you to guess.' (**December 1908**)

⊕ 'All thoughts are turned to London today. What will be the result of the second round with Crystal Palace? Oh that we could lift the veil and see!' (**1909**)

⊕ 'When the Burnley men found their feet, they had the time to take their bearings properly and they gave a Roland for every Oliver.' (**Crystal Palace game, 1909**)

⊕ The good form of the Burnley team was never better shown than in the last two matches against Bristol and Blackburn. They have been tough struggles between the "busy B's" and Burnley have hived the honey in splendid fashion.' (**November 1911**)

⊕ 'Boyle has been confined to bed with a very severe cold. Everyone will hope for the best, for a Cup tie without Boyle would be like Hamlet without the Prince!' (**January 1920**)

⊕ 'Five League games and still not a win! No wonder that "black care perches at the horseman's back" at Turf Moor.' (**September 1923**)

⊕ 'Dame Fortune, who has been flirting with Burnley during the whole of the season, appears to have jilted the club completely in the closing stages of the season.' (**1924**)

⊕ 'Easter has often proved the graveyard of hopes. Burnley have often been interred or refused resurrection at Easter!' (**1924**)

⊕ 'Though half a loaf may be better than no bread, when the whole loaf is wanted, and by virtue of all that is just, it belongs to any person, that person is justified in complaining if half of it is thrown away. That was the position of the Burnley team and the Burnley crowd on Saturday.' (**September 1924**)

⊕ 'The entire match was a tatterdemalion scarecrow garbed in a patchwork and threadbare suit of drab grey.' (**'Kestrel', Burnley 2 Blackburn Rovers 2, October 1928.**)

⊕ 'The fact remains that today Burnley is in a much worse position than it was at this time last season. And everyone knows what a terrible struggle Burnley had last season!' (**'Kestrel', 1929.**)

⊕ 'Once more Burnley's hopes were buried in the graveyard of Manchester City – buried and well pressed down.' (**Manchester City 4 Burnley 1, April 1929.**)

⊕ 'Burnley were made up of 10 comedians and amateur Peter Kippax!' (*Daily Express*, **October 1946.**)

⊕ 'With all deference to the gallant Fulham, the regular Filbert Street fans remember vividly the brilliant exhibition by Burnley, when they won here 6–2 on September 20th.

Leicester's football would have been too smart for the majority of sides, but Burnley's fast, smooth rhythm proved irresistible. Few will dispute the contention that no better blend of speed, grace and power has been forthcoming at this ground in post-war football.

Perhaps the most significant tribute was that given at half-time by the Leicester partisans, who swallowed their feelings at seeing their team 4–1 down, and cheered Burnley's masterly effort.'

(**Leicester City programme for the Burnley v Fulham Cup semi-final replay.**)

- 'Football is such a cruel game. Is it right that I have tears in my eyes for a team I don't support?' (A listener calling in on 606 after the Spurs League Cup victory in the last two minutes.)

REFEREES

- 'It would appear that referees and umpires are not always looked upon with favour at West Bromwich, otherwise surely it would not be necessary to provide an escort from the ground composed of members of the blue-coated gentry. It has been suggested to me that the gentleman referee, having an intimate knowledge of the treatment of these officials whenever they happen to go in the teeth of the West Brom spectators, cut his coat as it were, according to his cloth, and displayed a leaning to the home side, in order to save the possibility of any rough usage at the hands of the mob.' (**West Brom v Burnley, 1885.**)

- 'Nicol was reported for speaking strongly to a referee on a railway platform after a match. To most minds, a referee when once off the field has no power, but Nicol no doubt felt aggrieved at the penalty business. As a result Nicol was suspended for a fortnight, but the referee got off Scot-free!'(**1885**)

- 'Nobody was sorry when Mr Referee Lewis's whistle intimated that the farce was over.' (**1894**)

- 'Today Burnley would have beaten any team'. That was the remark of the referee, Mr H. Bamlett, after the game. (**Burnley 9 Crystal Palace 0, 1909.**)

RELEGATION

In March 1923 Burnley were fifth in Division One, and the *Burnley News* ran a piece headed 'The Spectre of Relegation!' Curiously, though placed fifth and only 12 points off the leaders (Liverpool), at the same time they were also 12 points off the bottom team (Oldham). In the end, the newspaper's fears almost came true when the Clarets finished just eight points off relegation and 22 behind the champions!

RELEGATED, WRONGLY

It was 21 December 1929 and Burnley were away at Leicester in Division One. There was nothing much at stake: Burnley were mid-table and creeping just into the top half. They had topped the table early on, and even now in December the team had still won more games than they had lost.

Unfortunately, Burnley lost the game at Leicester 4–3, but a 'goal' scored by Hutchinson for Burnley was disallowed by the referee, Mr Mee of Mansfield, because he believed that the ball had not crossed the goalline. However, a photograph taken of the incident by the *Leicester Mail* and reprinted in the Burnley press showed the ball clearly over the goalline. (Personally I still get annoyed – if not angry – every time I see the photograph in the library.)

The loss of this important point 'disappointed' (natural pun!) the Clarets very much, and Burnley slipped into the bottom half of the table. A fortnight later Burnley sold star forward Joe Devine (who had scored at Leicester) to struggling Newcastle United.

A bad sequence of results followed, and Burnley only won six games out of the remaining 22. The last match soon came and the position was grim at the foot of Division One. The bottom of the League appeared as follows:

	Played	Points
Newcastle United	41	35
Grimsby Town	41	35
Sheffield United	41	34
Burnley	41	34
Everton	41	33

On the last Saturday, Burnley had the hardest task of all the struggling clubs when they played against Derby, who were second from top. But on that crucial last day Burnley were superb, running out 6–2 victors with Joe Mantle getting a hat-trick. But, alas, in one great desperate effort, all five of the bottom teams won in fine style that day, with Sheffield United even winning 5–1 away at Manchester United! And in one of the closest finishes for years Burnley were relegated on goal average.

Burnley fans were left to contemplate two goals: one that counted and one that did not. They remembered how referee Mee had failed to see Leicester goalkeeper McClaren pull the ball back from behind his own goalline. A point at Leicester would have saved the Clarets. And just as bitter a pill to swallow was that ex-Claret Joe Devine scored the vital winning goal for Newcastle in their last game. Wrongly relegated! If only, if only, if only....then history might have been different.

RESERVES

Over the years the Burnley reserve team have been Champions of their League on six occasions: 1892–93 and 1893–94 North East Lancashire League; 1948–49, 1961–62 and 1962–63 Central League; and 1997–98 in the third tier of the Central League. The team were unbeaten during two seasons: 1892–93 and 1893–94. In 1893–94 they scored 119 goals in 18 games, an average of over six goals every game, while at the same time they only conceded 15 goals in 18 games.

ROBBIE'S UNDERPANTS

In one game in 2008–09, after Robbie Blake had scored, his celebrations included revealing his very distinctive pair of red underpants, emblazoned with the words 'Bad Beat Bob!' Obviously this meant something to poker players.

This led to the club shop being inundated with requests from fans for replica underpants, and I heard reports of hundreds of pairs being sold. The club probably made more money out of poker than Robbie did.

ROCHDALE RIVALS

During the dog days at Burnley (the seven seasons in Division Four, 1985–92) Burnley fans established a keen local rivalry with neighbouring Rochdale. There was no let-up between the rival supporters, and the games always attracted some of the best gates of the season at both grounds. As the rivalry grew, so did the gates! It started in 1985 with 4,241 at Turf Moor and 2,406 at Spotland, and ended in 1992 with 8,633 at Turf Moor and 8,175 at Spotland.

To set the scene: 'Rochdale – the very name sounds boring. It sounds like a bloody clog town and a mill town…it really is a one-eyed, one-horse town where nothing happens.' And those were the words of Rochdale Chairman David Kilpatrick. 'Where's Rochdale?' quipped Coventry City manager Noel Cantwell. In those days, the floodlights were so bad that Coventry refused to play a game under them.

Rochdale fans wore scarves that said 'Better than Burnley!' and they despised the arrogance of the newly relegated Clarets, who still thought of themselves as a First Division team, despite being in the Fourth.

Dave Thomas wrote, 'How were the mighty fallen! And how they at Rochdale resented us for being there, with our illustrious history, the remaining delusions of grandeur, the horror we expressed, our expectation that it was just temporary and short term, our clear feeling that we in no way belonged down there. In truth both clubs were pygmies at this time, but while Rochdale knew that, we didn't, as we filled their ground and took it over. And they disliked us even more for that, even though the gate receipts helped them tick over for another season.'

To sum it all up:

1985–86 – A 1–0 win at Turf Moor and a 0–1 defeat at Spotland. Honours were even though both teams were in the bottom half of Division Four.

1986–87 – Rochdale thumped the Clarets 0–3 at Turf Moor and for good measure they disposed of them in the League Cup. Burnley fans went home shaking their heads in morose disbelief. Burnley won 2–0 at Spotland, and with the advantage of hindsight if they had not won the Clarets would have gone out of the League and perhaps ceased to exist. At the end of the season both teams were in the bottom four of the Fourth Division.

1987–88 – Burnley won on Boxing Day at Turf Moor 4–0, but lost at Spotland 1–2. Burnley rose to the top half of the division, but Rochdale stayed in the bottom four.

1988–89 – In the first game of the season Burnley beat the Dale 2–1 at Turf Moor, but later lost at Spotland 1–2. However, the Clarets managed to knock the Dale out of the League Cup.

1989–90 – A dismal 0–1 defeat at Turf Moor led Ian Wood to write, 'Despite the opposition being down to nine men, we still manage to lose. It's enough to drive you to drink!' Rochdale supporters were ecstatic, while the Burnley fans were aghast at this ignominy. Dave Thomas wrote, 'In the list of the 10 lowest lowspots in Claret history, this is one of them.' It was worse than the 0–1 defeat at Spotland.

1990–91 – A 1–0 victory at Turf Moor was spoilt by a 0–0 draw at Spotland in the penultimate game. A win would have clinched promotion for Burnley. Both teams were now in the top half of the table.

1991–92 – Defeat at Spotland 0–1 was forgotten as the Clarets won promotion from Division Four. And whom did the Clarets beat in the last match they played in Division Four? Rochdale 3–1! The victory also stopped the Dale from reaching the Play-offs.

ROUGH PLAY

'The winning goal was the result of a faulty decision by referee, Mr Shallcross. I would not say for a moment that Mr Shallcross was biased in favour of either side, but I have yet to see Burnley get the advantage of such an incident, and I have missed only one match this season. I certainly cannot congratulate a good number of referees either on their fairness or their knowledge of the game, and I think I can say without question that the game as a whole was never worse refereed than the one I saw last Saturday. The system of selecting referees is altogether rotten!'
(**Fulham v Burnley, FA Cup, 1912.**)

Chapter Ten

S–T

(From Saying grace and Sea sickness to Transport problems and Trouble at Anfield)

THE 'S' TEAM

Strong

Smith (D.)   Smelt

Storer   Steel   Shannon

Stevenson (R.)   Shackleton   Smith (C.)   Steven   Summerbee

Subs: Sewell, Sommerville and Stevenson

SAYING GRACE

When asked to say grace at the dinner to celebrate the 50th anniversary of Jimmy McIlroy arriving in Burnley, the Revd David Wiseman said simply, 'For food, fellowship and football, we thank you Lord!' Later, in a tribute to Jimmy 'Mac', David said, 'Next to Jesus, in Burnley this man is God!' The audience stood and applauded to a man.

Meanwhile Paul Fletcher and Steve Kindon, who both do their fair share of after-dinner speaking, said that they now make more money out of talking about Burnley Football Club than they ever did playing for it. This is the 'grace' that they made up and which they use in the Burnley area:

'Thank you Lord for Gawthorpe Hall,
For Miller big and Flynn so small.
You were Burnley's almanac
With Adamson and Jimmy Mac.
Thank you Lord, for our Turf Moor
Harry's Road runs past its door.
You set the scene in '52
Thank you Bob Lord for Claret and Blue.'

SEA SICKNESS

Jimmy McIlroy recalls the story of how he and fellow Irish international Billy Bingham travelled back to England in the 1950s after an Irish match in Belfast. They were on the Belfast–Heysham ferry, and the boat was tossing to and fro. Jimmy was on the top bunk and Billy was lying on the lower bunk, groaning with every lurch of the ship. Eventually, Jimmy heard Billy mutter (or pray?) 'Please God, let this ship go down!'

SENDINGS OFF

In October 1973 Colin Waldron was sent off at Cardiff in an away League Cup tie. He was the first Claret to have been dismissed for more than five years. The last player to have been sent off was back in 1968. The culprit – Colin Waldron!

Ade Akinbiyi was sent off only minutes after making his debut against Sunderland in March 2005 as a sub. He lost his cool and headbutted a Sunderland defender. Akinbiyi had been injured since signing and so his debut was delayed…and delayed…and delayed until very late in the season. When at last he came on and lasted less than three minutes, the crowd was either in shock, or just fell about laughing at the absurdity of it all.

SEVENTIES FASHION

Tony Morley, the 1970s winger, was not too popular with the irascible chairman Bob Lord. Bob was very old fashioned and he could not abide players with long hair. And he certainly could not stand players wearing earrings. Morley grew his hair long, which Lord ordered him to have cut. Morley obliged by having one of the first skinhead haircuts ever seen at Turf Moor. Lord was aghast…and even more so when the short hairstyle revealed an earring!

THE SHOPKEEPER

My grandad used to take me to a shop on a side street just off Leyland Road in Burnley, where we would stand and look in the shop window. We never went in, but just looked in the window.

In the window was an old football painted in blue and white. I had never seen a painted football before and it fascinated me. It had a small card propped up against it which said, 'This is the football used in the FA Cup Final of 1904'. I did not realise at the time that blue and white were the colours of Manchester City and that they had won the Cup in 1904.

In goal for City that day was Jack Hillman, and my grandad used to proudly tell me that Hillman was the man who owned the small shop, just off Leyland Road. It meant little to me in those days when I was 'nobbut a lad', but it certainly meant a great deal to my grandad, who had seen big Jack Hillman play for Burnley hundreds of times. They even lived near each other 100 years ago!

And if only! If only I had gone in that shop just once then I too would be able to say with pride, 'I once met Jack Hillman.' But hindsight is a wonderful thing.

SING A SONG OF CLARET

'Of the community singing at Turf Moor, one can only say it was about as big a frost as the weather. The ordinary football crowd is too self-conscious to sing, and it is only when Cup tie fever raises the temperature that the Burnley crowd can let itself go sufficiently. The Burnley Lane Boys Band and their conductor did their best, as they always do.'
Burnley News, **January 1927**

'One recalls with pleasure, the community singing at Stamford Bridge last season for the Cup tie, when the great crowd of people sang lustily and at one period waved their song papers in unison, so that it was like a huge field of cotton grass waving in the wind. It was somewhat different from the half-hearted singing at Turf Moor last Saturday.

For one thing, Burnley folks are too self-conscious to sing, and in that direction they take their pleasures sadly. They have to be wound up by a huge crowd and a Cup tie before they sing well. And it is no use at all trying to get them to sing, unless there is a good band and a good conductor.'
Burnley News, **1927**

SIZE DOES NOT MATTER! 1.

Burnley's most famed half-back line was that from 1913–22 and was made up of Halley, Boyle and Watson. They were the bedrock of the 1914 FA Cup-winning team and the machine room of the 1920–21 side that won the League Championship and in the process went 30 consecutive League games undefeated. However, in an age of brute force and physical confrontation, it is often forgotten that George Halley was 5ft 8in, Tommy Boyle was 5ft 6in and Billy Watson was 5ft 7in.

SIZE DOES NOT MATTER! 2.

John Price, Brian Flynn, Brian Pilkington, Trevor Meredith and Adrian Heath.

SIZE DOES NOT MATTER! 3.

Burnley's forward line in 1923 read: Weaver (5ft 9in), Lindsay (5ft 5in), Cross (5ft 6½in), Kelly (5ft 6½in), Fisher (5ft 7½in).

Burnley's forward line in 1956 was even smaller: Gray (5ft 6in), McIlroy (5ft 8in), McKay (5ft 6in), Cheesebrough (5ft 7in), Pilkington (5ft 6in).

SIZE DOES MATTER!

'Turf Moor was the scene of a great football match last Tuesday, Tall Men v Short Men. In a report of well over 2,000 words, here are a few excerpts: "The skill of the Short Men was rewarded at last as everyone knew it would be. They scored a goal and the cheering which signaled this important event was simply deafening, and for some hundreds of yards was mistaken for rolls of thunder. Many horses in the town took fright and a great many people were frightened out of their wits. Other incidents of this memorable match may be recorded, but it is sufficient to add one. Photographers from all over the county volunteered to photograph the respective teams after the match and to pay a good round sum for the privilege, but as one of the players put it, they had not played to make millionaires out of struggling photographers, but to show how scientifically football could be played by men who had mastered the art."'

'The average height of the 'Long 'Uns' was 5ft 11in and that of the Lilliputians 5ft 4in.' Tall Men 3 Short Men 2
Burnley News

SKATING ON THIN ICE

'The match between Burnley and Glasgow Northern was not so well attended as one might have been led to expect. One reason being that skating was in full swing, and it took large contingents of regular visitors to the frozen sheets of water in the neighbourhood.'
1884

A TEAM FULL OF 'SMITHS'

Over the last 125 years the most common name for Burnley players has been 'Smith'. There have been 19 of them. They are as follows:

1882   Harry Smith, a local junior.
1885   William Smith, a local lad.
1904   Joseph Smith, from Keswick.
1904   Dick Smith, top goalscorer in his time, with a tally of 75 goals.
1905   Albert Smith, who played over 100 games.
1910   Philip Smith, from Chelsea.
1918   A. Smith, who played one wartime game.
1931   Ernest Smith, who played just seven games.
1932   Cecil Smith, a popular centre-forward who scored over 50 goals.
1933   Wilf Smith, from Blackpool.

1936	Bill Smith, from Crystal Palace.
1940	G. Smith, guest wartime player.
1940	Tom Smith, local wartime player.
1950	David Smith, later manager at Dundee and Torquay.
1959	Fred Smith, a fine full-back.
1977	Malcolm Smith, from Middlesbrough.
1989	Nigel Smith, from Leeds.
1994	Paul Smith, went to Hartlepool.
1997	Carl Smith, went to Worksop.

SMOKERS ANONYMOUS

During the 1940s and 1950s smoking was quite prevalent among the first team players, although trainer Billy Dougall tried to discourage the habit. Goalkeeper Jimmy Strong was a regular breaker of dressing room no-smoking rules and, prior to a game, smoke could often be seen curling up above the toilet door.

SO CLOSE!

⊕ For over three-quarters of a century Burnley fans have lived with the tales of our fathers and grandfathers about the 30 consecutive League games without defeat in 1920–21. (For me, it was probably the first thing I was ever told about the club by my grandad.) But there have been times when the club came close to beating their own record.

⊕ For example, after winning the last six games of 1971–72, the Clarets went the first 16 games of 1972–73 without losing. Then, after a defeat, another eight games without losing: 31 games and one defeat. Curiously, the defeat was against Orient (at home!) and they were struggling against relegation. The total run went to 37 consecutive League games, losing only twice.

⊕ In season 1981–82 the club played 30 League games and lost just once. Again the defeat was against a team struggling to avoid relegation – Exeter City. The total run went to 41 consecutive League games, with Burnley losing only twice.

SOUR GRAPES ON RELEGATION

'Since last week, something has happened – Burnley have again descended to the Second Division. Outside the town there has been very little sympathy expressed, and I doubt very much whether any was seriously felt. Why Burnley should be so unpopular, I don't profess to know.

The directors, I believe, intend to make an effort to carry on the club under League auspices, and those who really take an interest in the pastime will commend them for

their action, though on all sides the League system is condemned, and described as rotten from beginning to end. In my opinion, the sooner it breaks up the better for football, for its continuance on the present lines only means the breaking up of clubs.'
Burnley Express, May 1900

GET A SPADE!

Jimmy McIlroy tells the story of how, during one game in the early 1950s, Billy Morris went to the boundary wall to pick up a ball that had gone out of play (no spare balls or ball boys in those days). As he bent down to pick up the ball, a spectator leant over the wall and said, 'Morris, you should get a spade!' To which Billy said, 'Why?' 'To b…bury thissen!' came the curt reply.

SPONSORSHIP

These days, a club like Burnley could hardly exist without sponsorship. Currently, players, the programme, the Man of the Match, the ball, spectators' boxes, and a whole host of other things can be sponsored. This is separate from the official Club sponsors, Hollands Pies, and the official kit supplier, Errea. E.ON sponsor the FA Cup, Carling sponsor the League Cup and Coca-Cola sponsor the Championship. Perhaps the most curious are sponsorship for substitutes and that given for extra-time added on by the referee.

'SPORTING ACTION'

'It was a sporting action by David Taylor. Things looked ominous when Taylor had to retire through a collision with Etherington, the City right-winger, when Taylor protested against a remark made by a Burnley spectator with reference to Etherington.'
Burnley v Manchester City, 1922

THE STALWARTS

The Burnley club has depended for over 125 years on numerous stalwart players – not always the best, but those who gave it their all and were completely reliable. Many of them did not win much, but they were 'ever presents' in certain seasons. Those who achieved this honour the most have been:

Tom McLintock, defender	5 seasons
Joe Taylor, midfield	4 seasons
Fred Barron, midfield	4 seasons
Jimmy Strong, goalkeeper	4 seasons*
Alan Stevenson, goalkeeper	4 seasons

Brian Miller, midfield	3 seasons
Adam Blacklaw, goalkeeper	3 seasons
Billy Watson, midfielder	2 seasons
Tom Bamford, defender	2 seasons
Len Smelt, defender	2 seasons
George Bray, midfield	2 seasons
Tommy Cummings, midfield	2 seasons
Les Shannon, midfield	2 seasons
Martin Dobson, midfield	2 seasons
Leighton James, forward	2 seasons
Peter Noble, midfield	2 seasons
Billy Hamilton, forward	2 seasons
Tommy Hutchinson, forward	2 seasons**
Ray Deakin, midfield	2 seasons
Joe Jakub, forward	2 seasons

* Jimmy Strong played in four consecutive seasons without missing a game.
** Tommy Hutchinson played in every game from the time he arrived to the day he left. The seasons when the club had most ever presents have always been successful seasons – six players in 1972–73, three in 1946–47 and three in 1959–60.

STAN THE MAN

A book could be written (and has been) about the life of Stan Ternent. Here is a short rundown of some of the things he did:
He hit winger Glen Little over the head with a bottle.
He tried to knock out a Blackpool fan who spat at him.
He headbutted his own centre-forward in training at Bradford City.
He headbutted Birmingham centre-forward Bob Latchford.
He had a dressing-room fight with player Steve Doyle at Hull.
At Sheffield United he had a punch-up with United's assistant manager Kevin Blackwell outside the referee's room at half-time.
He threw flasks of soup back at the Burnley kitchen staff because they had no tops, only clingfilm.
(Full details can be found in Stan the Man by Stan Ternent and Tony Livesey.)

A STAR IS BORN

'In accordance with their policy of judicious building up for the future, Burnley FC have signed another young amateur centre-forward. He is Thomas Lawton, a Bolton boy, whose feats in junior football circles have attracted the attention of several League clubs.

[At] 15 years of age, he has enjoyed practically all the honours of schoolboy football, having captained his school team (Foulds Road Central School, Bolton), his home town, the Lancashire team, and also had three international trials with the England schoolboys.

In the last three seasons he has scored 520 goals. This promising young player is well endowed physically, standing just over 5ft 10in tall and weighing 11st 7lb. About a month ago, he had a run with Rossendale United's Lancashire Combination team, and scored three goals against Leyland Motors. He will probably appear in Burnley's West Lancashire League side on Saturday.'

Burnley Express, 20 February 1935

P.S. Tommy Lawton did play and scored two goals on his debut.

THE STAR BEGINS TO SHINE

'A magnificent performance by Lawton, a schoolboy international of exceptional promise, enabled Burnley A to round off a successful season last Saturday. All four goals for the home side were scored by the young centre-forward. Cool, precise, and always on the lookout for loopholes in the Bury defence, Lawton played a scientific game, and it is no exaggeration to say that most of the spectators spent the afternoon watching him alone.'

Burnley Express Burnley A v Bury A 4–1, May 1935

START TO FINISH…FIRST-TEAM PLAYING CAREERS

1. Jerry Dawson's first-team Burnley career lasted from 13 April 1907 until Christmas Day 1928 – over 21 years.
2. Leighton James's first-team career stretched from 21 November 1970 until 13 May 1989 – over 18 years.
3. Joe Jakub's first-team career at Burnley lasted from 24 April 1976 until 17 April 1993 – just 17 years.
4. Martin Dobson's first-team Burnley career lasted from 23 September 1967 until 10 March 1984 – over 16 years.
5. Arthur Woodruff's first-team career at Burnley lasted from 14 September 1936 until 19 April 1952 – over 15 years.
6. Billy Watson's first-team career at Burnley lasted from 3 April 1909 until 8 September 1924 – over 15 years.
7. John Angus's first-team career at Burnley lasted from 3 September 1956 until 21 August 1971 – nearly 15 years.
8. Tommy Cummings's first-team career at Burnley lasted from 18 December 1948 until 22 August 1962 – over 13 years.
9. Jimmy Adamson's first-team career at Burnley lasted from 10 February 1951 until 22 February 1964 – over 13 years.
10. Bob Johnson's first-team career at Burnley lasted from 5 January 1935 until 16 October 1948 – over 13 years.

11. Billy Morris's first-team career at Burnley lasted from 28 January 1939 until 4 October 1952 – over 13 years.
12. Steve Davis's first-team career at Burnley lasted from 25 November 1989 until 4 May 2003 – over 13 years.
13. Ronnie Hornby's first-team career at Burnley lasted from 25 December 1934 until 7 April 1948 – over 13 years.
14. Walter Place's first-team career at Burnley lasted from October 1886 until January 1900 – over 13 years.
15. George Bray's first-team career at Burnley lasted from 1 October 1938 until 29 September 1951 – 13 years.
16. Fred Barron's first-team career at Burnley lasted from 1 October 1898 until 1 April 1911 – over 12 years.
17. David Taylor's first-team career at Burnley lasted from 16 December 1911 until 26 April 1924 – over 12 years.
18. Joe Taylor's first-team career at Burnley lasted from 26 January 1895 until 18 April 1907 – over 12 years.
19. Jimmy McIlroy's first-team career at Burnley lasted from 21 October 1950 until 20 February 1963 – over 12 years.
20. Tom Morrison's first-team career at Burnley lasted from 3 March 1894 until 8 September 1906 – over 12 years.
21. Bob Kelly's first-team career at Burnley lasted from 15 November 1913 until 21 November 1925 – just 12 years.

And yet these playing careers pale into 'almost' insignificance when placed alongside the Turf Moor years of service, such as:

George Bray (1937–92) player, trainer and kit man for 55 years at Turf Moor.
Brian Miller (1952–96) player, coach, manager and chief scout for 44 years at Turf Moor.
Harry Potts (1937–79) player, manager and chief scout for 42 years at Turf Moor.
Ray Bennion (1932–65) player and trainer for 33 years at Turf Moor.
Billy Dougall (1926–58) player, trainer, physio and manager for 32 years at Turf Moor.

These are just a few of the loyal servants that I remember in my lifetime, as there have been many others over the years.

SUBSTITUTES

- In 1965–66 a whole new can of worms was opened for professional football in the UK when substitutes were first allowed.

- The first Burnley sub named was Sammy Todd in August 1965, but the first sub to be called upon was Ian Towers, the following week.

- ⚽ Three months later Len Kinsella made his League debut as a substitute (November 1965).

- ⚽ In October 1967 Willie Irvine became the first Burnley sub to score.

- ⚽ The number of subs was increased to two per match in 1986–87 (FA Cup only). This rule was extended to League games in 1987–88.

- ⚽ Andy Farrell was the first Burnley sub to score twice after coming on, in March 1991.

- ⚽ Andy Payton was the first Burnley sub to score three times after coming on in a League Cup game, in August 2000. Six years later, Gifton Noel Williams was the first to come on as a sub and score a League hat-trick.

The following is a list of those who have made most League appearances as a substitute:

Graham Branch	67
Ronnie Jepson	62
Paul Weller	62
John Mullin	52
Glen Little	46
John Francis	45
Bradley Maylett	45
Andy Payton	45
Andy Cooke	44
Demi Papadopoulos	39
Roger Eli	36
Paul Smith	35
Lenny Johnrose	32
Alan Moore	32
Andy Farrell	30
Kyle Lafferty	30
Graham Lancashire	27
Neil Grewcock	24
Chris McCann	23
Ian Moore	23
John Spicer	23
Mark Monington	22
Adrian Randall	22
Liam Robinson	22
Tony Grant	21
Lee Roche	21
Gordon Armstrong	20
Kevin Henderson	20
Ashley Hoskin	20

⊕ In contrast, David Williams was named as substitute goalkeeper for every one of Burnley's games in 1993–94. He sat on the bench as substitute goalkeeper for all 62 League, Cup and Play-off games, not once getting his boots or his gloves dirty!

SUPPORTERS' CLUBS

⊕ For many years there were no supporters' clubs at Turf Moor. This was mainly due to the club's policy in general, and the attitude of Bob Lord in particular.

⊕ However, over the last 30 years or so dozens of clubs have sprung up across the country (and the world). These include: Burnley Football Supporters, West Midlands Clarets, London Clarets, Accrington Clarets, Boundary Clarets, Rossendale Clarets, Central Lancs Clarets, Shooters Arms Clarets, Gordon Clarets, Craven Clarets, North Manchester Clarets, Earby Clarets, Colne Clarets, West Yorkshire Clarets and South West Clarets.

⊕ There are also Clarets clubs in Norway, and wherever in the world Clarets gather together.

THE FIRST!

Alex Lang was the first ever player to score a penalty for Burnley when he scored against West Brom in 1891. Three years earlier, in 1888, Lang had played in Burnley's first ever League game when they visited Preston. He was also captain that day. In 1889, Lang, the captain of 'Lang's XI', was the first Burnley captain to hold a major trophy aloft when his team beat Blackburn Rovers in the Lancashire Senior Cup Final. First team, first captain, first Cup winner, first penalty!

FROM ST HELENS TO BURNLEY

Two of Burnley's greatest-ever players were signed from St Helens Town: Bob Kelly and John Connelly. Kelly arrived at Turf Moor from St Helens Town in November 1913 for what was said to be the highest fee ever paid for a Lancashire Combination player. One newspaper described the 19-year-old Kelly as 'the most talked of player in Lancashire junior football circles – a second Buchan'. Many of those who saw him play said that Kelly was Burnley's greatest ever player until he left in 1925. Burnley chairman Bob Lord said the only time he ever cried was when Bob Kelly was sold.

Just over 30 years later, young John Connelly came from the same town to sign for the Clarets. He went on to help win the League Championship, play in the FA Cup Final at Wembley and play for England.

Legendary goalkeeper Bert Trautmann, ex-German POW, also played for St Helens Town after the war, and Burnley were first in the queue to sign him. That is until Manchester City sneaked in the night before the day that Burnley were due to meet him. The Burnley manager and directors were furious, and the rest, as they say, is history.

STATESIDE BOUND

Quite a few Clarets have journeyed to the US after leaving Turf Moor. They joined the following American clubs:
Tulsa Roughnecks (Doug Collins and Colin Waldron)
Denver Dynamos (Andy Lochhead)
Vancouver Whitecaps (Dave Thomas and Ray Hankin)
Minnesota Kicks (Willie Morgan)
Atlanta Chiefs (Colin Waldron)
Tampa Bay Rowdies (Tony Morley)
Portland Timbers (Willie Donachie)
Philadephia Fury (Steve Daley)

STRIKE!

'The Burnley officials are in a bit of a quandary as to how to get to London on Friday, in view of the coal strike.'
Clapton Orient v Burnley, March 1912

SUCCESSFUL SEASONS

☻ Like all football supporters, Burnley fans are always hungering for success – just a little, now and then! 2008–09 was in some ways the most successful season for many years. In January the Clarets were still in the League Cup and the FA Cup, as well as figuring well in the Championship.

☻ The last time that the club was still in two Cup competitions in January was in 1982–83. But, sadly, the club was relegated that season. Prior to that, the best year was in 1968–69 when the Clarets reached the League Cup semi-final.

☻ By far the best season since the war was 1960–61, when the club finished fourth in Division One and reached the FA Cup semi-final and the League Cup semi-final. They also competed in the European Cup.

☻ The first team actually won nothing that season – but what a season! Altogether they played 68 games – 42 Division One games, seven FA Cup ties, eight League Cup ties, four European Cup games, one Charity Shield game, four Lancashire Cup games and two close-season friendlies in Portugal.

THE 'T' TEAM

Thompson

Taylor (D.)   Taylor (J.)

Todd   Talbut   Thomson

Thomas   Toman   Taylor (G.)   Taylor (S.)   Towers

Subs: Thomson (H.), Thomas (W.), Thomas (M.) and Ternent

CLOSE TO TEARS

'Adam Blacklaw could have chosen to do any number of things when he received a back pass from Alex Elder in the dying seconds of extra-time in this electrifying FA Cup fourth-round replay at Anfield on Wednesday. He decided to boot the ball up field from the edge of his penalty area – and succeeded only in scoring a direct hit on Liverpool leader, Ian St John, lurking tenaciously little more than a couple of arm's length away. The ball rebounded past Blacklaw, St John flashed after it, and would undoubtedly have put it into the net had not Blacklaw in complete and utter desperation, rugby tackled him from behind.

A penalty of course, and left-back Moran put his side into round five with a safe, sure spot-kick, in a fantastic, sensational, last minute climax. That was the nightmare, freakish ending to Burnley's Cup hopes for another season – a finish that will live forever in the memory of 58,000 stunned spectators.

A tragic, terrible, careless mistake though by Blacklaw, who understandably enough, looked close to tears at the final whistle, only 20 SECONDS later.'
Burnley Express, Liverpool v Burnley, February 1963

TELLY TRIVIA

- John Kettley, who was born in Todmorden, has been an avid Burnley fan since 1960. He says, 'When I'm doing the weather reports on television or radio, I always try and drop Burnley in as often as I can – you have to don't you, really!' Perhaps best remembered was one Boxing Day forecast given by John on TV when a map of the UK was shown with only one place named – Turf Moor.

- Steve Kindon remembers the night when a particular episode of *Mastermind* was on TV. He was at home on his own, and, believe it or not, the contestant was answering questions on his chosen subject – 'The History of Burnley Football Club'. Then came the question, 'Who was it who scored for Burnley in both home and away games against Celtic in the Anglo-Scottish Cup?'. Steve relates how he ran around his living room shouting to an empty house, 'It were me, it were me, it were bloody me!'

⊕ The Clarets have long had links with northern soaps like *Coronation Street* and *Emmerdale*, with Len Fairclough, an old 'Corrie' character, a keen Burnley supporter. More recent soap personalities who are regular Clarets' supporters include Richard Moore, who played Jarvis the dustbin collector in *Emmerdale*. For years he wore a woolly hat in the series which had 'Burnley FC' emblazoned on it. The hat was eventually given away as a prize in a supporters' club draw.

⊕ Young Sam Aston, who plays Chesney on *Coronation Street,* is a keen Claret. More than once a Burnley shirt has been seen hanging on the wall in the Rovers Return.

THREE SPELL PLAYERS

For any player to have played for a club in three different spells is quite unusual. Five recent Clarets come to mind – Bryan Flynn, Leighton James, John Mullin, Steve Davis and Marlon Beresford. Back in the early days others to have had three spells with Burnley were Jack Hillman and Tom Morrison.

'3.33' (or 'THREE THIRTY-THREE')

In January 1996 Burnley fans organised a protest against the club's administration and board. The club was sliding gradually (we might say plummeting!) towards the foot of Division Four, and the team were in the middle of a run of seven games without a win. And so it was at 3.33pm on 10 February 1996, with Burnley at home to Crewe, that the Burnley fans united en masse and turned their backs on the game and the board for one minute. The board of directors responded. They did not resign. Instead, they sacked the manager, Jimmy Mullen.

PERCY THROWER, DAVE THOMAS AND BOB LORD

Not many players got the better of Bob Lord, but Dave Thomas did. By the time Burnley were promoted to Division One at the end of season 1972–73, Dave Thomas, who had played in a number of games for the Clarets at the beginning of the season, had been transferred to Queen's Park Rangers. By chance, when QPR played Burnley, Thomas was in the QPR side, and he learned from one of the Burnley team that the players had been paid a bonus for promotion depending on appearances. Thomas was clearly owed money, and he enlisted the help of his PFA rep to claim it.

Terry Venables accompanied him to the tribunal and together they faced the committee and the intimidating Bob Lord, who argued that Thomas was not entitled to it, having already been transferred. Dave Thomas remembers that he was a bag of nerves but the committee decided in his favour.

Thomas, a keen gardener, was cock-a-hoop with the triumph. Afterwards he took Terry Venables out for a celebratory meal and he was delighted to see his great hero, the gardener Percy Thrower. But what shocked Dave the most was seeing his idol with a whisky in his hand in the casino area of the hotel!

AS TIME GOES BY

Fred Barron, Jerry Dawson, Billy Watson, George Bray, Billy Morris, Arthur Woodruff, Jimmy Adamson, Tommy Cummings, John Angus, Martin Dobson, Jim Thomson and Joe Jakub: 12 famous names at Turf Moor, stretching from the 1890s to the 1990s. But what have they all got in common – what makes them unique in the club's history? Answer: they all had long careers at Turf Moor, in which their League appearances each stretched over three decades.

For those curious, their decades were as follows: Fred Barron (1890s to 1910s); Jerry Dawson and Billy Watson (1900s to 1920s); George Bray, Billy Morris and Arthur Woodruff (1930s to 1950s); Jimmy Adamson and Tommy Cummings (1940s to 1960s); John Angus (1950s to 1970s); Martin Dobson and Jim Thomson (1960s to 1980s); and Joe Jakub (1970s to 1990s).

THE FINAL TEST

In 1897–98 Burnley finished as champions of Division Two, which meant that they then had to compete in the 'Test matches' – an early form of the Play-offs. Stoke and Blackburn were at the bottom of Division One and Burnley and Newcastle were at the head of Division Two. After three Test matches, the mini-league appeared as follows:

	Played	Points
Stoke	3	4
Burnley	3	4
Newcastle	3	2
Rovers	3	2

As can be seen, both Burnley and Stoke needed a point to qualify at the top, and they were to meet in the last match. The ground was in a shocking state, and had it not been the last day of the season, so the referee declared, the game would not have been played.

All in all, five balls were used, and the crowd continually kept possession of them whenever the ball went off the pitch. But let the reporter at the time take up the story:

'There was plenty of fun of its kind and it was heartily relished. The crowd on the popular side made several attempts to collar the ball and at last succeeded in doing so, so that to the ending, the referee called for another ball. And so the game was finished with alternate balls, for at every opportunity, the spectators protested in a practical manner by capturing the leather. Once it was put on the roof of the stand by one of the spectators, and somebody climbed onto the roof and threw it down among the struggling mass below. While on another occasion, the ball found its way into the River Trent. But the best bit of the day was when one of the linesmen attempting to prevent the ball from leaving the field of play, ran full tilt into a policeman, who went beautifully head over heels. It was indeed the tit-bit of the afternoon, and even the most indignant could not suppress his merriment.' (*Burnley Express,* **1898**)

As it was, everybody from both Stoke and Burnley went home happy, and Test matches were never tried again. (In fact, neither club gained anything by fair means or foul, because the following season the League took the opportunity to enlarge Division One from 16 teams to 18, including all the four teams which had fought out those final Test matches.) This was the only time that Burnley saved Rovers from relegation!

THESE WE HAVE LOVED

Over the years, Burnley have seen the best players. Some of them have been opponents, but just as many have been part of the team. For countless reasons, but mainly money, Burnley have let them go. These are just 20 of the hundreds of famous (and world-famous) players that have seen sold by Burnley: James Crabtree, George Beel, Jimmy McIlroy, Ralph Coates, Jimmy Ross, Bob Kelly, John Connelly, Dave Thomas, Jack Hillman, Louis Page, Willie Morgan, Brian O'Neil, Jack Bruton, Tommy Lawton, Steve Kindon, Martin Dobson, Jack Hill, Billy Elliott, Leighton James, Trevor Steven.

Every generation has had their favourites. It is tempting to muse that maybe Burnley would not be the club it is today if these players had not been sold? Or maybe they would have had a more successful club, if they had been kept?

THE THIRTY-FIRST GAME

After playing a League record of 30 consecutive League games in 1920–21, Burnley visited Hyde Road in Manchester on Easter Saturday 1921 to play Manchester City. The Clarets were beaten 3–0. This is an extract of the match report given in the *Burnley News*:

'If ever there was a team which could beat Burnley, it was a side such as the City who seemed to revel in that mud-heap of theirs, which it has never been my lot yet to see with a decent carpet of grass and the surroundings of which are redolent of desolation and dilapidation, such as are rarely found in the possession of a First League team today.

Utterly unsuited to accommodating a crowd of the dimensions which were expected on Saturday, it was no wonder that some regrettable scenes should occur.

All the surrounding house tops were packed with people, and the roofs of the stands were points of vantage from which a large number of people witnessed the game. The players' dressing rooms, which have had to be constructed since the old wooden stand was burnt down, accommodated many others, some of whom at one period drove their feet through the sky-lights and caused the players to think about their own safety.

At one corner of the field, the crowd swayed disconcertingly for a time, and ultimately the surging press at the top of the embankment exerted such pressure that there was a scene of the wildest confusion, and quite a number of those nearest the barriers were thrust forward and injured, causing several of them to be trampled upon.

At another part, there was a wild stampede and the crowd overflowed onto the field and took up position inside the barrier, till there was less than a yard from the touchline to the feet of the spectators. Then a portion of the crowd outside the walls managed to break in, and then to add to the troubles, part of the main stand caught fire during the progress of the game.'
Manchester City v Burnley 3–0, March 1921

And after the game...
'Rumours say that when the Burnley football team die, the mystic words "Three-Nowt!" will be found engraved on their hearts!'
Burnley News, **March 1921**

THIS IS YOUR LIFE

For my 50th birthday my wife planned a special *This is Your Life* evening for me – in Burnley of course. Among the special guests invited, totally unknown to me, were Harry Potts, Jimmy Robson, Ray Pointer and Jimmy McIlroy. I am pretty stoic on special occasions, but the presence of such heroes at my birthday party moved me tremendously. It was a pity about Jimmy McIlroy.

In those days he worked as a journalist, and he sent a letter describing how he was out of the country; nevertheless, he sent me his warmest good wishes for a happy night. Wow! Jimmy Mac writing to me?!

At the end of the evening, the MC asked if I had enjoyed the night? 'Wonderful!' I replied, still clutching my letter from the great man. It was then that the MC revealed that Jimmy had been sat there all the evening, revelling in my innocence!

To put the icing on the cake, Jimmy came forward, made a delightful speech and presented me with one of his Irish international jerseys. I have still got the photos and the jersey to prove that it all really happened.

Ten years later, my wife (God bless her!) and Jimmy Mac did it all again by being present at a secretly arranged birthday party for my 60th.

TODMORDEN HOTSPUR

The wife of a friend stopped me earlier this year and enquired if I was still following Burnley. 'Yes', I replied 'and next week I'm off to Tottenham for the Cup tie.' The following week, my friend reported back that his wife had told him I was off to Todmorden to watch Burnley in a Cup tie!

TRAINER'S TALES

For well over a quarter of a century, Jimmy Holland was physiotherapist for the club. He told many tales of his time with the players, 'On one occasion after a two-week stay in Bermuda, we returned travel weary through Manchester Airport. I have always been accident prone and walked through customs with an eyepatch covering an eye injury from when I had walked into a tree, and a sling supporting a broken arm I had picked up in a five-a-side match. The customs men were smiling at me, which worried me to say the least. It was only when I got to the coach that I discovered I had walked through customs and a packed Manchester Airport with a sign that said "I am a smuggler" stuck on my back.

On another occasion, I spent a full afternoon removing coral spines from the body of a player. He was out swimming with his roommate in a quiet bay in Majorca when a frantic cry of "Shark! Shark!" sent him clambering onto a coral outcrop. "Jaws" was a best-seller at the time and the injured player's roommate who had done the shouting (and will also remain anonymous) almost drowned himself in a fit of laughter!'

TRAINING

'I hear very good accounts of the men during their stay at Lytham, their behaviour being excellent. On Tuesday, the men walked to St Annes to see the stranded vessel. On Wednesday afternoon, they walked to Blackpool. On Thursday morning, they had a run and in the afternoon, two hours walking. Yesterday, they had skipping to finish the course. The men are in excellent spirits.'
Training for the Everton Cup tie, 1894

'Instead of going to Blackpool as intended, the players were taken into the country around Burnley and one is inclined to think it is not a bad choice. There are some bonny spots around here and the great thing is not to allow the minds of the players to become obsessed with the idea that they are training. Let them forget the field and the ball, and a good free and easy dinner and a walk is just the way to get them into condition.'
Burnley v Barnsley FA Cup tie, 1911

TRANSFERS

The start of the transfer system
It did not take Burnley long to enter the transfer market; in fact, approximately 28 days! In many ways it can be said that the international transfer market began with the Turf Moor team. When the club began in 1882 one of their very first games was against the local village of Read on 30 October 1882. The result was Read 7 Burnley 3.

A month later, the teams met again and Burnley won 5–0. How to explain the turnaround? We need to read the 'Correspondence Column' of the *Burnley Express* to discover the reason.

'Dear Sir,

The Committee of the Read Cricket and Football Club beg to call the attention of the Burnley Football Club with regard to the publication of the match at Calder Vale on Saturday, October 28th, as they procured the services of Messrs W. H. Moorhouse and T. Bury (Darwen), Lathom (Blackburn), Clegg (Enfield) and Waddington (Accrington) and never advised us. When we arranged the match, it was to play Burnley, and nor the whole of North East Lancashire, and in future, should any arrangements be made, we shall thank them to play as per agreement, and publish it accordingly.

J. Walmsley (Assistant Secretary)'

It was obvious that already the pressures of wanting to have a successful team were causing Burnley to look elsewhere for players, rather than fielding 'the locals'. Inside 12 months Burnley had turned their attention from North East Lancashire to Scotland.

The poaching of players caused great unrest north of the border, and Burnley scouts later told of those early days when it was a risky thing to go to Scotland searching for players. Many was the time that scouts had unsigned notes slipped underneath their hotel bedroom doors, warning them to 'get out of town, or else...!' On one occasion a member of the Burnley committee had to take refuge in a Dumbarton public house from a crowd of 500 men and women who had assembled 'to guard their own'.

One observer wrote at the time, 'The Scots crowded every single football team in Lancashire, and in one particular case, only a single Englishman was included in the team, and he was said to feel lonely.' That team was Burnley and that 'lonely Englishman' was Leonard Metcalfe. By 1892, Burnley had 64 Scots on their books.

The arrival of Tommy Boyle
'Burnley have made a rare capture in Boyle, the Barnsley captain and centre-half. But fancy signing a man on at four o'clock in the morning! There are some club managers who would not get up at that time for the best footballer in Christendom!'
Burnley Gazette, September 1911

The growth of transfer fees
Year	Transfer	Fee
1895	James Crabtree to Aston Villa	£250 English record fee
1901	Billy Bannister to Bolton	£300
1902	Jack Hillman to Manchester City	£350
1925	Bob Kelly to Sunderland	£6,500 English record fee
1928	Jack Hill to Newcastle	£8,000 English record fee
1948	Alan Brown to Notts County	£14,000
1950	Harry Potts to Everton	£20,000
1953	Billy Elliott to Sunderland	£27,000
1964	John Connelly to Manchester United	£56,000
1968	Gordon Harris to Sunderland	£70,000
1968	Willie Morgan to Manchester United	£117,000
1971	Ralph Coates to Tottenham	£190,000 English record fee

1974	Martin Dobson to Everton	£300,000
1975	Leighton James to Derby	£310,000
1995	Steve Davis to Luton	£750,000
2006	Richard Chaplow to West Brom	£1 million
2007	Robbie Blake to Birmingham	£1 million
2008	Andy Gray to Charlton Athletic	£1 million

TO BE CONTINUED...

'I will say this only vonce...'

The transfer of Ralph Coates to Tottenham in the early 1970s was like something out of a James Bond secret agent film as it was clothed in so much secrecy.

At the end of the 1970–71 season, manager Jimmy Adamson rang Ralph at home as, to keep fit, he was training in a local park. Ralph went shopping, came back and was about to cut the grass when a voice whispered over the garden hedge. It was the chief scout Dave Blakey, who told him to get into the house quickly because he could not talk outside. 'There are spies everywhere', he told Ralph.

Even in the house he could not tell Ralph much, but said there was to be a secret meeting on the M6. When Ralph picked up the phone to tell his wife Sandra, Blakey grabbed the phone out of his hand and said he must not tell anyone. Dave Blakey then phoned his own wife to pass on a message that they would be 45 minutes late for the secret rendezvous, and that he had made contact. Meanwhile, Coates thought that the whole thing was ridiculous.

He was even more convinced when Blakey sneaked Ralph into his car, except that it was not Blakey's car. Blakey had been to a local garage, left his own car there at the front, and on the pretext of a test drive, taken a car from the back of the garage for the journey to the Post Horn, a public house near Keele. At the Post Horn, they found it so full that the meeting with Spurs manager Bill Nicholson took place in the back of the car. Sandra, Ralph's wife, alerted to the events, had rushed home in order to accompany him. Ralph duly signed for £190,000.

Heads he goes...

When Paul Fletcher was sold to Blackpool, then managed by Stan Ternent, there was a haggle over the transfer fee. With Fletcher present in the room, Ternent offered £30,000 but Bob Lord wanted £35,000. It got to £32,500. Impasse. They therefore decided to toss a coin for the other two and a half. Ternent won. The deal was struck and Bob Lord never spoke to Paul Fletcher again.

'Goldfinger!'

When Steve Kindon arrived back at Turf Moor in the late 1970s from Wolves, to talk to Harry Potts and Bob Lord about signing for Burnley again, he had no intention of ever signing. He came out of politeness because he liked them both. 'How do I go there and avoid signing without upsetting anyone?' he asked his Wolves pals. 'Ask for a ridiculous wage that you know he'll refuse' was the answer.

Steve and Harry chatted for a while about everything except actually signing, and then Bob Lord appeared and took over the meeting. 'And how much do you want?'

asked Lord. Kindon made up a ridiculous figure, 'Fine' said Lord, 'and what else?' Kindon, amazed, thought of a few more things, and Lord answered in the affirmative to each. 'Come back to Burnley where we love you' he said imploringly. 'Sign here and you can keep my gold pen.'

Kindon signed. 'And now I'll have my pen back please', said old Bob.

Years later, after Bob had died, there was a knock at the Kindon's door. He still lived in Burnley though he now played for Huddersfield. At the door was Hilda Lord, Bob's widow. An astonished Kindon asked her in. 'I have something for you,' she said. 'After you signed for Burnley, Bob was telling everyone at our house how he had tricked you into signing by offering you his special gold pen, and then took it back off you.'

Thereupon, she took the pen out of her handbag and gave it to Steve. Steve still has the pen and it is one of his most treasured possessions.

A King's ransom
'I joined the Clarets for a King's ransom…fifteen thousand pounds. Bob Lord had offered 10 head of cattle and three pigs, but Peter Swales the Manchester City chairman thought they would bounce!' (**Mike Summerbee**)

Transfer fees received
The club have featured in record fees deals throughout the years, though this has fallen away more recently. It all began in 1895 when Burnley transferred local lad James Crabtree to Aston Villa for £250, an unheard-of fee in those days. Indeed, this was the first 'record fee' in England.

England goalkeeper Jack Hillman was sold to Manchester City for £350, and local lad Billy Bannister went to Bolton Wanderers in 1902 for £375. These fees were dwarfed in the 1920s when local hero Bob Kelly went to Sunderland in 1925 for £6,550. It was a national record fee, fitting for a national figure. Similarly, that record was broken in 1928 when Burnley and England captain Jack Hill was transferred to Newcastle United for £8,000.

The only other occasion, pre-war, when Burnley hit the transfer market big time was when youngster Tommy Lawton was transferred to Everton for £7,000. This was a then League record for a 17-year-old.

When club captain Alan Brown went to Notts County in 1948 the club received a Burnley record fee of £14,000. Two years later this was exceeded when Harry Potts went to Everton for £20,000. And three years later the record was broken yet again when Billy Elliott was sold to Sunderland for £27,000.

Over a decade passed before that figure was broken by winger John Connelly when he was transferred to Manchester United for £56,000. In the 1960s, players were sold in increasing numbers to balance the books, and in 1968 Gordon Harris went to Sunderland for £70,000. Six months later Willie Morgan followed Connelly when he too went to Old Trafford for a fee of £117,000, while, much to the hurt of local fans, idol Ralph Coates went to Tottenham in 1971 for £190,000.

And so it has continued – Dobson, James, Davis, Chaplow, Akinbiyi, Lafferty and more. There will be others!

Transfer fees paid

The club have always sold more than bought players due to the constant tight financial budget. The largest fees in the 'early days' were for players like Jimmy Ross and Alex Leake. Astute buys were those of Bert Freeman (£750) and Tommy Boyle (£1,150), both in 1911.

Bob Kelly was purchased for what was said to be 'the highest fee ever paid for a Lancashire Combination player'. But these figures were beaten after World War One when the club signed centre-forward Joe Anderson from Scottish club Clydebank for £2,000.

Now one of the leading clubs in the country, Burnley were able to attract some of the best players, none better than big Jack Hill, the Plymouth centre-half and England captain. He arrived at Turf Moor in 1923 for £5,000, which was the League record at the time. This fee remained a Burnley record until 1950 when manager Frank Hill brought the 18-year-old Jimmy McIlroy to Burnley from Irish club Glentoran for £8,000. It was not until August 1951 that the Turf Moor club hit the headlines again when they paid a club record fee of £25,000 for Billy Elliott, the Bradford Park Avenue left-winger.

Since then, Burnley have followed most clubs by entering fully into the transfer market, even being prepared to pay over £1 million for a player. Whatever would Bob Lord have said?

Nearly transferred!

One of the most prolific scorers of all time and a Liverpool legend, John Aldridge nearly signed for Burnley before he ever became famous. When he was an unknown at Newport County, the Burnley manager offered £40. Nothing happened, Aldridge flourished and Burnley were relegated.

TRANSPORT PROBLEMS

1. Everton v Burnley 1885

'On the way to Liverpool, the Burnley team had an unfortunate experience. The noon express from East Lancashire was 40 minutes late at Preston Junction and the railway officials had started the connecting train to Liverpool before its arrival. The players were placed in the dilemma that by taking the next train to Liverpool they would be landed at Exchange Street Station (three miles from the ground) 10 minutes after the match should start. A threat of demanding compensation was made and Mr Nield, the courteous stationmaster, arranged that the 11 should go by the 2.15 express to Southport, and afterwards be taken by the same train especially to Liverpool.

By this means, Exchange Street Station was reached about 3.50 and cabs took the team to the ground which was reached at 4.30. The game was not as exciting as the journey and was lost 4–0!'

2. More transport problems! (This was the infamous Forest versus Burnley game in 1900 when Burnley were relegated)

'The Burnley players left Burnley at 11.20 for Manchester. When they arrived at the other Manchester station, it was found that an accident had taken place and the saloon by which the North East Lancashire contingent were to travel had been damaged. This necessitated a delay of about one hour and the consequence was that the train did not reach the Lace capital till late and the team could not get to the Forest ground in time for the 5.15 kick-off.

Occupants of the grandstand urged the Forresters to play up, shouting out that they wanted Burnley out of the First Division.

The fateful match over, the players had to dress and get to the station hurriedly, otherwise they would have been too late for the homeward train. When they landed at Manchester, they cabbed across the city, but the train to Burnley had gone. And so the men came on to Ramsbottom and then joined the train which does not come any further than Accrington. However, those in charge of the party persuaded the officials to allow the train to come on to Bank Top, arriving in the small hours of the morning. Bank Top was all in darkness and locked up.

Of course the committee cannot be blamed for railway unpunctuality and railway accidents, but if they had started an hour or two earlier to ensure having time to cover the journey, they would have done as they ought to have done. The men would have been none the worse for an hour's leisure after the tedious ride. The mismanagement in their last outing of the season is a fitting climax to a series of blunders.'
Nottingham Forrest v Burnley, April 1900

3. More trouble with trains!
'Burnley's visit to Leeds did not begin well at all. The Railway Company had not seen fit to put a saloon on the 9.29 train, by which it had been arranged the team would travel. Rather did they choose to travel by the 11.37 on which a saloon could be put.

Just before the time for the train to leave Manchester Road station, a heavy goods train passed through in the direction of Towneley, and it was generally expected that some delay would be caused. But there was general consternation when word reached the station that the goods train had run off the line a bit further up, and traffic would be delayed considerably.

After a time, passengers were told to cross over to the other side of the station, as traffic would be conducted on a single line till the obstruction was cleared away. But it was not until 12.15 that a big train-load of Burnley followers, about 700 in number, including a saloon full of members of the Wesley Brotherhood on a visit to their old friend, the Revd J.E. Mattinson – left the Manchester Road Station.

And what a slow journey it was to be sure. For the match commenced at 2.15, or was timed to, and the finger of the clock had passed the hour of two, when Leeds was eventually reached. Taxi cabs had been telephoned for from Low Moor, but they failed to put in an appearance, and the team had to make a dash, capture what hansoms they could commandeer – in at least one case they commandeered one which had been engaged by someone else – and drive to the field, late enough to make the club liable to a fine.

Meanwhile the crowd swarmed into cars en route for the field. The Leeds Corporation must be a "business like" Corporation for they "did it on" Burnley all right by charging them double.'
Burnley Express, **Leeds City v Burnley, November 1911**

197

Stuck in traffic

Paul Crichton was Burnley's regular goalkeeper from August 1998 until September 2000. He played a total of 82 games altogether and was an ever present in season 1999–2000. One day, on the way to the McAlpine Stadium in Huddersfield, Paul was stuck in traffic and failed to arrive at the ground in time. Manager Stan Ternent had no choice but to play Greek Nik Michopoulos for his first League game. Nik had a wonderful debut, Burnley won the game 1–0, and Nik went on to play 92 League and Cup games for the club.

As for Paul – he never played for the Clarets again.

The first double-decker

In October 1926 photographs appeared in the *Burnley News* of the first double-decker tram to travel up Yorkshire Street under the Culvert to Turf Moor.

'Sulphurous tunnels'

'Journeys to places like Birmingham, Leicester and Derby were the order of the day and except in the case of Derby, it did not appear to trouble the players at all. The Derby trip was dreaded because of the run through the sulphurous tunnels in a saloon which was generally at the end of the train, and which rocked terribly going down. The result can only be imagined!'
Burnley News, 1932

TROUBLE AT THE TURF

1. Tony Kay played for Sheffield Wednesday and then Everton in the 1960s. In an era of hard men, Kay was one of the toughest. He, like his Everton colleague Jimmy Gabriel, was a McIlroy fan, but that did not stop him taking McIlroy out of a game with a bad tackle. At half-time, as they left the field, Bob Lord came down the tunnel telling people how he was going to give Kay a good hiding. Kay heard all about this and told his manager Harry Catterick 'that if Lord came anywhere near him, then he would be the one to get a good hiding.'

2. 'In 1967 I asked for a transfer from the club. The game was changing so much and I felt that the city clubs with the buying power of big gate receipts would soon begin to dominate the First Division.

Unfortunately, my request to leave the club did not go down too well either at management or boardroom level. But my mind was made up and I felt I had to leave Burnley to benefit my career. My wanting to leave the club was before Freedom of Contract, and I soon found myself in a predicament with the club refusing my transfer request and my game and relationship with the club deteriorating. The lowest ebb came when the club refused to let me play in any of the sides and banned me from the training ground.'
Willie Morgan

TROUBLE AT LEEDS UNITED

'Don't let them intimidate you' said manager Jimmy Adamson to the Burnley team before the epic 1974 League clash against League leaders Leeds United. 'It's alright for you boss, sat in the dugout. We've got wives and families to think about!' said Duggie Collins. That was the day that Frank Casper's knee was shattered, along with his career.

TROUBLE AT PORTSMOUTH

'In my first season we played Portsmouth at Fratton Park. They were a top-class First Division side in those days, due in no small measure to the skills and drive of the legendary Jimmy Scoular. He was a Scottish international wing-half with thighs like tree trunks; they did not come any tougher than Jimmy – as I was to find out.

Going up the left-wing flat out, Scoular came across and caught me with a tackle that sent me over the line, the grass verge, the running track, and over a low fence into the crowd. With no subs in those days, I was thrown back into play 10 minutes later after the shock treatment of the cold sponge.

Jimmy had not even been spoken to by the referee, and with play going on, he sidled up to me and snarled: "Listen, you little Fenian Irish bastard, that's nothing to what I'll do next time." In my innocence – and terror – I quickly spluttered, "But I'm a Protestant!" To this day, I can still see the anguish on Jimmy's face, "Oh God son, I'm sorry. Did I hurt you?" he blurted out.'
Jimmy McIlroy

TROUBLE AT ANFIELD

Liverpool's Tommy Smith was a legendary hard man in the 1970s. Jimmy Greaves, in his book *The Heart of Football*, tells a story about Smith and Burnley's Steve Kindon. 'Steve Kindon played for Burnley' says Greaves, 'and Steve was so quick he could have raced pigeons. He was a teenager when he first played for Burnley at Anfield and his pace began to get the better of Tommy Smith. Time and time again, he would push the ball past Smith and leave Smith for dead. He was beginning to make Tommy look a bit of a chump, which Tommy naturally objected to, especially in front of his own crowd.

So Smith, fed up of all this, decided to take matters into his own hands and threatened Kindon that if he did it again he would break his leg. Kindon, young and green around the gills, was rattled and went up to referee Clive Thomas and told him of the threat.

"Ref, ref, that Smith is gonna break my leg if I go round him again!"

Clive Thomas was well versed in the banter between players and gave him his advice, "Really, in that case, I wouldn't go round the outside of him again, if I were you son. Now get on with it.""

Chapter Eleven

U–V

(From Ukulele and Unenviable records to Victorian verses and Violence)

'U'

'U' is unbeaten run undone,
The bastion has fallen,
To Barnsley! Why Barnsley?
A game not lost but stolen.

An open goal missed, own goal scored,
The soccer gods are fickle,
This vanquisher of Premier sides
Left in a pretty pickle.

Would promotion be so great, being
Repeatedly defeated,
The joke team of the Premier League,
Merely Barnsley repeated?

Yet a win is always so sweet,
Defeat bitterly tasted,
Not three points lost, but on Barnsley
Those were three points wasted.

So please forgive the poet who
To rancour is resorting,
For this was his first game for months
And leaves him quite unsporting!!

Dave Alton

This was written after the 1–2 home defeat by Barnsley on Boxing Day, 2008.

UKULELE

The 1970s centre-forward Paul Fletcher, currently chief executive at Burnley FC, is a well-known after-dinner speaker. He is also an accomplished ukulele player and a fully paid up member of the George Formby Appreciation Society.

UNENVIABLE RECORDS

It is 77 years and 11 League games since Burnley last won at Barnsley.
It is 46 years and 10 League games since Burnley won at Manchester City.
It is 47 years and 10 League games since Burnley won at Manchester United.
It is 38 years and five League games since Burnley won at Chelsea.
It is 45 years and 14 League games since Burnley won at Notts Forest.
It is 40 years and seven League games since Burnley won at West Brom.

Unsuccessful sequences
Runs since the war without a win in League games only:
1.= Brian Miller was manager for 18 consecutive games (1979–80 and 1980–81).
1.= Steve Cotterill was manager for 18 consecutive games (2006–07).
3.   Harry Potts was manager for 16 consecutive games (1978–79 and 1979–80).
4.= Jimmy Adamson was manager for 14 consecutive games (1970–71).
4.= Joe Brown was manager for 14 consecutive games (1976–77).

UNSOLVED DEATH

A mysterious and unsolved death occurred concerning Burnley Football Club in the early years of the last century. Spen Whittaker was the Burnley manager in 1910, and with Burnley due to play Manchester City and a new player to be urgently registered, Whittaker decided to take the overnight train to London to register him in time for the game.

Late on a Friday night, Whittaker left for London on the 2am train from Burnley. He was seen to be asleep in his compartment by a fellow traveller, but when next he looked, Whittaker was gone and the compartment door was open as the train hurtled along.

The alarm was raised and the body of Mr Whittaker was found by the trackside, still alive, but with severe head injuries. He regained consciousness briefly, but was unable to explain how he had fallen out of the carriage. He died at midday on the Saturday.

Nobody has ever found out what happened, but it is guessed that half awake, he opened the carriage door thinking it led into the corridor of the carriage. If the train was travelling at speed, the wind may well have dragged him out and flung the door wide open as he held on to it.

The game was played, and his death was announced during the game, which ended 3–3. A 'shilling' fund was started for his wife and three children, and within days over 1,000 shillings had been collected.

'UNTOUCHABLES!'

In season 1920–21 the players of Burnley Football Club established a League record that was to stand for more than 80 years. The record was that Burnley had played for 30 consecutive League games, 16 at home, which were all won, and 14 away, five victories and nine draws. The run began on 6 September 1920 and lasted until 25 March 1921 – more than six months without tasting defeat.

A commemorative plaque outside the home dressing room at Turf Moor still proudly recalls the remarkable achievement and serves as a reminder to today's players of an outstanding sequence of matches.

It was not until season 2003–04 that the record was finally surpassed, by Arsenal, who went through an entire season of 38 games unbeaten.

The record is still well worth recording – it still takes the breath away as you read down the results!

6 September	Huddersfield	h	3–0
11 September	Middlesbrough	h	2–1
18 September	Middlesbrough	a	0–0
25 September	Chelsea	h	4–0
2 October	Chelsea	a	1–1
9 October	Bradford	a	3–1
16 October	Bradford	h	1–0
23 October	Tottenham	a	2–0
30 October	Tottenham	h	2–0
6 November	Newcastle	a	2–1
13 November	Newcastle	h	3–1
20 November	Oldham	a	2–2
27 November	Oldham	h	7–1
4 December	Liverpool	a	0–0
11 December	Liverpool	h	1–0
18 December	Preston North End	a	2–0
25 December	Sheffield United	h	6–0
27 December	Sheffield United	a	1–1
1 January	Preston North End	a	3–0
15 January	Blackburn Rovers	h	4–1
22 January	Blackburn Rovers	a	3–1
5 February	Aston Villa	h	7–1
9 February	Aston Villa	a	0–0
12 February	Derby County	h	2–1
23 February	Derby County	a	0–0
26 February	Bolton Wanderers	h	3–1
5 March	Bolton Wanderers	a	1–1
12 March	Arsenal	h	1–0
19 March	Arsenal	a	1–1
25 March	Manchester United	h	1–0

No wonder the plaque is headed 'REMARKABLE RECORD!'

'UP THE CLARETS!'

For well over 25 years, I had waited for someone to write a book about my beloved Burnley Football Club. But no one did, so I decided to do it myself. Not that I had ever written a book, but for three years, from 1970 to 1972, I worked at it. I wrote and wrote and wrote. Until in the end, I had in the words of the Burnley librarian Richard Caul, a veritable 'Encyclopaedia Clareticca!' My title was far more obvious. I called it *Up the Clarets!*.

After three years, all I needed was a piece about Bob Lord; I had a chapter about him, but I just needed an interview with the man himself to give it a personal touch with a few good quotes. So I rang up his secretary and arranged an appointment one Monday morning. I got to Turf Moor bright and early, very excited to be meeting Mr Lord and going into the club's offices.

However, the man on the door refused me entrance, saying that Mr Lord was not seeing anyone that day – even if I did have an appointment. I protested suitably, but to no avail. I returned to my car and cried. My club! My granddad's club! My Dad's club! The club I had supported from Workington to Wembley! And the only book ever written about the club. It seemed the chairman would not even talk to me, even if I had travelled over 50 miles to get there.

As I sat there, I looked at all the pages I had written about Bob Lord and tore up the lot. Not a word of it was ever included in the book! In 1972, the club were struggling in Division Two, but Mr Caul said, 'Stick with it! They'll come good and then we'll get a publisher'. In between time, Burnley FC offered me £70 for the entire work – over 100,000 words!

The following season, 1972–73, the Clarets won promotion and I was asked by Robert Hale & Co. if they could publish my book *Up the Clarets!* By 1974, it was a sell-out. There are times when the club do not deserve the lifelong support they get from their unquestioning fans.

US

The first season back in Division One was 1973–74, and the first game played was at Bramall Lane where Sheffield United were playing the Clarets. And I was over 6,000 miles away in San Francisco. (During the summer of 1973 I was serving at a church in California on a pastoral exchange.) I expressed disappointment to one or two of the members of my church in San Francisco that I should miss the big opening game.

On the following morning, Sunday 26 August, I was conducting morning worship. One of my members, Chuck Peterson, was the editor of the *San Francisco Chronicle* and unknown to me, he drove across the bay (some 25 miles or so) to his office to pick up the morning edition.

During a pause in the service (halfway between prayers and a hymn) he stood up and announced that he had the paper, but did not understand the result. He said it read 'Sheff United 0 Burnley 2'. The news was greeted by a bewildered silence from the congregation and a Lancashire sounding 'Whoopee!' from the pulpit.

VALUE FOR MONEY?

In 1889–90 the club lost a lot of fans in the town when they raised admission charges from fourpence to sixpence. These days, that may not appear too much, but in 1889 it was a fair amount and letters poured into the local press objecting to the extravagant and exorbitant charges, 'especially as we are not winning anything!' said one annoyed correspondent (the club were in the middle of a run of 19 League games – over a year – without a win).

More fuel was added to the controversy by the fact that Rovers, Preston and Everton only charged threepence, while at Turf Moor, to watch the least successful team in Lancashire, it cost twice as much.

Burnley v Canadian XI, November 1891
'If the gate was a "four penny one", people could not expect to see "saxpenny play" – at least that seems to be the Scotch idea!'
Burnley Express

VICTORIAN VERBOSITY

⊕ Reading match reports in Victorian days is an education in itself. The ball was more often referred to as 'the leather' or 'the sphere', and players were 'kickers of the leather'.

⊕ The home side were usually described as 'the ground team' or 'our boys', while the opponents were 'the enemy'! The full-time whistle was described as 'the call of time' and classical scholarship often crept into match reports: 'The game between Burnley and Clitheroe was well contested from the Alpha to the Omega'. (*Burnley Express,* 1883)

⊕ The Burnley defence was looked upon as 'the Burnley Citadel', while a good crowd would be described as 'the large concourse of spectators'. And some things we may never quite know what was meant. Especially concerning 'screws' and 'scrimmages'. Phrases like a 'neat screw' or a 'tight screw' or 'screwing the leather' were commonplace, while 'scrimmages' seemed to take place near the goalmouth and goals were often credited to 'scrimmage'.

⊕ There was always something quite delightful in the reporting, such as 'the Burnley goal was rather frequently visited' (**1883**) or 'the match was spoiled in many ways by the visitation of Jack Frost and his bride Lady Snowflake, for it to some extent interfered with the game, while financially it was, I should imagine, a very decided frost.' (**1888**)

⚽ Every game had its unique description, and one comment reflected both a scholarly background and a knowledge of the British Empire. 'The ground was a veritable Slough of Despond and at the conclusion of the game, the players looked like a band of Zulus'. (**1882**)

⚽ 'On Saturday, the Blackpool team paid a visit to Turf Moor in order to try conclusions with our premier team.' (**1895**)

⚽ Northwich Victoria were described as 'the kickers of the sphere from the cheese county!'

VICTORIAN VERSES

Burnley's great rivals in the early years were always nearby Padiham, and for several seasons Padiham held the upper hand. This was until 13 December 1884 when Burnley came out top, victors by 4–0. The following 'funeral card' was published in the local press the following week.

R.I.P.

Lament of the Padiham Footballites on Burnley winning by four to nothing, Dec 13th 1884.

Alas for Padiham players
Renown for them has gone,
The Burnley lads have thrashed them
By four clear goals to none.
For several years the former
A good and well trained band
In summer or in winter,
Have held the upper hand.

But now alas no longer
Can Padiham claim the name
Of being the best hands at
Our national winter game.
The Scottish Burnley players
Have shown them how to play
Tho' Padihamites were saying
Four to one on I'll lay.

The game was well contested
And each man he did try
To score against his opponents
And oft at goal did shy.
But 'twas only at the last half

After all was said and done
That Padihamites discovered
They'd lost by four to none.

Then from the team's supporters
There rose a mighty shout
Which could be heard at Burnley
Or somewhere thereabout.
In an hour from the finish
'Twas impossible to roam
And find a Padihamite.
Each had journeyed to his home.

In 1898 Burnley had their first FA Cup run of any note. Previously, they had lost 12 of the 18 Cup ties they had played. But in season 1897–98 they reached the quarter-finals, where they met Everton at Turf Moor. 'The most important event ever decided at Turf Moor admits no doubt' said the local press. 'The team are in good spirits and as fit as a fiddle. Let's hope they play a merry tune.'

Mr J. Bradshaw of Yorkshire Street, Burnley, penned the following verses:

Play up, my boys, you've nought to fear,
This is the best match of the year.
If you win this, you then will steer
Into your true position.

Let Haddow stir between the sticks,
Let's have no namby pamby tricks,
May all his fisting and his kicks
Be done with true precision.

Let Morrison his partner feed,
Dash down the wing and take no heed,
Shoot at the goal with lightning speed,
As he has done before, sir.

Let Captain Ross keep up his play
And shoot at goal in his old way.
If he does this, we'll win the day.
He's best shot in the nation.

Let Billy Bowes determined be
Then we some brilliant play shall see
There's none can get the ball like he
When he is that way minded.

> If Burnley chaps will just play up
> They perhaps may win the English Cup
> If this comes off, we all will sup
> To their heroic victory.

Alas, there was no 'heroic victory' and the Turfites lost 3–0. The loss was blamed in the local paper on the fact that Burnley had lost the toss and Everton chose to play down the slope with the wind on their backs. They scored three goals within six minutes, and Burnley finished the game with only 10 men.

VIOLENCE

Midlands violence – West Brom v Burnley, 1890s

'As the players returned to the dressing room, they were followed by the crowd and Morrison was struck. During the progress of the match disgusting language was used towards the Turfites. This is not Burnley's first such experience at West Bromwich Albion.'

Teesside violence – Burnley v Middlesbrough, September 1920

'The opposition saw to it that Anderson got well punished, and a fist to the jaw was one of the penalties.'

North East violence – Sunderland v Burnley, 8 January 1955

I was at Roker Park in Sunderland for a third round Cup tie in 1955, and it was the first time I experienced crowd violence. I had gone with a school friend and I carried, as I did at every game in those days, my claret and blue football rattle. We were stood on the terraces an hour before kick-off when we became surrounded by a group of teenage Sunderland fans. Rather menacingly, they moved towards Keith and I and they seized my rattle. I noticed that one of them had a large pocket knife, which rather scared me.

Without saying much, this lad with the knife calmly used the blade to unscrew the screws holding my wooden rattle together. Then he threw the screws away into the crowd and, with a smile, handed me back numerous pieces of coloured wood, which were previously my rattle. I might have been scared, but I was silenced.

London violence – Spurs v Burnley (1960s)

It was the early 1960s and forward Arthur Bellamy was just starting to get a game in the first team. Arthur, who later became the groundsman at Burnley's Gawthorpe training centre, was, and still is, not much more than 10 stone when dripping wet. In one of his very first games at Tottenham, he was getting some really rough treatment from legendary half-back Dave Mackay, who was as tough as teak, had a chest like a barrel, tree trunk legs and ate nails for breakfast. Nobody messed with Dave Mackay.

But Burnley manager Harry Potts did. Incensed at the treatment his young skinny inside-forward was getting from the merciless Mackay, Harry, wearing his famous old raincoat, strode up to Mackay in the tunnel at half-time, grabbed him by the top of his shirt, pinned him against the wall and ordered him to lay off his young player who was just starting out in the game. 'You don't forget a thing like that' says Arthur Bellamy today.

Scottish violence – Burnley v Celtic (1970s)

The worst night of violence ever seen at Turf Moor was in September 1978 when Celtic came to Burnley to contest the Anglo-Scottish Cup. Celtic supporters arrived in Burnley in their thousands from the early morning onwards and almost took over the town. Although there were few if any reports of violence on the streets, it was a far different matter at the game. Burnley took the lead through a Steve Kindon goal and it was then that the trouble began.

In those days, the Longside was a standing terrace and half of it was given over to away supporters. Other Celtic fans were standing at the Bee Hole End behind the goals, leaving a mass of Burnley fans sandwiched in their half of the Longside. Bottles were hurled at the Burnley fans, fighting erupted, and then the railings were uprooted and used as spears, and they too were hurled over at the Burnley supporters.

Hundreds of fans escaped onto the pitch, the game was stopped, and the players were taken to the dressing rooms as the scenes continued. It was suggested that one Celtic player, and one Burnley player, Steve Kindon, should go onto the pitch to appeal for calm.

'Just one small problem boss', Kindon replied to Harry Potts. 'It was me that scored the goal!' The scenes of violence were so bad that it was on national TV news.

Turf Moor violence 1 – Burnley v Oldham, January 1920

'Tommy Boyle fell on top of Dolphin, who had been involved with Jones the Burnley full-back the previous week, and he broke bones in Dolphin's shoulder. Billy Watson caught Bradbury on the instep, and he had to go off too. Oldham now had nine men….now ball or man was their motto, and they usually chose the man. Nesbitt received several bad kicks, and once Lindley luckily escaped being kicked on the head with a back-heeler, as he bent down to pick up the ball for a throw-in.'
Burnley News

Turf Moor violence 2 – Derby County v Burnley, March 1920

'Personally, I do not think that Boyle looks quite fit, but for all that I regretted the action he took with regard to Peart on one occasion. One Burnley player has just finished two months suspension for retaliation, and the fact that Boyle had been kicked did not justify him seizing Peart by the throat.'
Burnley News

Turf Moor violence 3 – Burnley v Derby County, February 1921

'Anderson, in one of Burnley's rather infrequent raids, after 10 minutes of play, attempted to tackle Lawrence, the Derby goalkeeper, who had the ball. The goalkeeper swinging round, caught Anderson in the face with his elbow, and in the stomach with his knee, and laid him out. He had to be carried off and attended to, and for a long time after his return, he staggered about like one completely dazed. A second time he was bowled over with a knock on the head, and then finally, about

10 minutes from the final, he was struck with the ball in the stomach, and had to be carried off for the rest of the game. Thus, for the fourth time in the last six games, and for the third consecutive Saturday, Burnley finished the game with 10 men.'
Burnley News

Turf Moor violence 4 – Burnley v Portsmouth, 1929

'After the trainers had been called on to attend to five players in the first 20 minutes – three of Burnley's and two of Pompey's – the referee thought fit to intervene and he called the players together and intimated to them that the next man guilty of rough play would have to seek refuge in the dressing room.'
'Kestrel'

Turf Moor violence 5 – Gordon Harris v Jimmy Adamson

It was 1963, and it was no secret that there was no love lost between Jimmy Adamson, the 1962 Footballer of the Year and assistant England team manager in Chile, and the burly, fiery Gordon Harris. Jimmy, for all his elegance and culture, was also tough, and in a training session in the gym playing five-a-side was quite rough on Gordon Harris.

He upended Harris once and Harris was not best pleased. He upended him again and laughed as Harris showed his displeasure. 'Bomber' Harris waited his chance and in the next tackle upended Jimmy. As Jimmy came down, Harris caught him with a beautiful punch which laid Adamson out on the floor with blood trickling from his face. Harris quietly turned round, left the gym and went home.

Turf Moor violence 6 – Graham Branch v Derby County

It was 27 August 2005 and Burnley were beating Derby County 2–1 at Turf Moor when, after 55 minutes, Derby full-back Marc Edworthy was on the receiving end of a shockingly high kick routine by Burnley's Graham Branch. It took place near the corner flag, and Branch later claimed that it was accidental. As a Burnley fan, let me say that everyone on the ground winced.

Branchy was extremely lucky to get off with just a booking, but after a very long delay Edworthy left the field with a severe facial injury, which caused him to miss the next few games. Justice was done, and seen to be done, five minutes into the 11 minutes of added time which the referee allowed when Rasiak equalised for Derby.

This has gone down in Derby as one of the 10 worst tackles in Derby County's history, clashes for which the perpetrators are never forgiven.

Chapter Twelve

(From War and Wardrobes to X marks the spot!)

A 'W' TEAM

<pre>
                    Waiters
            Woodruff   Winton
        Walker   Waldron   Watson
  Weller   Wright   Waddle   Weaver   Waterfield
</pre>

Subs: West (A.), West (D.), Walton and Wharton

'W'

'W' was to be for Wembley,
A Claret triumph again
And BURN-ER-LEE beneath the arch,
But instead it's White Hart Lane.

Forty-five glorious minutes,
The Clarets cause was supreme,
But it took less than half the time
For Spurs to destroy the dream.

A Burnley header missed the post,
By a ball's width, that's all,
A Burnley header inside the post,
A fourth conceded; own goal!

The ember of hope still smoulders,
Though not a result they'd choose,
With the tie now seemingly lost
Clarets have nothing to lose.

It's just three goals that's required
As long as Spurs do not score,
What a victory that would be,
A famous night at Turf Moor.

However unlikely it seemed,
And against all the odds,
Three goals scored, two minutes to go…
How fickle the soccer gods!

Dave Alton
(Reflecting on the two semi-final games against Tottenham)

WAR

The threat of war hung heavy over England at the time of the 1914 FA Cup Final as Burnley played Liverpool. King George V was the first monarch to attend the Final, and it has often been suggested that he did so as a political gesture to unify the British people in a time of crisis.

Undaunted, after the Final Burnley proceeded with their pre-arranged close-season tour of…Germany! Earlier in the season of 1913–14, the club had received the following letter from the Deutscher Fussball Club in Prag: 'We ask courteous if you were not willing to come on the continent for 14 days in the time from middle May to June 1, and 6 plays in this time in diverse towns, and what you wish for travel compensations. We are praying you send us answer by return of post and sign with exquisite respect. D.F.C.Prag.'

Very few teams could have resisted such an offer (if the understood it!) and so, in the close season of 1914, Burnley made their first overseas tour, an 18-day visit to Austria, Hungary and Germany. During their six games Burnley beat Berlin 2–1, and were the last team to visit Germany before hostilities commenced, returning to England less than a month before the outbreak.

From all reports, it would seem that hostilities began during the tour, as the club returned with 13 of the players on the injured list. Only goalkeepers Dawson and Sewell returned unscathed from the conflict!

In 1916 the club helped the war effort by sending out footballs and jerseys to the men fighting in France. By 1917, Alf Lorrimer and William Pickering had been killed in action; Tommy Boyle had been hit with a shell in France and was in hospital; ex-player Jimmy Hogan was a prisoner of war in Austria; Levy Thorpe returned home badly wounded in the knee; and Charlie Bates, ex-player and first team trainer, had been a prisoner in Germany for four years. Two Burnley reserve players, Harry Langtree and William Johnson, were also World War One fatalities. In 1919 Teddy Hodgson died from kidney trouble, which had developed while he was serving with the Allied army of occupation in Germany in 1918.

'The Football League have announced that today's matches will take place unless there is war, in which case it is unlikely that the Government will allow big gatherings of people.'
Burnley Express, 26 August 1939

Wartime appearances
The players who made most appearances for Burnley during World War One were:

Dick Lindley	132
Jerry Dawson	78
Bert Freeman	76
Billy Nesbitt	73
Harry Hastie	72
Bob Kelly	72
Tommy Boyle	63
Eddie Hodgson	62

Wartime goals
Leading goalscorers during World War One were:

Bert Freeman	39
Eddie Hodgson	39
Dick Lindley	37
Bob Kelly	26
Billy Nesbitt	23

Wartime appearances
The players who made most appearances for Burnley during World War Two were:

Arthur Woodruff	243
Tommy Gardner	216
Bob Brocklebank	189
Ronnie Hornby	112
Jimmy Strong	103
Peter Kippax	97
Alick Robinson	96
R. Webster	80
Harold Rudman	75
R. Snowden	67
Len Martindale	61

Wartime goals
Leading goalscorers during World War Two were:

Bob Brocklebank	77
Tommy Gardner	46
Harry Jackson	45
Peter Kippax	44
Ronnie Hornby	26

R. Bright	19
George Knight	18
Billy Morris	15

Forty-nine players 'guested' for the Clarets during the war. These were players registered with other League clubs, who were stationed near Burnley and made themselves available to play. These included Reg Attwell (West Ham), Jackie Chew (Blackburn) and Jimmy Strong (Walsall), who all went on to have fine careers at Turf Moor.

Among those who played for Burnley during the war were Jack Bray (Manchester City) an English international, Cyril Sidlow (Wolves) a Welsh international, Jack Fairbrother (Preston), who won an FA Cup-winners' medal with Newcastle United in 1951, and Frank Soo (Stoke), the famous Chinese player.

WARDROBES

Was it commentator Stuart Hall who gave Burnley left-winger Steve Kindon the nickname of 'the flying wardrobe'? It somehow seemed appropriate.

While on the subject of bedroom furniture, Burnley actually had a player on their books in 1980 called Micky Wardrobe. He played just the one game, as a substitute when he came on in the home game against Carlisle in April 1980. He was later transferred to Stockport County.

'A WARM PAIR!'

'Followers of the Manchester City club believe that Ross and Meredith will make one of the finest wings in all creation, and there is no doubt that they will become a warm pair.' *Burnley Express* (Written after the transfer of Jimmy Ross to Manchester City in March 1899.)

THE WEATHER

'The presence of our Northern friend, the ice king, was not the only element of frost in connection with the tie between Burnley and Astley Bridge. The proceedings were a "decided freeze".' **1886**

'The clerk of the weather has recently distributed the rain drops in a most unfair manner and nowhere has he shown his spite so much as in this district and more especially towards football players and enthusiasts. There is conclusive evidence that if possible, he would wash Turf Moor out of existence!' **1885**

'A very unusual occurrence was witnessed at Turf Moor yesterday afternoon on the occasion of the annual encounter between Burnley and Halliwell. The game was started while the rain came down in torrents, and play progressed under very adverse conditions – the rain increasing in volume and was little short of a deluge. After playing for about five minutes, young Brady scored for Burnley, and directly afterwards the teams left the field, the visitors leading the way.

Some few minutes later, Mr Massey, the president of the club, interviewed the teams, and they positively refused to come onto the field again. Mr Massey promised the spectators checks for Saturday's match, the announcement being well received. There was a good attendance, the stand of course, being packed.' *Burnley News,* **26 December 1888**

Burnley and fog 4 Villa 0

Things were not going well for Burnley in 1888–89. It was the first League season, and the club were next from the bottom when the most famous team in the land, Aston Villa, came to Turf Moor. To the amazement of every one in the country Burnley went on to win 4–0! What was the reason? Why the sudden improvement in the struggling Burnley side? The secret behind Burnley's success was that on the way to the game three Aston Villa players got lost in a Manchester fog while changing trains and the team were only able to field eight men.

Fog bound

Fog was a common feature of Lancashire 100 years ago, as witnessed by this quaint report. 'Thank goodness yesterday was not today. We hope that today will be as far from yesterday, as yesterday was from July! It would give us a shock to wake this morning and find that we could not find which was the opposite side of the street. But the fog has begun to lift.' **Burnley v Barnsley, FA Cup, 1911**

Manchester's green fog

'Burnley were hunting the elusive at Derby on Saturday, but they did not manage to find it. The Turf Moor side had a somewhat exciting time in making the journey. The fog was settling down when Burnley was left, but on arriving at Manchester, a thick green fog had let down the curtain on the day, and night had changed places with noontide.

Inquiries from the station authorities revealed the fact that the Derby train had been suspended on account of the fog, and the players had to quickly tumble out of the train saloon into the cold air, mount cabs, and drive from Manchester Victoria to the Central station. Mr Catlow had to chase after Watson who was due to arrive at Victoria station from Southport somewhere about the time as the rest of the team, but he secured him, put a Pressman on the right road, and turned up smiling at the Central station at the right time.

Manchester was soon left to its unenviable company, the fog, and for a long time the sun shone. But Derby made its presence felt a good few miles before it was reached in the shape of a grey mist. It shrouded everything and though not of the green colour of the Manchester fog, it was sufficient to kill football for the day.

Derby is one of those towns where they always have a band on the field and one duly arrived. And from somewhere out in the unknown and unexplored bank of fog, it sardonically commenced to play *Will 'o the Wisp.* Later it tooted forth a fantasia with *Home Sweet Home* as the predominant pattern. Whether it was spontaneous or from malice afterthought, there was certainly humour in the music.

Meanwhile the referee made several anxious visits out into the unknown regions. Sometimes the fog lifted a little and when a hint of blue sky showed through the fog, a Derby enthusiast eagerly pointed to it, but had his enthusiasm choked by a cool and calculating Lancashire man, who regarding him with somewhat of scorn said: "Aye, but wer' not laikin up theer, tha knows!"' ***Burnley Express*, 1911**

'B......Brigadoon!'
It was just as bad in the 1960s, as recalled by Jimmy Greaves, who came over by coach from Manchester with the Tottenham team. Looking down from the 'Bull and Butcher' at the top of Manchester Road, he said that Burnley 'looked like bloody Brigadoon, appearing out of the mist!'

Weather abandons game at Turf Moor
'After a gruelling battle with a storm lasting over an hour and a quarter, the extreme cold combined with the terrible ground conditions and the sweeping rain triumphed and led to the curtailment of the Burnley reserves match with Sheffield Wednesday reserves at Turf Moor. Five players collapsed in the space of two minutes, and a quarter of an hour from the end, the game was abandoned.

One does not remember such a scene as that of last Saturday, when players had to have their clothing cut from them, as they were too helpless to pull off the clinging garments. After they had stripped, they went into water so hot that others in the room who were helping, jumped aside when the hot water splashed them, though the players themselves could not feel the heat. Some of them would have blistered themselves without knowing it, had they been left to themselves.

What a terrible day Saturday was! Cold, persistent, biting! Half-time came and there was almost a revolt in the dressing rooms as trainers struggled to get their teams back on the pitch...' ***Burnley Express*, November 1929**

WELL TRAVELLED

Adeola Akinbiyi has played with 11 different League clubs, as has Andy Gray.
This is nothing as compared to goalkeeper Paul Crichton, who played for 14 clubs, including Burnley, between 1986 and 2001.

But top of the 'travellers' is goalkeeper Marlon Beresford, who has had 15 different clubs, *plus*. 'Plus?' Plus three stays at Sheffield Wednesday, three stays at Burnley, and two each at Northampton, Middlesbrough and Luton! He was last heard of at Oldham Athletic, after an amazing 21 moves. It is a wonder he keeps still on his goalline.

WEMBLEY DOUBLE

Andy Farrell is the only player in Burnley's history to play for the club twice at Wembley. He was in the Burnley side which lost to Wolves in the 1988 Sherpa Van

Trophy Final. Six years later he came on as substitute in the Second Division Play-off Final of 1994, against Stockport.

WHAT A DIFFERENCE A SEASON MAKES

The contrast between 1925–26 and 1926–27 was remarkable. After 17 games and only three victories in 1925, the Clarets were bottom of Division One. Twelve months later, after 13 games in 1926–27 (and only two defeats), the Clarets topped the League.

To follow the two seasons to their end, in 1925–26 the Clarets eventually escaped relegation by a single point, while the following year, after their splendid start, the club finished fifth, nine points behind champions Newcastle.

WHAT IF…?

Football is a game of 'what might have beens' and the history of Burnley Football Club is no different. The last 125 years have been punctuated with events that changed the course of the club's history. But, what if…?
Burnley had not sold Jimmy McIlroy in 1963?
Burnley had not beaten Orient in 1987?
Burnley had not sold Bob Kelly in 1925?
Burnley had defended against Hamburg, instead of trying to win away? (1960)
Jimmy McIlroy had not missed four games through injury in 1961–62?
Colin McDonald had not broken his leg in Dublin in 1959?
Burnley had not signed Cliff Britton as manager in 1946?
John Haworth had not been appointed manager in 1910?
Burnley had not won re-election in 1903?
Burnley had not sold Martin Dobson in 1974?
And there have been many more.

WHO'S THE PLAYER?

Most older football supporters are familiar with 'Spot the Ball' competitions, but in the 1920s the *Burnley Express* ran a 'Who's the player?' competition. Several players would be pictured in action, but one would have his face blanked out. The reader who could guess the player won £1 10s for his efforts.

WHO WOULD HAVE THOUGHT IT?

In the 18 seasons between 1946 and 1964, Burnley, Spurs and Wolves between them finished in the top four 23 times…Burnley five times, Spurs eight and Wolves 10. Who would have thought that after these three teams had dominated English football for more than a decade, none of them would ever win the Division One title again? Indeed, in the space of 12 seasons, all three teams were relegated – Wolves in 1965, Burnley in 1971 and Spurs in 1977. How are the mighty fallen?

THERE'S ONLY TWO WILLIE MORGANS!

Contrary to general opinion, Burnley once had another Willie Morgan. The first Willie was a local boy, born in Burnley in 1896. He was a left-half, who deputised for Billy Watson six times in 1921–22, as the great team began to break up. He did the same four times the following year, and again for a further 18 games in 1923–24.

And then, just as his career was beginning to blossom, Willie's dreams of fame and success were shattered when he suffered a broken leg after a collision with a Sunderland forward. He never played senior football again. It could have all been so different for Willie the first. His form had taken the Clarets to the FA Cup semi-final, but without his presence in the team, Burnley were beaten 3–0 by Aston Villa in the big game.

Personally, I got to know this Willie very well in the 1970s, when he occasionally attended my church in Poulton-le-Fylde. He was a delightful little man. And as for Willie the Second – we all know his story!

WIND

'Over a long course of years, one does not remember a game being played in such a gale. There have been periods in a match when the wind has been high at one time or another, but it was wind all the time on Saturday, of a force which is imaginable only to those who witnessed the game, and the consequence was that some queer pranks were played by Sir Boreas. He roared and raved in an alarming fashion, and the game was accompanied by a rattling and banging of anything loose which at times made one feel that part of the grandstand was going by the board, or that the flag pole, after all its swaying and rocking, would at last collapse.

They are evidently accustomed to high winds in Bradford, judging by the small arsenal of footballs present, and though the ball was as often out of play as in, no time was lost on that account, for immediately one sphere sought to dawdle with the elements on the other side of the stands, another was discharged from the battery, a messenger was dispatched after the truant, and so it went on and on.'
***Burnley Gazette*, Bradford Park Avenue v Burnley, 1911**

HEADS OR TAILS?

'The wind played many queer antics, the first being when the coin was tossed up, and the captains had to run 15 yards down the field to find it when it dropped. On another occasion, Dawson took a goal-kick, and after the ball had travelled a few yards from

him, the wind carried it up, and then blew it back over the crossbar for a corner-kick.'
Bury v Burnley, January 1916

WINNING PROGRAMME NUMBER

For well over 10 seasons in the 1940s and 1950s, Burnley's match programme had a winning number. Each programme was numbered differently, and as an encouragement to buy a copy the winning number was announced each week at half-time. (The winner usually got a prize of £1).

For 18 months or more, my father would always get the right number before it was announced! '25252' he would say, followed by the loudspeaker announcement, 'The winning programme number is 25252!' Or maybe he would suggest '7851'. And sure enough, within minutes the same number was announced. It became a half-time feature for all the people stood nearby as they asked him what it would be this week?

Sometimes he would give a choice of numbers, expressing maybe a little doubt in himself. Not once was he ever wrong! 73195 or 31952 or 7352? 'The winning programme number is 7352!' came the announcement. I pestered him for well over a year, until one day he told me quietly, 'It's the date.'

So 25252 was the 25 February 1952 or 7851 was the 7 August 1951 or 31952 was the 3rd of whatever 1952. Of course, he never had the winning programme. And he never ever told me how he had discovered the secret. Good old Dad!

A PIECE OF WET HISTORY

'Rain fell rather heavily while the general meteorological outlook was far from reassuring, but happily the water demon kept out of the way, until the closing phases of the game. Then however, the process of emptying his can commenced in right good earnest.

The Committee have complied with the order of the League in providing a net and though none of the goals were disputed, it proved useful in preventing goals being claimed when the ball went near the posts.'
Burnley v Aston Villa, October 1891

WORLD CUP CLARETS

⊕ Five Burnley international players have taken part in World Cup Finals over the years – one Scot, three Irishmen and a single English player.

⊕ The first time that Burnley ever had a player competing in the World Cup Finals was over 50 years ago, when Scotsman Jock Aird, the Burnley right-back, played in Switzerland in the 1954 World Cup Finals. Sadly, Scotland lost both games, against Austria and Uruguay, and were eliminated. Curiously, Jock was played out of position in both games, playing at left-back rather than in his usual right-back spot.

- 1958 saw two of Burnley's most famous internationals competing in the World Cup held in Sweden. They were goalkeeper Colin McDonald in the England team and inside-forward Jimmy McIlroy in the Northern Ireland team.

- Colin McDonald played in all four of England's games (drawing three and losing one) and was eventually voted the best goalkeeper in the tournament.

- Meanwhile, Jimmy 'Mac' was going one better as his country reached the quarter-finals. During the competition Northern Ireland won two, drew once and lost two. They could well have gone further, but for the weight of fixtures: all five games were played within 11 days.

- 1982 saw two of Burnley's Irish internationals, Billy Hamilton and Tommy Cassidy, playing in the World Cup Finals in Spain. Billy was one of Northern Ireland's heroes, as his team won through to the quarter-finals, winning once and drawing three times. Billy's two goals against Austria earned him worldwide fame, and by scoring in this game he is currently the only Burnley player ever to score in the World Cup Finals. In the victory over Spain, Billy was also joined by fellow Claret Tommy Cassidy. However, after playing five games within 17 days, Northern Ireland were beaten in the quarter-finals.

WORLDWIDE CLARETS

The fans' website 'Claretsmad' has a record of the different countries where Clarets fans live. So far, the total runs to 57 different countries – from Australia to Austria, the Bahamas to Bulgaria, Canada to China, Germany to Guam, Italy to Indonesia and from the US to the United Arab Emirates. All this support for a little town in Lancashire!

WORST FA CUP RUN

Between 1904–08 Burnley played six FA Cup ties, drawing one and losing five.

X MARKS THE SPOT

Over the years, 'X' has meant a variety of things for football fans. Obvious ones are the cross where you thought the ball was in 'Spot the Ball' competitions, and the cross you made on your pools coupon, signifying your forecasted fixture.

It has come to mean a drawn game, as in '1 for a home, 2 for an away and X for a draw'. But for the first 50 years of League football, an X was placed against the home team in a fixture to denote which was the home team, e.g. Blackburn 1 x Burnley 3 (October 1922). It is only in more recent years that the home team has been put first in the fixture.

Chapter Thirteen

Y – Z

(From Yawn and YMCA to Zelem and Zenith)

'Y'

'Y' is a night at York City
Almost two decades ago,
When thousands travelled from Burnley
To witness the come-back show.

Half a decade from the abyss,
That brink the club teetered on,
Just one game from oblivion,
Lose – and the Clarets were gone.

But then, just five seasons later,
Another great commotion,
Again a single, vital game,
This time, though, for promotion.

Jimmy Mullen's Claret army,
Five thousand strong at least;
Counting all who claim they were there,
That would greatly be increased.

Who now can recall Blackstock's goal?
For when the score is reckoned
It's John Steele Deary's leveller,
John Francis with the second.

But, those goals were seven weeks shy
Of when they should have been scored,
Triumph delayed by tragedy,
A death should not be ignored.

Trainee on the Longside roof,
Retrieving a ball, when he
Fell through and died on the terrace;
Remember Claret Ben Lee.

The night that relaunched the Clarets
To the Premier League, maybe,
Is a night to be remembered,
Along with Claret Ben Lee.
Dave Alton

(Looking back to promotion at York, and ahead to the Premier League, and not forgetting a tragedy at Turf Moor).

YAWN?

The club's motto for the season 2008–09 was 'A New Dawn'. With plans to redevelop the ground, adding a cinema and a hotel at a cost of around £20 million, hopes were high for promotion as well. But after the club had lost their first two games of the season, many fans renamed the season 'The New Yawn!'

YMCA

In 1882 the Young Men's Christian Association held a meeting with the curate of St Peter's Church in Burnley, the Revd M.W. Hill presiding. It was decided to form a rugby club under the title of the YMCA, playing at Calder Vale, but the name of the club was soon changed to that of an earlier club called Burnley Rovers. In May 1882 it was decided 'that the club in future play under Association rules'. By the time they played their first game in August 1882 the club had dropped the term 'Rovers'.

YOUNGSTERS!

- David Thomas was 16 years and 220 days old when he made his Division One debut for Burnley (v Everton, May 1967). Tommy Lawton was slightly younger at 16 years and 174 days when he made his debut (v Doncaster Rovers, March 1936), but this was in Division Two.

- Other youngsters to play for the Burnley first team have been Eric Probert and Jason Harris. Eric Probert was 16 years and 287 days old when he made his debut against Arsenal on 30 November 1968. In Eric Probert's second match, against Spurs on 29 March 1969, he became the youngest Claret (17 years and 40 days) ever to score in a First Division match.

- However, when Tommy Lawton scored his first goal (also in his second game, but two goals and playing away), against Swansea on 4 April 1936, he was only 16 years and 180 days old at the time.

- Jason Harris was 16 years and 331 days old when he made his League debut (v Lincoln, 22 November 1986).

'Z'

And finally it's Z, for Zeal,
The passion felt day by day
By supporters who expect it
From the players in their play.

This will be demonstrated by
Obvious Zip and Zest,
A winger with a Zig-Zag run
Is considered to be best.

While consulting the Zodiac
Is probably not much use
In influencing results, but
How about prayers to Zeus?

A Zen approach might be better
With calm total and complete,
Nothing disturbs tranquillity,
Not even a home defeat.

Or is it that just being a Zombie,
A hapless fool of the fates,
A dimwit who doesn't understand;
If so, Ewood awaits.

Because when hope is at Zero,
And all seems gloom and despair,
However Zollistic he is,
A Claret is always there.
Dave Alton

'ZEBRAS'

It was in 1911 that Burnley stopped playing in green and started wearing claret and blue, thus becoming 'the Clarets'. This was a move by manager John Haworth, who adopted the colours of the current League champions, Aston Villa. But far more successful than Villa then were Newcastle United, who had won three titles in five seasons. If Burnley had adopted their colours, they might have been called the 'Zebras'!

ZELEM

There have not been very many professional footballers since the war whose names have begun with 'Z', but the Clarets had one of them, Peter Zelem. Peter played for Chester, Wolves and Preston before arriving at Turf Moor in 1987, and he was one of the eight new faces to be seen in the first game after the 'Orient' crisis. Altogether he played in 17 games and scored two goals for the Clarets.

ZENITH

When has been the zenith of Burnley Football Club? There are two nominations: the years from 1914 to 1922 and those from 1959 to 1963. In both of these eras, Burnley dominated English football, and there is much that is parallel between the two periods.

In both periods, the club finished champions, runners-up, third, fourth and reached the FA Cup Final. Both teams had great captains – Tommy Boyle and Jimmy Adamson; both teams had a genius of an inside-forward – Bob Kelly and Jimmy McIlroy; and both teams were scattered with international players.

But there were differences. The 1914–22 era encompassed World War One, and it can only be wondered what heights the team might have reached but for the war. The 1914–22 team also won the Cup, while our later heroes finished as runners-up.

Other differences include: when the 1920–21 team won the title they achieved 59 points, while the 1959–60 team 'managed' 55 points. On the other side, the 1920–21 team scored 79 goals and 72 the following season, while the 1960–61 team scored a century in a season, and did it again the following year. This was a different game though, just as we would never expect a team to score a century of goals these days.

But for me (brought up on the 1959–60 team), the thing that swings the decision is the '30 consecutive League games without defeat' in 1920–21, which is rarely equalled or beaten to this day, over 80 years later. Imagine playing from September to March without losing? Seventeen consecutive home victories. And the 'Halley, Boyle 'n Watson' dream team also won the FA Cup.

Maybe my Dad was right after all?

Or maybe the zenith is yet to come?

P.S Recognising that the game of football these days is on a totally uneven playing field (due to millionaires and finance etc), maybe these days, after Burnley's recent promotion, are the zenith? Let us enjoy them.

Answers
1. Bert Clewley Freeman
2. Tommy Wilkinson Boyle
3. Jack Marshall
4. Joe (Jakub)
5. Colin Agnew McDonald
6. Fred Taylor (1947) and Fred Smith (1963–70)
7. Karbassiyoon and Papadopoulos
8. Painter and Pointer. Peyton and Payton
9. Cox, Eli, Gow, Lee, May
10. Eddie Hodgson in 1919
11. 102 in 1960–61
12. 29 in 1970–71
13. Four
14. 29 by Willie Irvine in 1965–66
15. Seven